Concepts and Careers in Physical Education

second edition

Robert D. Clayton
Colorado State University
Fort Collins, Colorado

Joyce A. Clayton

with contributions by

William W. Bolonchuk
University of North Dakota
Grand Forks, North Dakota

Donald Buchanan
Mankato State University
Mankato, Minnesota

Laurna Rubinson
University of Illinois
Champaign, Illinois

56636

Burgess Publishing Company
Minneapolis, Minnesota

ACKNOWLEDGMENTS

The second edition of this text has undergone numerous changes from the earlier one. In the six years between the initial thought of this project and its completion, many individuals have given their time and talents and should be thanked publicly.

Professor William Bolonchuk of the University of North Dakota provided the first impetus to the project by cooperating in establishing the skills testing program described in Chapter 7. Subsequently, Professor Jean McCarthy of Mankato (Minnesota) State University provided students in his Tests and Measurements classes the opportunity to gather and use skills test data. In addition, Professor McCarthy has critically reviewed several chapters.

Without help from prospective physical education majors at Western Michigan University, Wayne (Nebraska) State College, Ball State University, University of North Dakota, and Mankato State University, the test data would be woefully incomplete. Over 1200 students have taken or given the various tests outlined in this text, or have worked in the research laboratory. Karen Eberhard of the University of North Dakota established the computer programs which enabled the quick and accurate establishment of norms. These persons deserve special recognition.

Jill Binstock, Cheryl Davey, and Barbara Gifford have typed various parts of the manuscript; ultimately, it is these persons that deserve credit for its completion.

If we have unwittingly omitted acknowledgment for usage of any material in this book, we sincerely apologize.

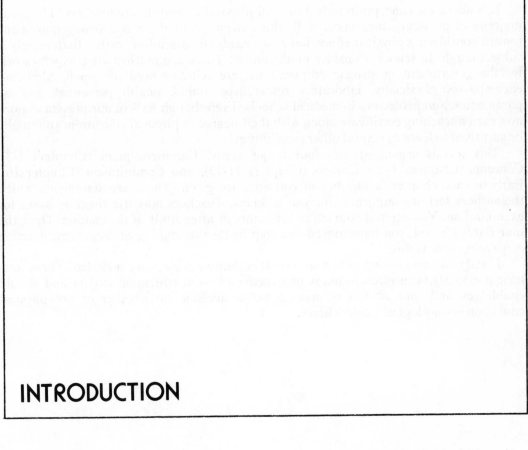

INTRODUCTION

This text is designed for students who are considering a career in physical education. While a few might understand the wide scope of physical education, most are aware only of the teaching and coaching aspects. With these thoughts in mind, the purposes of this text are:

1. To describe and illustrate the purposes of American physical education, the knowledges of science and society which contribute to this discipline, the career possibilities available to professionals, and the characteristics and responsibilities of successful physical educators.

2. To outline a program whereby the student's qualifications for the profession can be examined both by self and the advisor, with the intent of comparing these results with other current physical education majors and with successful professional persons in the field.

If these two purposes are reached, the ultimate goal is attainable — to have each student make the correct decision as to whether he or she should (and could) continue the training necessary to become a successful physical educator.

Two misconceptions should be explained at the onset. Many persons scoff at physical education majors, describing them as semiliterate athletes who are not smart enough to major in any other field. Perhaps some, but not very many, fit this description. You will soon discover that courses such as "underwater basketweaving" are nonexistent, and that the majority of your courses (such as motor learning, sport and society, anatomy, physiology of exercise, kinesiology, tests and measurements) are rigorous, challenging, and informative.

It is also a misconception to feel that all physical educators are teachers. The great majority of physical educators now fit this category, but there is a strong movement toward considering physical education as an academic discipline, rather than merely a subject taught in school. Consider mathematics. There are mathematicians who work for the government or private corporations, are self-employed, or teach. Medicine encompasses physicians, laboratory researchers, public health personnel, nurses, paramedics, and professors in medical schools. Even though 85% of our present majors now earn a teaching certificate along with their degree in physical education, you might be surprised to learn of several other possibilities.

This text is organized into four major areas: Commencement (Chapters 1-3), Concepts (Chapters 4-10), Careers (Chapters 11-15), and Commitment (Chapter 16). Early in each chapter, a number of concepts are given. These are statements which the authors feel are important for you to know. Teachers may use them as bases for examinations. You can test yourself either before or after study of the chapter. Once the material is learned, you have moved one step further in making an important decision concerning your future.

Finally, this text is unique in that several evaluative devices are included. These tests have previously been given to many prospective physical education majors and should enable you and your adviser to make a better decision on whether or not physical education is your logical career choice.

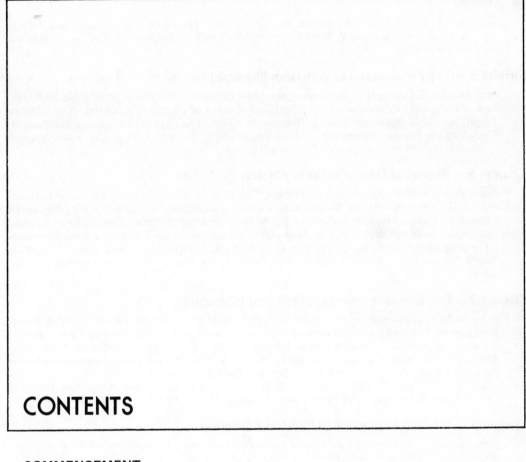

CONTENTS

CHAPTER 1

FIRST CONSIDERATIONS

INTRODUCTION

Some students who read this text have just begun college careers, and are justifiably confused by the terms used to describe various aspects of this new environment, to say nothing of the entire organization of the school. Regardless of your previous college experience, if you are reading this particular section, you are undoubtedly an undergraduate student; that is, you have not yet earned a Bachelor of Science or a Bachelor of Arts degree. Either of these degrees usually requires taking certain courses, earning satisfactory grades, and accumulating a certain number of credits. This process customarily takes four years. In the sections that follow, details of the process will be explained so that you need not remain silent when friends talk about general education, GPA, consent, the bulletin, the dean, and other such terms.

CONCEPTS TO BE GAINED FROM THIS CHAPTER

When you have mastered the material in this chapter, you will be able to demonstrate comprehension[1] of this concept:

---

[1]Your instructor will indicate the procedure by which you might demonstrate comprehension of this concept. It may be written examination (short essay, multiple-choice, true-false, matching, or completion questions), class discussion, written composition, or other means. The standard of performance will also be established by the instructor.

1. A well-prepared person has extensive knowledge about a chosen school and field of study. This would include information about:
   a. Terms commonly used in colleges and universities
   b. Rationale for general education courses
   c. General education and physical education major (or minor) courses required at a particular school
   d. Role of advisers
   e. Organization of a particular school, down to the faculty level
   f. Number of faculty members in the department (division)
   g. Name of the chairperson of the department (division)

TERMS

Regardless of the area or subject, there are common terms that must be understood by the student. The remainder of the text discusses many such terms which relate specifically to physical education, but this chapter will discuss the specialized language of colleges and universities.

Prerequisites are requirements (courses or experiences) that must be satisfied before certain other courses can be taken. For example, algebra must usually be taken before trigonometry. It is quite common for *consent of the instructor* to be listed as the prerequisite, which indicates that before enrolling in the course, you must get the instructor's permission. The primary practical problem with prerequisites is that students quite often overlook them! Should you fail to meet the prerequisites of a course, and do not have the instructor's consent, you must then drop the course. This is usually costly, and causes a schedule problem.

Credits are numerical points given for each class taken; the number of credits is usually related to the number of formal hours spent in the class per week. Thus, a three-credit class meets three hours per week. Laboratory courses (i.e., nonclassroom courses) generally meet twice as often as classroom courses for the same number of credits. This implies that laboratory hours do not require as much time for outside study, and thus do not merit the same credit as classroom course. Physical education students, along with music and art students, customarily spend more time in actual class meetings than the credits would indicate.

Ordinarily, *grades* are given for courses taken. In the majority of colleges, each grade is awarded *honor points* (A=4, B=3, C=2, D=1). Dividing a student's total credits earned into the honor points yields the *grade point average*, or *GPA*. For example, a student takes 15 credits, earning 10 credits of A and 5 credits of B: 10 credits $\times 4 = 40$, 5 credits $\times 3 = 15$. The GPA is 3.67 ($55 \div 15$). The GPA is probably the single most important record you will accumulate in college. It is the common standard for comparing students, and is checked by prospective employers or graduate schools. A recent trend is to permit some courses to be taken on a *credit - no credit* system. In these instances, a student who successfully passes the course receives credit but no letter grade. Students who are required to take a particular course and are apprehensive about the final grade usually are pleased to use this option.

A school year is divided into *quarters* (from 10 to 11 weeks long), or *terms* or *semesters* (usually 15 to 16 weeks). Regardless of the word used, the length of time spent determines the number of credits earned. An average load is 15 to 17 credits under either system, with 180 credits (quarter system) or 120 credits (semester system) being the usual minimum number required for graduation. When all requirements (credits earned, satisfactory GPA, required courses taken) are satisfied, a degree is awarded.

The Associate in Arts degree may be earned after two years of study, while four years of study (perhaps including two at a community college) generally yields enough credits for the bachelor's degree.

Since course requirements, rules, and regulations change frequently, schools print an annual or biannual *catalog*, or *bulletin*. Because of these changes, students usually have the option of meeting the requirements printed in the year they enter college, or the year they plan to graduate. The college catalog or bulletin represents your contract with the school, and obviously should be consulted at periodic intervals.

A term you will encounter early in college is that of *general education* courses. Sometimes called *liberal education* courses, they are required on the premise that part of a good education is to become more knowledgeable about the entire environment, not merely a chosen field. Rightly or wrongly, these courses are not especially popular with students.[2] General education courses normally account for about one-third of the total credits required for graduation. Sometimes these required courses are established by state law, but usually faculty and students have jointly cooperated in their formulation. The following list shows the common categories of general education courses, with a few specific examples of courses found in each:

Communication skills — English, composition, speech, etc.

Natural sciences — biology, chemistry, physics, etc.

Social sciences — sociology, economics, history, etc.

Humanities — philosophy, literature, music, art, etc.

There is a strong trend toward making general education more *elective*, which means that the student has some choice in course selection. For example, the general education requirement might be "Select 12 credits from the Social Sciences." This gives you the option of selecting from whatever courses are considered part of the social sciences at your particular school (not all schools have the same combination of courses in each category). It is quite common to require general education courses as prerequisites to courses in the major, so judicious selection may reduce the number of credits you would need to meet all graduation requirements.

Other terms that must be understood deal with majors and minors. A *major* implies that a student has decided to do a great deal of college work in one particular area, with the thought that this concentration will be of value in later life (usually as a vocation). Many readers of this text are considering physical education as a possible major. If so, about 30%-40% of the credits required for graduation would come from physical education and its related areas. A *minor* indicates that the chosen area is of secondary importance; it usually requires 15%-20% of the credits for graduation. In physical education, there are many common requirements for either a major or a minor, so you might begin as a minor and then change to a major (or vice versa) with a minimum amount of program change. Depending upon your future plans, you may wish to secure a double major, or two minors. The current bulletin of your school will give details of every program available.

At this point, it might be wise to acknowledge that students are often disappointed

[2]Faculty members hear complaints about general education courses. The following comment, written by a senior majoring in political science, might be of interest.

"Now I know that general education is a pain in the neck at times, and one asks himself, 'Why am I taking this stupid course?' The answer is that employers want a person with a broad liberal arts background. On the other side of the coin a person cannot be a businessman, nurse, etc., 24 hours a day. General education is designed to give you a well-rounded background in things that will probably help you enjoy other aspects of life also." (James Endres, letter to the editor, Mankato State University *Reporter*, Dec. 2, 1971, p. 3.)

when they are not allowed to take a large number of courses in a major during their first year of college. You should realize that about a third of all students change majors at least once in their college career, and this is most apt to occur in the freshman year. By taking primarily general education courses and sampling several courses in the proposed major, you will make a good start toward meeting general education requirements and obtaining a more realistic view of your chosen field.

An area of general concern is the selection of elective courses. Since the required credits in general education plus your major will seldom equal the total required for graduation, you will have to elect additional courses. If you plan to teach, the state certification laws require that you take *professional education* courses (psychology of learning, growth and development of children, student teaching, etc.). These normally constitute 15%-20% of the graduation credits. Should you be taking a nonteaching major, you obviously will have a greater number of elective courses. It might be wise to select electives from one or two areas and thus complete one or two minors, rather than select only from courses recommended by classmates.

Finally, consider the role of *advisers* — the persons who serve as the link between you and the school. They can inform you of the latest curriculum changes or when certain courses are offered, indicate how to better profit from your years at college, and offer counsel on problems related to school and life in general. The main duty of the adviser is to know you well enough to help you meet your objectives. Some students feel that an adviser is unneeded — that they can graduate without such help. Some do graduate without help, but a surprisingly large number of students spend more time and money than needed merely because they fail to seek/or heed their advisers.

ORGANIZATION OF THE COLLEGE OR UNIVERSITY

Because of the great number of possible majors and minors, colleges and universities are divided into various segments designed to meet the role assigned to them by society. The great diversity of size, location, financial resources, and personality of leaders means that no two colleges or universities are organized precisely alike. The major features of all schools are reasonably close to those shown in Figure 1-1.

The person in charge of the institution is the president (or chancellor). He or she has a group of advisers to aid in making top-level decisions, with a Vice-President for Academic Affairs (or Dean of Instruction) being designated as the person primarily responsible for academic concerns. The typical college or university is organized into three to eight major segments called schools, divisions, or sometimes even colleges. Each represents a major area of concern, such as education, medicine, business, law, liberal arts, or industrial technology. In some institutions, physical education is one of these major segments. Most physical educators would consider this the ideal organizational structure. The top person in each major group is usually a dean.

In institutions where these major groups are composed of several different areas (for example, the School of Education might include elementary and secondary education, special education, physical education, and counseling), one further segment is needed. This final group is called a *department*, and is usually led by a chairperson or department head. A group of faculty members compose the department in which you intend to major. In theory, these individuals function as a team to carry out the aims of the department, the school or division, and the institution. Historically, many institutions have had separate physical education departments for women and for men. For various reasons, a recent trend has been to combine these departments.

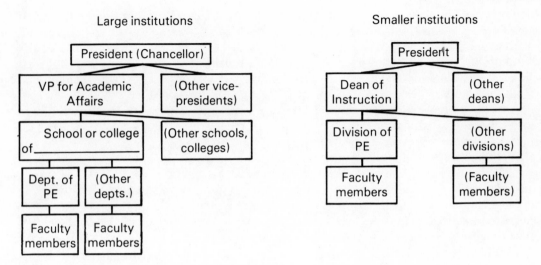

FIGURE 1-1. Typical organization of colleges and universities.

Statements for Class Discussion

1. If you can pass a course without meeting the prerequisites, why worry about them?
2. There should be no minors in physical education. If a student is not interested enough to major, then he or she shouldn't take physical education.

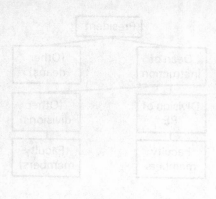

FIGURE 1. Typical organization of colleges and universities.

COMMENCEMENT

CHAPTER **2**

SELECTING PHYSICAL EDUCATION STUDENTS

INTRODUCTION

This text is usually read as a student begins to study the academic discipline of physical education. The term "academic discipline" is probably new — and strange — to you. Few people closely relate the words "academic" and "physical education," and "discipline" implies punishment to most persons. No doubt you think of physical education as a particular class you took in high school. There it was considered a "subject," as were mathematics and English. At this particular moment, you must be thinking that working in physical education (probably teaching and/or coaching) is your goal. Perhaps it will be, but you should know more about physical education as an academic discipline, and about your strengths and weaknesses, before making a definite commitment. Likewise, most departments would like to know more about you before accepting you into their program. This chapter details the purposes of this text, provides definitions for such terms as "academic discipline" and "physical educator," and examines the rationale for a selection program. It begins with a listing of concepts which should guide you in your study.

CONCEPTS TO BE GAINED FROM THIS CHAPTER

When you have mastered the material in this chapter, you will be able to demonstrate comprehension of these concepts:

1. Because of its purposes, this text may be helpful both to the student and to the discipline of physical education.

2. Certain terms (physical education, physical educator, AAHPER, selection program, screening program) must be understood in order to intelligently discuss why and how prospective physical educators should be selected.
3. Several schools have various selection programs for physical education majors, but none precisely follow AAHPER recommendations.
4. Regardless of selection devices used, probably a combination of student self-selection and departmental screening is best.

PURPOSES OF THIS TEXT

This text is designed for students who are considering a career in physical education. While a few students might understand the wide scope of physical education, most are aware only of the teaching and coaching aspects. With these thoughts in mind, the purposes of this text are:

1. To describe and illustrate the purposes of American physical education, the knowledges about science and society which contribute to this discipline, the career possibilities available to professionals, and the characteristics and responsibilities of successful physical educators.
2. To outline a program whereby the student's qualifications for the profession can be examined both by self and an adviser, the intent being to compare these results with other current physical education majors and also with successful professionals in the field.

If these two purposes are reached, the ultimate goal is attainable — to have each student make the correct decision as to whether he or she should (and could) continue the education necessary to become a successful physical educator.

WHAT IS PHYSICAL EDUCATION?

This chapter will make you aware of the procedures advocated by some colleges and universities as they select physical education students. You will be asked to judge the merit of these procedures. That this might be better done, you should understand that physical education is more than a gym class, it is more than playing games, it is more than doing vigorous calisthenics and sweating. Physical education goes beyond coaching athletic teams and teaching people to dance. As a matter of fact, physical education does not always take place on the playing field! Our definition, later amplified in Chapter 5, is that physical education is

1. an *academic discipline* which attempts to
2. *investigate* the *uses* and *meanings* of
3. *exercise, games, sports, athletics, aquatics, gymnastics,* and *dance*
4. to *understand their effects*
5. *on* and *for*
6. *individuals* and *groups*.

In other words, physical education is the study of the many concepts and knowledges which relate to people and their movements.

WHAT IS A PHYSICAL EDUCATOR?

Characteristics of physical educators (according to critics) include being overmuscled, being semiliterate, and being an athlete who would find it difficult to major in any other field. Other characteristics include being concerned about people, being outgoing, being skilled in many sport activities, being knowledgeable about the human body. All these characteristics lead to the development of stereotypes — a mental picture of what people must be like if they are members of a particular group. You have a favorable stereotype of a physical educator in mind, or you wouldn't be reading this text now. The stereotype we would like you to visualize is a person who possesses such a

1. *breadth* and *depth* of knowledge
2. concerning at least *one key concept* of *human movement*
3. that he or she can function as a *scholar*, a *researcher*, and/or a *professional educator*.

At this point you are probably uncertain what we mean by a scholar or a researcher; you are probably more concerned with the absence of the terms *teacher* and *coach*. A greater discussion of this definition is given in Chapter 5.

TERMS RELATED TO SELECTION PROGRAMS

Before we can discuss the material in the remainder of this chapter, you must understand these terms.

1. AAHPER — American Alliance for Health, Physical Education and Recreation. Members include college students who are preparing to work in health, physical education, or recreation; teachers at all levels; and other professional workers.
2. Selection program — the process of deciding which *potential* physical education majors have the desirable physical, mental, and social qualities that indicate they probably will successfully complete their educational program.
3. Screening test — some type of physical, mental, or social-emotional examination which aids a department in estimating how suited a person is for *continuing* education in the area of physical education. (Quite often, a screening test is a shortened form of a longer test. An example would be a basketball test consisting of field-goal shooting, dribbling, and passing, or a teacher aptitude test consisting of some of the questions from a longer personality test.)

FACTORS ENCOURAGING A SELECTION PROCESS IN PHYSICAL EDUCATION

Selection programs are widely used in such academic disciplines as medicine, law, and teacher training. It should be the responsibility of physical education departments to do likewise. The problem has always been, however, that no one admission test, no one personal interview, no one screening device is 100% accurate. But, faulty as selection programs might occasionally be, it must be remembered that in the long run they benefit both the student and the discipline.

First and foremost among the factors encouraging a selection process is the simple fact that there is a surplus of both men and women physical education teachers. Granted, there are careers other than teaching in which physical educators are needed, but even allowing for those who don't teach, there is still a surplus. This being true, departments must provide some means by which the better qualified students are encouraged to remain, and the others shown alternative career possibilities.

Secondly, departments know much more than they previously did about the physical skills and knowledge of beginning physical education majors. For example, we know that the average beginning major can make a certain number of foul shots in basketball (females — 2 out of 10, males — 4 out of 10). (See Chapter 7, Tables 7-7, 7-8, and 7-9.) We know that the average beginning physical education major scores 42 points out of 60 in Form 2B of the AAHPER Knowledge Test. (See Chapter 9, Table 9-2.) Comparison between your scores and the average gives some means by which a selection might be made.

Third, the great influx of community college students has caused departments to lose one of their best means of selection — that of knowing a person for a period of one or two years and being able to informally encourage or discourage him or her.

Finally, maximizing learning is the aim of education. One way to achieve this is to permit students to waive courses, or to earn credits by examination. Knowledge of a student's background, skills, and knowledge will help meet this aim.

AAHPER RECOMMENDATIONS CONCERNING SELECTION PROGRAMS

Many departments in colleges and universities satisfy themselves in some way that the students majoring in their area meet certain competence standards. Sometimes these standards are related only to grades received in high school courses, but often (as in foreign language, music, drama, art, industrial arts) students are expected to possess minimum performance skills as they begin their study. A selection program evaluates all students, selecting some and rejecting others.

AAHPER has provided guidelines to physical education departments in regard to selection. In one publication (AAHPER 1948, p. 21), departments were urged to ensure that students have a wide variety of personal skills in physical education activities. Another publication (AAHPER 1962, p. 53) was more definite, suggesting that for admission to the program, a student should give evidence of good health, above-average physical development, special skill attainments, and desirable personality attributes. It further states that, at the completion of their training, physical education majors should have skill in archery, badminton, baseball, basketball, football, golf, gymnastics, speedball, social dance, softball, square dance, swimming, tennis, track and field, and volleyball (AAHPER 1962, pp. 69-70).

Their latest statement (AAHPER 1974, pp. 24, 36) is consistent with earlier thoughts but with one new criterion. The most successful professional preparation programs assess students in at least these three areas: 1) ability to move effectively, 2) physical fitness level, and 3) physical skill in a number of sport activities. However, there is now widespread support for assessing a student's: 4) ability to work successfully with persons of all ages. This criterion implies that a student's personality, leadership skills, and human relations aptitude are just as important as the motor skills mentioned above.

CURRENT PRACTICES IN SELECTING PHYSICAL EDUCATION MAJORS

With the use of screening tests, it is possible for physical education departments to select majors who best meet the qualities deemed necessary for success in that field. But what have departments actually done in the selection process?

Dale Nelson (1965) found that almost all of the American physical education leaders he polled favored having a physical proficiency requirement for beginning physical education majors. (Those who did not favor such a requirement felt that it does not always indicate teaching ability.) There was disagreement among the leaders as to exactly what skills should be tested and what level of proficiency should be required. Certain areas were mentioned by most of the leaders: team sports, individual sports, rhythms, and aquatics. They indicated that two other desirable requirements were some type of physical fitness test, and participation in varsity or intramural sports.

Marcinko (1966) asked heads of 59 university and college physical education departments about the selection program at their school. Out of these schools, 37 did not test freshman majors, while 13 did. Of this latter group, 12 schools tested them in basic skills only, while the last gave both basic skills and knowledge tests. Additionally, 6 schools tested all freshmen, both majors and nonmajors. Thus, 19 of the 59 (32%) schools gave some type of a physical skills and/or knowledge test to entering major students. Marcinko indicated that there was a great variation in the tests given and he concluded, "There is a *need* for some kind of standardized test which all schools can use and national norms by which all could compare their physical education students." (Marcinko 1966, p. 27.)

Munch (1969) surveyed 12 colleges and universities in the United States that were judged to have a "degree of excellence" in their undergraduate male professional preparation programs. He concluded that the directors of these schools favored both subjective and objective evaluation procedures when selecting prospective majors. The factor that was most favored for selective admission was the student's command of the English language, both oral and written. Even though only 2 of the 12 schools required tests of motor ability, physical fitness, etc., the directors desired such devices. These tests would be developed by the specific institution and used for predicting success in both the professional activity courses as well as later success in the profession. The major personal quality favored for selective admission was the applicant's determination to succeed, with the second highest quality being the student's curiosity and/or inquisitiveness. A sincere desire to help others through physical activities as indicated by professional attitude, and/or a balanced physical education philosophy, was judged almost as important.

Richardson (1965) described a selection program used at Denver University. Personal qualifications expected of physical education majors were excellent health, evidence of weight control, the 60th percentile on the AAHPER Fitness Test, and acceptable dress and manners. Among additional requirements, male majors were to demonstrate competence in fundamental movement skills, wrestling, gymnastics, aquatics, five individual or dual sports, and four team sports.

Resick (1965) has written about the selection and retention program used at Kent State University. The physical education department decided that four factors should be known about their major students: the presence or absence of any physical or mental deficiencies; their knowledge of activities; their participation experience in athletics, intramurals, and professional groups; and their sports skill (judged after taking activity courses).

Dowell (1965) described a similar program at Arkansas State College. In this instance, there were three factors in the selection phase — participation experience in athletics, intramurals and professional groups; competency in a motor ability test; and evaluation of the students by a review board of staff members after they had taken some major courses.

Paul and Welch (1968) outlined the selection and retention program at Eastern Carolina University. Their staff had decided upon five criteria: physical fitness and motor ability scores, weight control, attitude ratings, basic skills grades, and general academic record.

While not a formal department selection program, the men's physical education staff at the University of Iowa listed the qualities they deemed desirable for male physical educators. The 22 different qualities which were listed could be put into these three broad categories: 1) academic aptitude; 2) physical aptitude and skills background; and 3) personality and empathy factors. (Casady 1970.)

BASIC COMPONENTS OF A SELECTION PROGRAM

The sources cited above indicate that a selection program is advocated by AAHPER. Such a procedure has been developed in certain schools, but each is structured differently. This difference is to be expected, as each department has a different view as to what levels and what kinds of competence might be desirable and feasible in their particular instance. In this diversity, there is general agreement on two components of a selection program: 1) measurement of physical fitness; and 2) measurement of skills in several commonly taught activities.

However, consider how Barbara Nelson (1971) summarized the problem inherent in selection programs. She reported that in 1964-65, freshman women majors at the Ohio State University were given a series of four physical tests and three scholastic aptitude tests. In 1970 the files of these former freshmen were checked, and separated into those who had graduated (N=23) and the nongraduates (N=80). The scores on each of the seven tests were checked and were found to be of little help in predicting which students would "succeed" (i.e., those who would graduate). Nelson concluded her report by saying, "Perhaps the selection process lies in the informed choice of the student herself. Until more tests appear for this purpose, adequate advising, involvement in the department, early field experience, and the availability of academic and financial aid might make it possible for students to screen themselves by clarifying and acting upon their own goals" (Nelson 1971, p. 197).

Thus, we are convinced that physical fitness and physical skills tests are *not* the only attributes that should be evaluated, and we are convinced that it is *not* the responsibility of the physical education department alone to make the selection. Accordingly, Chapter 3 presents the outline for a self-selection program, whereby you and the department are given opportunities to examine the results of several evaluative devices. When you finish this chapter, you should be much more certain of your future role in physical education.

Bibliography

AAHPER. 1948. *Report of the National Conference on Undergraduate Professional Preparation in Health, Physical Education, and Recreation.* Chicago: Athletic Institute.

_____. 1962. *Professional preparation in health education, physical education, and recreation education.* Washington, D.C.: AAHPER.

_____. 1974. *Professional preparation in dance, physical education, recreation education, safety education, and school health education.* Washington, D.C.: AAHPER.

Barrow, H. Classification in physical education. *The Physical Educator* 17 (Oct. 1960):101.

Baumgartner, T. A., and Carlson, R. P. Screening and evaluation procedures for undergraduate majors at Indiana University. *JOHPER* [1] 45 (May 1974):83-84.

Bowen, J. C. In view from the outside. *JOHPER* 45 (June 1974):29-30.

Brynteson, P. AAHPER's number one priority should be standards. *JOHPER* 43 (Mar. 1972):32.

Casady, D. R. Qualities in high school students for future physical education majors. *Iowa JOHPER* (Apr. 1970):22-23.

Dowell, L. J. Professional preparation: Selection, retention and recommendations. *The Physical Educator* 22 (Oct. 1965):101-4.

Fisher, M. J. Assessing the competence of prospective physical education teachers. *The Physical Educator* 29 (Oct. 1972):93.

[1]*JOHPER (Journal of Health, Physical Education, and Recreation)*: after 1974, changed to *JOPER (Journal of Physical Education and Recreation)*.

Hoffman, H. A., et al. Selective admissions: A first step in professional preparation. *JOPER* 46 (Oct. 1975):29-30.

LaPlante, M. But what can we expect? *The Physical Educator* 23 (Dec. 1966):149.

McCarthy, J., and Clayton, R. Baseball academy: Implications for professional preparation. *JOHPER* 44 (June 1973):6-7.

Marcinko, J. J. To test or not to test. *The Physical Educator* 23 (Mar. 1966):26-28.

Marshall, J. M. The role of the physical education selection committees. *The Physical Educator* 27 (May 1970):70.

Munch, L. R. 1969. *Selection and retention procedures for undergraduate male physical education majors.* Doctoral dissertation, Springfield College (Mass.).

Nelson, B. Predicting success in the college physical education major program. *The Physical Educator* 28 (Dec. 1971):196-97.

Nelson, D. O. Proficiency evaluation in physical education activities. *The Physical Educator* 22 (May 1965):65-67.

Paul, T. L., and Welch, J. E. Selective retention of physical education major students. *The Physical Educator* 25 (Oct. 1968):114-15.

Resick, M. C. The second look. *The Physical Educator* 22 (May 1965):70.

Richardson, D. A start in selective retention. *JOHPER* 36 (Jan. 1965):34-35.

Welch, J. E. Proud to be a jock. *The Physical Educator* 30 (May 1973):87-88.

Wilson, B., et al. Measures of stereotypes toward college women physical education majors. *The Physical Educator* 31 (Oct. 1974):140-42.

Wilson, R. Competency testing. *JOHPER* 35 (Feb. 1964):33-34.

Student Activities

1. Assume that your responsibility is to select 25 freshmen physical education majors, and that each of the 25 is to graduate and be a success in some phase of our discipline. What items would you use in your selection program?
2. Not all schools have the facilities or staff to conduct an effective selection program. If your school does not have such a program, interview one faculty member to find out the reasons.
3. Talk to fellow students who have transferred from community colleges or other four-year schools. Did their previous school have a selection program? If so, was it considered by the students to be reasonable and fair?

Statements for Class Discussion

1. What one item in a selection program is the most important? Be able to defend your answer.
2. Who should have the primary responsibility in the selection process — the department or the student? (That is, should the department be able to forbid a person to major, or should a student be allowed to major despite the department's desires?)

COMMENCEMENT

CHAPTER **3**

BEGINNING YOUR
SELF-SELECTION PROGRAM

INTRODUCTION

Chapter 2 discussed the rationale of selection programs; it concluded with the thought that perhaps two views — yours and the department's — might be desirable. The objective of this chapter is to outline how the remainder of the text can be used for your self-education. As you have noted, the authors indicate by concepts what you should gain after studying each chapter. Of more importance, however, is for you to become aware of your capabilities and interests in the psychomotor, cognitive, and affective domains related to physical education. This knowledge will enable both you and the department to make a more sound judgment as to your career potential in physical education.

This chapter begins with definitions of important terms. Then six desirable attributes of physical educators are discussed. Ways of evaluating each of the six — interest, biological development, knowledge, motor skill development, personality, and attitude — are briefly described, and their reference in future chapters is noted. Finally, descriptions of various periodicals are given, so that you might begin to read about the many aspects of the discipline of physical education.

CONCEPTS TO BE GAINED FROM THIS CHAPTER

When you have mastered the material in this chapter, you will be able to demonstrate comprehension of these concepts:

1. Certain terms (the three educational domains, evaluation, validity, reliability,

15

motor skills, test items, objective and subjective evaluation and raw scores) must be understood before a successful selection program can be undertaken.

2. A tentative evaluation of the desirable attributes of a physical educator can be made as the remainder of this text is studied.
3. Reading scholarly, scientific, professional and technical periodicals is essential to becoming a competent physical educator.

DEFINITION OF TERMS

Until a person understands the terms, it is difficult to speak the language! This is true in every aspect of learning. Thus, the following terms should be studied before you proceed in this area.

1. *Domain* — As used in education, a general term which sets the boundaries of thought and study. For example, the "affective domain" relates to feelings, and not to knowledge of facts nor to the physical skill of hitting a ball. There are three domains which will be discussed in this text — psychomotor, cognitive, affective.
2. *Psychomotor domain* — Indicates the mind-body relationship that is present in virtually all physical movements. An example of a psychomotor skill is your ability to hit a pitched ball.
3. *Cognitive domain* — Indicates the knowledge and understanding of facts, ideas, and thoughts that a person "knows" intellectually. Your ability to correctly answer a question is primarily a cognitive skill.
4. *Affective domain* — Indicates the feelings, attitudes, and values that a person possesses. Your ideas about sportsmanship are examples of elements of the affective domain.
5. *Evaluation* — A procedure to ascertain how competent a person may be. Evaluation may be based on one or a number of factors tested in a variety of ways.
6. *Validity* — Means truthfulness. In evaluation procedures, the question is asked, "Does the test measure what it is supposed to measure?"
7. *Reliability* — Means consistency. In evaluation procedures, the question is asked, "Does the test yield the same results (when given under similar conditions) each time it is administered?"
8. *Vocational interest inventory* — A test (usually written) in which a person indicates what types of things (jobs, leisure activities, hobbies) he or she would like to do. These answers are then matched against possible vocational choices.
9. *Motor skills test* — A test designed to measure the psychomotor skill ability of a person in a particular sport. It may be a screening test, or it may include every single element of the activity.
10. *Test items* — Parts of a test. For example, a serving test might be one item of a volleyball skills test.
11. *Objective evaluation* — The process of precisely determining the capacity, distance, speed, etc., of a student in a particular test item with some type of measuring device. Timing the 100-yd. dash with a stop watch and counting the number of correct answers on a true-false knowledge test are examples of objective measurements.
12. *Subjective evaluation* — The process of judging the skill of a person in particular test item or entire activity. Watching a person run 100 yds. and classifying that person as efficient or competent in running ability would be a subjective judgment.

13. *Raw scores* — The actual (or first) result obtained in scoring a test. For example, when a student successfully makes 6 out of 10 free throws, the raw score would be 6. A score of 78 on a written test would be a raw score.

DESIRABLE ATTRIBUTES OF A PHYSICAL EDUCATOR

It would be easy to list desirable adjectives (trustworthy, loyal, etc.) as necessary attributes of a good physical educator, but the same general list would apply to almost every role in life. However, there are at least six specific attributes that physical educators should possess. These are described below, and then summarized in Table 3-1.

1. A most important attribute is *interest* in physical education as a career. All prospective majors say that they have a great interest in the field. Sometimes this interest is based on hero-worship of the high school physical educator or coach. Or the reason "I like to work with children" is given, without the speaker realizing that there are dozens of possible careers that involve working with children. You will be given a chance to evaluate your interest in physical education in at least three ways:
   a. Taking, and having proper interpretation of, a *vocational interest inventory*. No doubt sometime in the past several years you have taken one of the many inventories that are available. However, if you haven't had such a test in the past year, it might be wise for you or your instructor to make arrangements with the counseling center of your school to do so as a part of your introduction to physical education. Remember that while these tests possess validity and reliability, they are not absolute indicators. But honest answers on your part will tell you where you are right now, and this is the first step in a meaningful self-evaluation.
   b. Reading and submitting reports on *articles* related to various chapters of this text. At the end of each chapter, you will find a list of references which pertain closely to that topic. Perhaps your instructor will assign a certain number to read. Even if he or she does not, you can make a reasonably accurate subjective judgment of your interest in physical education by doing some reading in this area. If these readings seem like busywork, or are tasks put off until the last minute, your interest may not be as high as that of an enthusiastic, eager learner. (A simpler test is to see if you can read just one article in a periodical without finding two or three others of equal interest!)
   c. Participating and reporting on a physical education field experience (school classes, Little League coaching, working for the government) which has great attraction for you. Chapters 11, 12, and 13 mention several possible vocations related to physical education, many of which are not teaching. Your instructor might ask you to actually gain experience in working with people in a situation of your choosing. This should be an assignment that is both interesting and meaningful if your interest in physical education is as high as it should be.
2. The attribute of *biological development* is important for a physical education major. Chapter 6 discusses this as one of the concepts of American physical education, and then presents the details of the AAHPER Youth Fitness Test. Should you take the test, you can compare your scores with other potential physical educators.
3. *Motor skill development* is what most students think physical education is all about. How well you can perform the many activities which are a part of our program should be known as you begin your education, and may be evaluated

by psychomotor skills tests. These tests are composed of skills which are part of the activity (in football, passing for accuracy or punting for distance). Most serve as objective screening tests, although some are subjectively judged by an expert. Chapter 7 explains the rationale behind these motor skill tests and gives details for many. By using your raw scores, you can compare yourself with other prospective physical education students. It may not be possible for your school to give all the tests, but the directions are complete enough for you to perform most of the items on an informal basis by yourself or with one or two other interested majors.

4. *Knowledge* certainly is desired of prospective majors. This implies more than knowing the rules of basketball. There is a national knowledge test in physical education, based upon the physiological, psychological, sociological, and mechanical principles of movement. These principles are taught in a good school physical education program. Scales are available which will permit you to compare your score with such groups as 12th graders, undergraduate physical education majors, and graduates in physical education. Chapter 9 will describe the test more fully.

5. *Personality* is a key attribute in the success of any of us. Counseling centers have the trained personnel to administer and interpret any of the several available personality tests. Unfortunately, the validity of such tests is open to question, and you should view the results of the tests as guides, rather than as absolute indicators. In Chapter 11, scores are shown for majors in some of the tests; if possible, your instructor will permit you to make comparisons. If it is inappropriate for you to do this as part of a class, then perhaps you can make an individual appointment with your school's counseling center for such an appraisal.

6. Finally, your *attitude* toward physical education as a career can be shown by the action you take after reading this text, especially Chapter 16. This last chapter asks you to make a decision. Will you decide to major in physical education? If so, this means joining professional groups, beginning to build your professional library, and participating in out-of-school professional activities. Perhaps your decision will be to minor in our discipline or pursue the coaching certificate. Actions which should be started now to better prepare yourself are outlined. Of course, the decision could be to seek your career elsewhere.

TABLE 3–1. ATTRIBUTES AND EVALUATIVE DEVICES DESCRIBED IN THIS TEXT.

ATTRIBUTES TO BE EVALUATED	EDUCATIONAL DOMAIN	EVALUATIVE DEVICES	WHERE DESCRIBED IN TEXT
1. Interest	Affective	1.a. Vocational interest inventory	1.a. Chapter 3
		b. Read articles	b. Chapters 6-15
		c. PE field experience	c. Chapters 11, 12, 13
2. Biological Development	Psychomotor	2. Youth Fitness Test	2. Chapter 6
3. Motor skill development	Psychomotor	3. Skills tests	3. Chapter 7
4. Knowledge	Cognitive	4. Knowledge test	4. Chapter 9
5. Personality	Affective	5. Personality tests	5. Chapter 11
6. Attitude	Affective	6. Essay	6. Chapter 16

PROFESSIONAL PUBLICATIONS

There are several publications devoted exclusively to matters of concern to physical educators, and others which publish articles of general interest. Most of these periodicals are the sources you will study if your college or university has a good academic physical education program.

TABLE 3–2. USEFUL PERIODICALS FOR PHYSICAL EDUCATORS.

MAJOR THEME	TITLE OF PERIODICAL	COMMENTS
Scholarly	*Quest.*	Most unusual publication in our field. First, it is jointly published by two separate groups (National Association for Physical Education of College Women, and National College Physical Education Association for Men). Secondly, it is intended to whet the intellectual appetite — that is, to present ideas and thoughts that cause the reader to think about the basic questions confronting physical education.
Scientific	*Journal of Physiology. Journal of Applied Physiology.*	Published by groups other than physical educators. Deal with exercise physiology topics.
	Journal of Sports Medicine and Physical Fitness.	A project of the American College of Sports Medicine. The group is of recent origin in the U.S., although sports medicine has long been regarded as an important part of European medical and physical education groups. The *Journal* is not written for the beginning physical educator, but perusal of even one issue will indicate how the physician, physiologist, and the physical educator should work as a team.
	Journal of Motor Behavior. Journal of Motor Learning. Perceptual and Motor Skills. Journal of Applied Psychology.	Published by groups other than physical educators, but contain articles basic to the understanding of motor learning.
	International Review of Sport Sociology. American Journal of Sociology.	The *International Review* is published by persons interested in sport and society. Both contain material of a sociological nature basic to our discipline.
	Research Quarterly.	This is a quarterly journal published by AAHPER for the express purpose of presenting research reports in HPER. In fact, most of the articles are in the physical education discipline, with considerably less in health and recreation. The majority of the articles are the reports of theses and dissertations done by graduate students, but the percentage of articles written by those who are considered research workers is constantly rising. (Continued on p. 20)

TABLE 3–2 CONT.

MAJOR THEME	TITLE OF PERIODICAL	COMMENTS
Scientific (cont.)	*Research Quarterly (cont.)*	Articles on physical fitness, exercise programs, and teaching methods were quite common until the late 1960s, but research studies related to motor learning, sociology of sport, psychology, etc. are just now appearing. As a beginning student, you will not find the *Research Quarterly* easy reading; the comprehension of statistical terms is difficult at this point. Nevertheless, careful reading of the abstracts which appear with each article will familiarize you with the general outline of the report and its conclusions.
Professional	*Journal of Physical Education and Recreation. (JOPER)*	This is a monthly (9 publications per year) of AAHPER. Each issue contains articles pertaining to the special interests of HPER and teaching problems, coaching situations, and new developments in school and community programs. Advertisements of new products and books are a part of each issue. Student membership in AAHPER includes a subscription to *JOPER*.
	The Physical Educator.	A quarterly publication of the men's professional physical education fraternity, Phi Epsilon Kappa, sent to all PEK members. Articles are mostly related to teaching or philosophical problems in physical education, although health and recreation are not excluded. The style of writing and content generally appeal to students, and many students report that this is their best source for practical teaching tips.
	The Foil.	Published quarterly by the women's professional sorority, Delta Psi Kappa. This journal is essentially similar in style and content to *The Physical Educator.*
	Update.	This is a special newspaper published by AAHPER nine times per year. It contains mostly news about meetings and reports to members, and is sent to all AAHPER members.
Technical	*Athletic Journal. Coach and Athlete. Scholastic Coach. Mentor. Dance Magazine.*	These are published by private companies. They contain "how to do it" articles in dance and in coaching.
General interest	*Sport. Sporting News. Sports Illustrated. WomenSports. Sportswoman.*	Published by private companies. Contain an excellent sampling of how sport (in all aspects) is an influence in American life.

Bibliography

Owen, R. C. A record of physical education majors' participation in co-curricular and extra-curricular activities. *The Physical Educator* 28 (Mar. 1971):27.

Turner, E. R., and Williams, H. P. Library vandalism and the physical education villains. *JOHPER* 44 (Feb. 1973):39.

Student Activities

1. Investigate your school library to see which of the periodicals mentioned in this chapter are available. (Actually find them on the shelves, not just their listing in the card catalog.)
2. Investigate your school library to see how each of these sources is useful to physical educators:
   a. *Reader's Guide to Periodical Literature*
   b. Education index
   c. ERIC (Educational Resources Information Center)
   d. Microcards in HPER (now called Microform Publications in HPER)
3. Investigate your school library to see what other periodicals, besides the ones listed in the chapter, are available in these disciplines:
   a. physiology
   b. psychology
   c. sociology
   d. anthropology
   e. history

Statements for Class Discussion

1. The most important attribute of a beginning physical education major is _____ .
2. The most important attribute of a professional physical educator is _____ .
3. If physical education and athletics really improved a person's character (i.e., honesty, sportsmanship) there would be very little library vandalism.

CONCEPTS

CHAPTER **4**

A BRIEF HISTORY OF
AMERICAN PHYSICAL EDUCATION

INTRODUCTION

Several books have been written about the history of American physical education. This short chapter will summarize the highlights of five eras, in the hope that you will gain insight into the historical background of modern physical education. You will discover that history has a way of repeating itself. For example, the 1960 emphasis on physical fitness was but another swing of the same pendulum. The current emphasis on movement education is an outgrowth of the natural program advocated in the early 1900s. The participation by females in athletic competition in 1976 has its genesis long before Title IX. Knowledge of the past can help in understanding the present and forecasting the future.

In April, 1960, *JOHPER* featured an article called "This Is Our Heritage." The basic format of this article is adapted for presentation here. You may wish to read this article in its entirety.

Historical material as presented in this chapter probably seems related only to the cognitive domain — that is, it provides facts and dates by which you gain knowledge. Actually, we hope that the affective domain is also dealt with, because an appreciation of history provides much help in shaping your views and philosophy. Historical facts must be synthesized into current knowledge and situations. Only then can the best possible decisions be made.

CONCEPTS TO BE GAINED FROM THIS CHAPTER

When you have mastered the material in this chapter, you will be able to demonstrate comprehension of these concepts:

1. Play, games, dance and sport (collectively called physical education) have been a part of American life since 1620.
2. To remain essential to American education, physical education has had to change with the times. This includes changes in:
   a. the objectives of the program
   b. the activities taught, supervised, and coached
   c. the professional preparation of physical education teachers
   d. the role of athletics in the schools
   e. emphasis on physical fitness, both school age and adult
   f. participation by girls and women in athletics

RECREATION, GYMNASTICS, AND CALISTHENICS (1620-1865)

The beginnings of physical education in the United States were very modest and informal. While various European nations (especially Germany, Sweden, and Denmark) had evolved specific programs geared to their needs, no one system of physical education came to this country with the colonists. In early colonial days, New England was the only section of the country without games; this is usually attributed to the strict Puritan beliefs. The Dutch (in New York) and the English (in Virginia) certainly did not frown on recreational activities of a physical nature, although there was no organized movement as such. Because the aim of education was popularly considered the "3 R's," the few schools which were established provided no place for physical education or recreation. The first record of any school encouraging sports for recreation's sake was Samuel Moody's Summer School in Massachusetts.

When the academies began to appear in the Eastern seaboard states, scholastic physical education appeared. The founders of these institutions believed that good health was a prerequisite for a good life, that a person should be able to participate in sports, and that shorter school hours provided ample time for sports. These reasons, along with the influence of prominent European leaders who favored a planned physical education program in schools, led to the inclusion of physical activities in the daily life of students. Because physical education came after school, these private institutions did not attempt to control this activity; instead, it was left to the students.

It can truthfully be said that immigrants and immigration were responsible for the ultimate inauguration of physical education in the public schools. When the Round Hill School in Massachusetts was established in 1825, the founders believed so strongly in physical training that they hired a German gymnastics instructor named Beck to supervise the students in this activity. Beck was the forerunner of the early foreign instructors, who worked primarily in the Northeast. However, the main impetus in the field of physical education was a result of the great immigration of Germans to this country. Because they spoke little or no English, they tended to live together in cities and to establish their own societies. The most prominent of these societies was the United Turnverein of North America. Although this movement had three aims (intellectual enlightenment, sociability, and physical development) the latter seemed to be most important. Prior to the Civil War, membership in this organization numbered 10,000 and a training school for leaders was established. (There are "Turner" groups active in certain cities and towns of the United States today. In most cases, they are noted for their outstanding gymnastic programs.)

It has been mentioned earlier that some schools in the East had "tolerated" recreational sports as an after-school activity. A growing belief in the value of physical activity led to the passage of a law in Boston in 1853 that all children in elementary school must have a daily period of physical exercise. Because teachers were not trained to lead the activity, this rule was not enforced. In 1855 the city of St. Louis reported that some physical education was taking place in its schools. Because gymnastics was a regular part of the curriculum in many European countries, it was only natural that the immigrants to the United States brought pressure upon local school boards to include it in the school curriculum.

During the Civil War (as has happened during subsequent periods of war in the United States) the physical weakness of American youth was cited as a main reason for physical education's inclusion in the school curriculum of every city and town. While this argument was primarily directed to boys, other persons were advocating increased physical training for women. Dio Lewis argued that German gymnastics discriminated against age and sex, and that only his system (as taught in his Normal Institute for Physical Education in Boston) would properly develop both boys and girls. While he was unpopular with fellow workers in the field, it must be noted that he was the motivating force behind the adoption of physical education in school curricula during the period 1860-1865.

Through the years, many outstanding women leaders in the field have made significant contributions. The forerunner was Catherine Beecher who, as early as 1828, advocated physical education for women. She founded two private girls' schools, and is considered to be the first native American to formulate a comprehensive gymnastic system adapted to American needs. The inauguration of any particular movement cannot be credited to her, but she is to be remembered as the earliest proponent and crusader of physical education for women in the United States.

GYMNASTICS AND MEASUREMENT (1865-1900)

This period in American life can generally be termed one of "education for nationalism." The heavy immigration, the westward movement, the growth of centralized government, and the industrial development of the country all combined to ensure that life would not remain static. Education underwent profound changes — widespead free schooling, the thought of compulsory education, tax-supported high schools, expanded curriculum in natural and social sciences, child labor laws, and the idea of social education as a proper aspect of the curriculum. The aims of education included the broadening of the scope of training, the inculcation of social ideals, and an emphasis on vocational subjects in high school.

Physical education had definite aims during this era, as listed by Sargent (1906, pp. 66-71).

1. Hygenic: the consideration of the normal proportions of the individual, the anatomy and the physiological functions of various organs, and a study of the ordinary agents of health such as exercise, diet, sleep, air, bathing, and clothing.
2. Educative: the cultivation of special powers of mind and body used in the acquisition of some skillful trade or physical accomplishment, such as golf, swimming, or skating.
3. Recreative: the renovation of vital energies to enable the individual to return to his daily work with vigor and accomplish his tasks with ease.
4. Remedial: the restoration of disturbed functions and the correction of physical defects and deformities.

After the Civil War, battle of a different sort (but of almost equal vigor) developed among professional workers. This was over the relative merits of the Swedish gymnastic system versus the German system. "The Swedish system was supposed to have a scientific basis in studies of human anatomy, whereas the German gymnastics had been a more spontaneous movement" (Nixon and Cozens 1947, p. 31). Actual debates were held, with neither side conceding. School administrators were caught in the middle of this issue, since their physical education specialists were usually trained in only one system. Eventually, it became common to see apparatus of both systems in school gymnasiums — German horses, bucks, parallel and horizontal bars, and the Swedish stall bars, booms, climbing ladders, poles, and balance boards.

While the argument between advocates of the German and Swedish systems raged, other issues were being considered. During the Civil War, military training had almost exclusively replaced physical education in colleges and universities. This influence spread to high schools and was continued in some cases long after the war.

In 1889 a physical training conference was held in Boston which was to have great influence upon the program of physical education for many years. Unfortunately some of this influence is felt even today. At this meeting, the educators in attendance proposed a number of conditions which were to be met by a physical education program if it was to be incorporated as a part of the regular school curriculum. In effect, they said that such a program must require very little time, must be inexpensive, must not demand specially trained teachers, must conduct its activity in the classroom (because activity carried on outside the classroom could not be educative), and must not require apparatus. This was accepted by physical educators at that time, and while we no longer believe that education occurs only in the classroom, the idea of "10 minutes per day of calisthenics taught by the classroom teacher (grades K-6)" still hinders an effective program in some localities.

A very important development for later physical education occurred during this period, and may be termed "tests and measurements." While the specific techniques may no longer be used, the concept that scientific tools and procedures should be employed in physical education remains. Anthropometric measurements and strength testing were vigorously supported by such pioneers as Hitchcock and Sargent; these were "mainly for anatomical and physiological science and to allow the student by annual comparisons to see what his development might be"(Van Dalen 1953, p. 416). The period from 1885 to 1900 was the "golden age" of anthropometric measurements, with thousands of students from elementary level through college being measured.

The relationship of athletics and physical education began to be discussed. During the period now under consideration, there was no relationship between these two areas, either at the college or high school level. Athletics were after school and semiorganized. The prevailing attitude toward athletics in public schools was that they were unnecessary, since all the children had chores to do which consumed their excess energy.

A great influence on the curriculum in physical education was the preparation of teachers in this field. Earlier mention has been made of Dio Lewis' school in Boston and the Normal School of the Turnverein movement. Several private schools were founded in this period, the most notable being Sargent's school in Cambridge, Anderson's school in New Haven, the YMCA in Springfield, Massachusetts, and the Boston Normal School of Gymnastics. All of these schools had different training procedures and curricula. Eventually, the students seemed to develop an appreciation for other schools and systems. Thus by 1900 the bitterness which marked earlier years had largely disappeared.

Another development which was to greatly influence curricula in later years was the organization of various professional groups. In 1885 the forerunner of the American Alliance for Health, Physical Education and Recreation was formed. This group is now regarded as the national voice for all physical educators.

State legislation making physical education compulsory was initiated in 1892 in Ohio. California had such a law in 1886, but it does not seem to have been enforced.

Facts regarding the date of the exact passage of such legislation in the older states are not consistent among several sources; it is known, however, that Ohio, California, North Dakota, Wisconsin, and Idaho were among the earliest states to pass compulsory physical education laws. The forces behind these laws included interest groups in the various states: the Turnverein, the Women's Christian Temperance Union (WCTU), and various professional teacher organizations.

Although the number of professionally trained workers in physical education was small during this era, at least four stand out as true pioneers. Dr. Edward Hitchcock of Amherst College conducted the only organized college program of physical education up to 1865. All students took his classes, which were aimed at hygienic and recreational purposes. He was a medical doctor, and was the first physical educator to be appointed as a full faculty member in an American college. His main interest was anthropometry. Dr. Dudley Sargent, another medical doctor, established what was termed the "Sargent System" of physical education. This was actually a combination of Swedish and German gymnastics, plus sports, athletics, and measurement. His two distinctive contributions were in the field of teacher training and in the invention of numerous exercise devices which the user could adapt to his own strength. W. G. Anderson, M.D., was the instigator of the American Alliance for Health, Physical Education and Recreation, and was very influential in teacher preparation. Amy Morris Homans was originally drawn into teacher training because of a strong conviction of the need for trained women teachers. She became head of the physical education department at Wellesley College and exerted a strong influence on teacher training for many years.

ATHLETICS, DANCING AND TESTING (1900-1930)

This three-decade period saw the United States enter a world war, rise to unprecedented economic heights, and then plunge into a great depression. The physical education movement was vitally affected by each of these major developments. It was also affected by the scientific, developmental, and social education movements which began to assume prominence. The social education movement was the most influential, promulgating the idea that the school should be a miniature society with a flexible curriculum.

Physical education was gradually moving away from the foreign systems of gymnastics toward what was called the "New Physical Education." Hetherington (1910) defined the four phases of the educational processes for the new physical education as follows:

1. Organic education — a process to develop vigor. This refers to nutrition and elimination as well as physical development.
2. Psycho-motor education — the process that develops power and skill in neuromuscular activities.
3. Character education — the development of moral, social, and spiritual powers.
4. Intellectual education — the child learns by doing, especially through play.

The profession faced increased challenges from several directions. With the new century came a determined effort to bring athletics and dancing into the physical education curriculum as an acknowledged part of education, not as merely something for school children to organize and conduct for themselves after school hours. This presented a challenge to the gymnastics devotees to protect their heretofore unquestioned monopoly of the program. The "battle of the systems" now gave way to a new conflict of gymnastics versus dancing and athletics (Lee and Bennett 1960, p. 39).

The athletic movement (and the playground movement which was to come very shortly) were indications that professional workers were revolting against formalism in educational training. Because the athletic movement (and the recreation movement also) were fostered to capture the immediate interests of youth, it is small wonder that gymnastics began to lose favor. The games that were being played after school began to be taught as a part of the regular physical education program. While on the surface the new program appeared to be an improvement over the formal gymnastic system, the fact was that the pendulum started to swing too far, and professional workers began to divide into camps again. Williams (1949, p. 177) reported on the state of confusion by saying:

> Thus, for more than three decades after 1889, examples of the two types of physical education in the school could be found; one, composed of artificial exercises, arose in response to a group of ideas wholly foreign to the traits, characteristics, and needs of American boys and girls, and which were justified by those who proposed them on the grounds of correction of defects, acquirement of health, or promotion of discipline. . . . The other was represented by the extreme development of competitive athletics which arose as a natural activity of youth, stimulated by the commercial and advertising values of games, and without the educational leadership which such an activity should attract.

The entry of the United States into World War I meant that the usual wartime programs of fitness replaced the traditional program. While this was advantageous in that it permitted a change to a new program after the war, it certainly did not help professional workers conduct the most efficacious program for all concerned.

Measurement in physical education, as we understand it today, dates from 1920. Strength testing declined during this era, while athletic achievement tests, classification tests, cardiovascular tests, motor ability tests, and character-rating tests all began their development from crude methods to refined tools useful to the profession. This phase was handicapped by the lack of sufficiently trained personnel.

The leaders of this period — Luther Gulick, James McCurdy, Thomas Wood, and Clark Hetherington — are neatly divided into two groups. Gulick and McCurdy were both associated with the YMCA college at Springfield, Massachusetts, and were the links between the "gymnastics" past and the "New Physical Education" future. They were scholars as well as teachers and served as the acknowledged leaders of the profession during this time. Wood and Hetherington were philosophers, in the sense that they visualized a purpose for physical education above the common "perspiration and muscle building" concept that prevailed. Wood began his opposition to all foreign gymnastics systems around the turn of the century, while Hetherington's influence began in 1913.

REORIENTATION AND FITNESS (1930-1960)

The continuing years of the depression brought about an increased unwillingness to include physical education in the curriculum of the public schools. Fortunately, because of the tremendous support given by AAHPER, physical education remained very much a part of the school curriculum. This support took the form of the publication of a pamphlet which was distributed by the thousands, distribution of more than 20,000 copies of the April, 1933, issue of *JOHPER* to school personnel, and the formation of a national publicity committee.

During the years 1930-41, physical education continued to change more in theory than in actual practice. Although there was less extreme emphasis upon gymnastics, the general economic situation prevented schools from securing additional equipment or facilities to keep up with the latest philosophical thinking. An oversupply of physical education teachers enabled schools to select better personnel. The fact that many states sharply upgraded educational requirements for teachers meant that those imbued with current philosophies of physical education were usually selected as replacements for traditionally trained teachers. Van Dalen (1953, p. 472) reported that in 1930 few states required more than one year of training for physical educators; by 1940 all but a few required two to four years of work.

The aims of physical education continued to be modified during this era. The thoughts of Wood and Hetherington were adapted by Williams and Nash, both of whom went beyond the old concept of gymnastics for the development of strength and vigor. A new aim, preparation for leisure time, was advocated and readily accepted, especially since the economic hardships made enforced leisure time available for many. The value of active participation in athletics (for boys) was stressed, but not for the moral qualities, as before; the thought was that the adjustment students had to make to social situations was even more important. Athletic participation for girls and women was advocated by very few citizens and even fewer women physical educators. In fact, Mrs. Herbert Hoover's assertion that athletic competition was unladylike was so influential that female athletes had less opportunities than before. During World War II physical fitness was stressed, but this was the first wartime period where there was no large substitution of military training for physical education.

Physical education in this era may be summarized by the following statement:
Physical education is a way of education through physical activities which are selected and carried on with full regard to values in human growth, development, and behavior. Because it is a phase of the total educational program, physical education aims for the same general goal that gives purpose to all the other learning experiences of the school — the well rounded development of all children and youth as responsible citizens in our democratic society (Streit and McNeely 1950, p. 136).

The scope of the physical education curriculum broadened considerably during this era. Calisthenics, rhythmic movements, apparatus, tumbling, athletic contests, team games, swimming, lifesaving, mass games, dance, tennis, golf, handball, and others were all properly included in the program. Because the emphasis had shifted from the word *physical* to the word *education*, any activity which properly provided for this could be included. Most high schools had a wide variety; it was common to find 15 different activities offered to students during their high school years. However, a great many school systems continued the emphasis on boys' sports at the expense of offering a variety of activities. By state law, schools had to have physical education classes, but many times these were free play sessions.

A report on the low physical fitness level of American children, published in 1953, signalled the beginning of a return to one of the original aims of physical education. Although usually not considered a valid fitness test by most experts, the Kraus-Weber Test was the impetus for President Eisenhower's creation of the President's Council of Youth Fitness. Ironically, AAHPER was not invited to attend — participants were national sports figures and physicians. Eventually AAHPER was asked to devise a national fitness test, which was done in 1957.

To recount the influences of all the prominent persons in physical education for this period of time would be a monumental task. J. F. Williams and J. B. Nash have been mentioned in earlier passages as proponents of different aims of physical education. Both of these men were true leaders of this period, and Williams especially was responsible for the greatly increased emphasis on social and carryover values. Today, the writings of C. H. McCloy and Delbert Oberteuffer are studied with interest in the area of philosophy and objectives of physical education. In examining the development of intramurals, Elmer D. Mitchell stands supreme. The field of scientific measurement finds Van Dalen (1953, p.473) listing no less than 23 "capable research workers."

McCloy is generally regarded as their leader during the period under discussion; T. K. Cureton and Peter Karpovich are also noteworthy in the area of research and are probably next in rank.

LIFETIME SPORTS, FITNESS AND AN ACADEMIC DISCIPLINE (1960-1977)

Continuing the emphasis upon fitness, President Kennedy changed the name and aim of Eisenhower's council to the President's Council on Physical Fitness. Millions of Americans of all ages were tested with the Youth Fitness Test, and thousands earned one of the various awards offered by the council. This test was given to both American and foreign students; comparisons on this basis were usually unflattering to Americans! Schools with outstanding fitness programs were recognized. LaSierra High School (Carmichael, California) achieved national prominence with its establishment of rigorous standards[1] for the white, red, blue, gold, and purple fitness levels. Fitness also became more evident in girls' programs, but to a lesser extent than in boys' programs. Several adult physical fitness programs achieved popularity, beginning with the Canadian Air Force 5BX Program, and continuing with jogging, aerobics, and cycling. Much advertising time and space was donated to the fitness cause.

The Lifetime Sports Foundation became operative in the mid-1960s. This group was composed of sporting goods companies and sporting groups (e.g., National Bowling Proprietors Association). They each contributed money both to print materials which would help teachers do a better job in training people in certain lifetime sports (bowling, golf, archery, tennis), and to conduct workshops in which teachers could actually participate in a training program conducted by a master teacher.

Athletics was attacked and supported with equal vigor by many groups. The taxpayers' reluctance to support school bond issues caused some school boards to curtail or suspend athletic competition. Certain national authorities (including prominent physical educators) called for a "new" athletic program which would do away with what they considered overemphasis on a few major sports. On the other hand, the demand for coaches grew so great that special coaching certificates were offered by many colleges. There was an increase in the number of junior varsity teams sponsored by schools in a wider variety of sports (such as gymnastics, ice hockey, bowling, and skiing) so that more students might become participants.

The increase in sport teams in the 1970s was unique in one respect. Athletic opportunities for girls and women doubled and tripled in many schools. Before this time women physical educators had advocated "play days" rather than interschool competition. The "new" physical educators felt that athletics could be as beneficial to girls as to boys, so they began to request "equality of opportunity." They were greatly aided by the government's passage of the Higher Education Act. Title IX of this document (effective July, 1975) gave legal impetus to the struggle, and it is safe to say that there will be equal opportunities for males and females in the foreseeable future.

The boom in athletics also extended downward. Little League baseball, Pop Warner football, Biddy Basketball, and age-group track and swimming are examples of flourishing sports programs for both boys and girls.

Up to this point, the historical facts mentioned have all related to the practical application of physical education to the well-being of society. The early emphasis on health as a goal, then games, athletics and dancing, then leisure activities, then back to fitness — all of these are professional in nature. Up until 1964, little attention was given

---

[1]Example (boys): three trips up and down on vertical pegboard, 20 pull-ups, 62 push-ups, 26 bar-dips, 2 arm hang for 3½ minutes, carry person of own weight for 1½ miles.

to the relationship of physical education to other disciplines. It was at this time that physical educators began to initiate the research and reflective thinking that characterize an academic discipline.

The American College of Sports Medicine, patterned after similar well-established European groups, attempted to motivate physicians, health educators, and physical educators into becoming much more aware of the mutual role of medicine and the health sciences. Similarly, groups of sport psychologists and sports sociologists were formed. All of these movements served to focus attention on physical education as an academic discipline as well as a profession.

Bibliography

Allen, S. History's greatest athlete. *Sportswoman* 1 (Spring 1973):12.

Bennett, B. L. Curious relationship of religion and physical education. *JOHPER* 40 (Sept. 1970):69.

Betts, J. R. Home front, battlefield and sport during the Civil War. *Research Quarterly* 42 (May 1971):113.

Boyle, R. H. The report that shocked the president. *Sports Illustrated* 3 (Aug. 15, 1955):38.

_____. The bizarre history of American sports. *Sports Illustrated* 16 (Jan. 8, 1962):54-62.

Cady, S. Bibliography on the Negro in sports. *JOHPER* 42 (Feb. 1971):70.

Cantwell, R. America is formed for happiness. *Sports Illustrated* 43 (Dec. 29, 1975):54-71.

Coursly, L. N. Anita J. Turner — Early black female physical educator. *JOHPER* 45 (Mar. 1974):71-72.

Gerber, E. W. Early professional preparation curriculum in the United States. *The Physical Educator* 29 (Mar. 1972):38.

Hetherington, C. Fundamental education. *National Education Association Proceedings and Addresses* (1910):350-77.

Kroll, W., and Lewis, G. The first academic degree in physical education. *JOHPER* 40 (June 1969):73-74.

Langston, D. Sports on stamps. *JOHPER* 39 (May 1968):38-39.

Lee, M., and Bennett, B. This is our heritage. *JOHPER* 31 (Apr. 1960):25-85.

Lee, M., and Hackensmith, C. W. Notable events in 150 years of physical education. *JOHPER* 42 (Nov.-Dec. 1971):79. (See also later *JOHPER* issues for other such articles.)

Lewis, G. M. The muscular Christianity movement. *JOHPER* 37 (May 1966):27.

_____. John Richards Betts and the beginning of a new age in sports history. *JOHPER* 43 (Mar. 1972):81.

Little, J. R. Charles Harold McCloy: Ten years hence. *The Physical Educator* 27 (May 1970):57.

Lucas, J. A. Thomas Wentworth Higginson: Early apostle of health and fitness. *JOHPER* 42 (Feb. 1971):30.

Lynde, R. E., and Taylor, S. J. Literature of physical conflict. *The Physical Educator* 28 (Oct. 1971):143.

Mealy, R. The "battle of the systems." *The Physical Educator* 29 (May 1972):66-69.

Means, L. E. A report on Operation Fitness — U.S.A. *JOHPER* 31 (Nov. 1960):71.

Nixon, E. W., and Cozens, F. W. 1947. *An introduction to physical education.* Philadelphia: W. B. Saunders Co.

Park, R. J. The philosophy of John Dewey and physical education. *The Physical Educator* 26 (Mar. 1969):55.

_____. Joseph Neef and William Maclure: Early pioneers in American physical education. *The Physical Educator* 31 (Mar. 1974):23-26.

Parker, F. Sport, play and physical education in cultural perspective. *JOHPER* 41 (Jan. 1970): 29-30.

Patterson, P. Physical education in early Minnesota schools. *JOHPER* 42 (Feb. 1971):69-70.

Redmond, G. A plethora of shrines: Sport in the Museum and Hall of Fame. *Quest* 19 (Jan. 1973):41-48.

Sargent, D. A. 1906. *Physical education.* Boston: Ginn and Co.

Smith, R. Centennial: Moses Coit Tyler's "The Brawnville papers." *JOHPER* 41 (Mar. 1970):71.

Spears, B. 'Building up character has been my aim': A glimpse of the life of Mary Hemenway. *JOHPER* 42 (Mar. 1971):93.

Streit, W. K. Pioneers of physical education in Cincinnati, Ohio. *JOHPER* 42 (Sept. 1971):69.

_____, and McNeely, S. A. A platform for physical education. *JOHPER* 21 (Mar. 1950):135.

Thaxton, N. A. Tuskegee Institute — Pioneer in women's track and field. *The Physical Educator* 29 (May 1972):77-79.

Twenter, C. J. History speaks, but who listens? *The Physical Educator* 29 (May 1972):89.

Van Dalen, D. B.; Mitchell, E. D.; and Bennett, B. L. 1953. *A world history of physical education*. Englewood Cliffs, N.J.: Prentice Hall.

Vanderzwaag, H. Sports concepts. *JOHPER* 41 (Mar. 1970):35-36.

Wagner, A. A basic concept of physical education. *The Physical Educator* 21 (Dec. 1964):169.

Welch, J. E. The influence of sports on the Amherst plan of physical education. *NCPEAM Proceedings* (1962):124-28.

_____. The impact of Edward Hitchcock on the history of physical education. *The Physical Educator* 24 (May 1967):54-56.

_____. The six Pratt brothers — Laymen extraordinary in the history of physical education. *NCPEAM Proceedings* (1969):80-90.

_____. Edward Hitchcock and the early years of AAHPER. *JOHPER* 44 (Feb. 1973):50-54.

Williams, J. F. 1949. *The principles of physical education*. Philadelphia: W. B. Saunders.

Wilson, C. They had a dream. *The Physical Educator* 26 (Dec. 1969):173.

Zuckerman, J., et al. The black athlete in post bellum nineteenth century. *The Physical Educator* 29 (Oct. 1972):142.

Student Activities

1. Many colleges and universities offer master's and doctor's degrees. One of the requirements for either degree is a research project called a thesis or a dissertation. Look in the library card catalog under "Physical Education — History" for any thesis or dissertation which was done at your school. Read any one.

2. Examine related periodicals (history, sociology, etc.) for articles about early physical education. Read one or more.

3. There are several recent books on physical education history. Determine what is available in your library and read a chapter in any one.

4. If you are taking an English, history, economics, sociology, or political science course and must do a term paper, consider some aspect of physical education as your topic. Some possibilities are: Physical Fitness; Importance of Sport in the U.S.; Spectator Problems in Athletic Events; Fitness Fads (Calisthenics, Jogging, Aerobics, etc.); Charles Atlas: A Physical Educator?; Title IX and It's Implications on Sport; Is Fishing Part of Physical Education?

Statements for Class Discussion

1. The aim of physical education in school is to have fun.

2. There are valid reasons that women's participation in athletics should increase.

3. Some early physical education movements contributed significantly to today's physical education philosophy; others detracted from it.

4. The separate development of physical education and athletics in early times has contributed to today's separation of these two programs in many schools.

CHAPTER **5**

THE FOUNDATIONS OF AMERICAN PHYSICAL EDUCATION

INTRODUCTION

This chapter will outline the reasons we describe physical education as an academic discipline, the relationship of a profession to a discipline, and the body of knowledge that constitutes physical education. This chapter serves as a guide to Chapters 6-10, which discuss in detail each of the five major areas in the body of knowledge physical educators must study.

CONCEPTS TO BE GAINED FROM THIS CHAPTER

When you have mastered the material in this chapter, you will be able to demonstrate comprehension of these concepts:
1. Physical education meets the two accepted criteria of a discipline.
2. After adequate education, physical educators may become scholars, researchers and/or professional educators.
3. Because of specialized and narrow education, some persons become technicians rather than scholars, researchers and/or professional educators. Being paid to teach does not necessarily make one a professional educator.

THE DISCIPLINE OF PHYSICAL EDUCATION

The term physical education is thought by many to be an inaccurate description of our field. *Physical* implies that the mind and the body can be divided, while *education*

33

seems to infer that we are concerned primarily with some branch of teaching. There is no doubt that the public considers us in this light, feeling that physical education is a school subject, that athletics and physical education are synonymous terms, that homework is seldom required to pass our courses, and that playing games is our trademark. We admit that these characteristics are somewhat true, but the description of what we study, investigate, and teach is much broader.

In a very influential article, Henry (1964, p. 7) said that an academic discipline may be characterized by two major criteria:

1. It is an organized body of knowledge collectively embraced in a formal course of study.
2. The acquisition of such knowledge is assumed to be an adequate and worthy objective, without any demonstration or requirement of practical application.

We contend that physical education does meet these two criteria. We say that there are a number of facts, concepts, ideas, and hypotheses that an educated person should know. These are more than merely knowing how to play volleyball, or knowing the rules of ice hockey. They deal with why body development is so important, how learning to move efficiently affects mental learning, and when it is appropriate to build new facilities so that more people can participate. In short, physical education is a formal course of study utilizing the sciences of kinesiology, physiology, psychology, and sociology.

Rarick (1967, pp. 51-52) expands on Henry's comments by illustrating some of the areas which are part of our body of knowledge. He says:

1. Physical education as a discipline is concerned with the mechanics of human movement, with the mode of acquisition and control of movement patterns, and with the psychological factors affecting movement responses.
2. Physical education is concerned with the physiology of man under the stresses of exercise, sports, and dance and with the immediate and lasting effects of physical activity.
3. The historical and cultural aspects of physical education and dance occupy a prominent place in our discipline. The roles of sports and dance in the cultures which have preceded ours and in our own culture need to be fully explored.
4. Lastly, in physical education we are aware that man does not function alone. Individual and group interactions in games, sports, and dance are an important area, one which needs our attention.

Henry and Rarick are among many who support the rationale for a discipline of physical education. In 1965 a conference of distinguished physical educators was held in Chicago, the purpose of which was to consider physical education as an area of study and research. The group indicated that disciplines evolve around a central core of interest, and that for physical education, this central core consisted of study and research of man, with ". . . particular reference to his ability to move, the ways in which he utilizes his ability, and the ways in which his use of this ability is related to other aspects of his functional organization" (Metheny 1967, p. 75). These ideas were grouped into one concept called "movement as a function of man." The conference concluded that certain kinds of movement experiences and behavioral patterns (such as exercise, athletics, dance, gymnastics, sports) were the foundations of what is called physical education. These movements serve to interrelate man and his environment.

As you might expect, not all physical educators would precisely agree on the fundamental position that physical education is a discipline. Ulrich and Nixon (1972, pp. 11-13) maintain that physical education is a subdiscipline related to human movement, and would picture it as shown in Figure 5-1.

FIGURE 5-1. The discipline of human movement phenomena contains at least these nine subdisciplines.

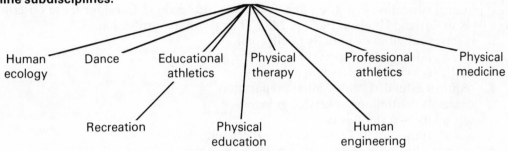

Adapted from C. Ulrich and J. Nixon, *Tones of theory* (Washington, D.C.: AAHPER, 1972), p. 12. Used by permission.

Ulrich and Nixon point out that physical education ". . . focuses on the development of human movement through various pattern processes to help the individual identify his nature, his potential, and his limitations" (Ulrich and Nixon 1972, p. 11). They further indicate that physical education is related to all other subdisciplines mentioned, and shares a part of the focus of each.

Whether we are a discipline or subdiscipline is really not as important as whether or not we "know where we are going." Franklin Henry's article caused wide comment because it came from a person who was noted for scientific and not philosophic writings. Henry said that physical education could draw some substantive content from general courses in those areas such as physiology, psychology, etc. which are basic to our field. But, he said, "This field of study, considered as an academic discipline, does not consist of the *application* of the disciplines of anthropology, physiology, psychology, and the like to the study of physical activity. On the contrary, it has to do with the study, as a discipline, of certain aspects of anatomy, anthropology, physiology, psychology, and other appropriate fields" (Henry 1964, p. 7). He also pointed out that while development of personal skill in motor performance might be a worthy objective, it is not to be confused with the academic field of knowledge.

Regardless of other differences, all physical educators agree that the interaction of man and his movement is our primary area of interest, and that we cannot merely borrow facts, and ideas from existing disciplines. We must support our own discipline through an organized program of study, research, and professional activity.

For years, physical educators have considered themselves professionals, i.e., members of the teaching profession. But professional activity is just one part of our focus. Paddick (1967) indicated that there were three types of activity found in a body of knowledge: 1) scholarly, 2) research, 3) professional. The aim of scholarly activity is to understand the subject matter, while the aim of professional activity is to render a service to others. Scholarly activity works within the subject matter, while professional activity applies knowledge to a particular problem faced by others.

Henry's second criterion indicated that a discipline might not have practical application, and it is with this point that a decided change of opinion has occurred within the ranks of physical educators. This "practical application" test influenced all professional preparation; the feeling was that if it didn't relate to teaching, it was not really appropriate to physical education. Now, many departments are recognizing that physical education majors may do other things than teach. This new development will make the discipline much more respected, needed, and demanding.

IS PHYSICAL EDUCATION A PROFESSION?

If physical education is a discipline, is it also a profession? Consider these criteria, given by Robbins and Hughes (1967, p. 243). They say that a profession:
1. involves activities essentially intellectual
2. commands a body of specialized knowledge
3. exalts service above personal gain
4. requires extended professional preparation
5. demands continuous in-service growth
6. sets up its own standards
7. has a strong, closely knit professional organization
8. affords a life career and permanent membership

It is clear that a profession is somewhat different from a discipline. A discipline exists so persons may study and learn, may examine all the facts and theories in a particular body of knowledge. A profession, while having its foundations in these areas (as indicated in items 1 and 2) exists to apply these knowledges by serving others (item 3). The profession advances in service to others by making sure that its members become more knowledgeable in various ways (items 4-7).

For years, teaching has been considered a profession by most people. Ideally, it does meet the criteria given. Therefore, a properly trained teacher of physical education may be considered to be a professional educator. But since a profession is based on the development of an intellectual body of knowledge, it is obvious that physical education needs different types of workers. Some of us spend our careers investigating and reporting the results of theoretical, idealistic, and scientific inquiry, while others deal with the application of these results as a service to others. To us, the profession of physical education (i.e., teaching) is a specialized part of the discipline of physical education.

DEFINITION OF PHYSICAL EDUCATION

In an earlier chapter, our definition of physical education was given. As you might expect, there are numerous definitions of physical education, each one similar and yet slightly different. Most of the older (i.e., before 1965) definitions indicate that physical education is the guidance of man's physical activity, the goal of which is to develop desirable physical, social, emotional, and intellectual traits. The material presented in this chapter uses this meaning. However, we are attempting to show that guidance of physical activity (e.g., teaching a person how to perform a physical skill) can be best done *after* the various concepts of our discipline have been studied. Our earlier definition still stands: "Physical education is an academic discipline which attempts to investigate the uses and meanings of exercise, games, sports, athletics, aquatics, gymnastics, and dance to understand their effects on and for individuals and groups." In other words, physical education is the study of the many concepts and knowledges which relate to man and his movements. The application of this study may be to teach others how to move more efficiently, but efficient movement is one end result, not the only area of concern.

DISCIPLINE OR PROFESSION — WHAT DIFFERENCE DOES IT MAKE?

You may be discouraged by the seemingly endless discussion of a discipline, a profession, and the repeated definition of physical education. But these are vital matters to you and your future. One of the past problems in our field is that some have said that physical education should be a science; that is, we should devote our energies to discovering new ways to perform a skill, new ways to strengthen muscles, new ways to discover new facts. Others have said we should call our work an art, using what knowledge we have to teach others better ways to move and to perform skills. If physical education is defined as a discipline which studies the uses and meanings of many forms of movement upon both individuals and groups, it logically follows that the nature of physical education involves various kinds of workers — scholars, researchers, and teachers. Thus, some physical educators are primarily scientists (i.e., scholars, researchers) while others are primarily professional educators (i.e., teachers or performers).

DEFINITION OF A PHYSICAL EDUCATOR

Earlier you were given our definition of physical educators: persons who possess breadth and depth of knowledge and skill concerning at least one key concept of vigorous human movement so they can function as scholars, researchers, and/or professional educators. Under this definition, professional dancers or athletes are physical educators. Athletic coaches are physical educators. Teachers of physical education are physical educators. Motor learning professors, who devote their time to laboratory research involving how animals (including humans) learn to perform, are physical educators. To be sure, the majority of physical educators are educators in the sense that they can perform effectively in one or more of the aspects of human movement and that their major effort is devoted to instructing others about human movement. In summary, a physical educator must be extremely knowledgeable about at least one key concept of vigorous movement, but does not necessarily have to be an educator.

THE BODY OF KNOWLEDGE IN PHYSICAL EDUCATION

In 1967 Fraleigh presented a model of the academic subject matter which should compose the discipline of physical education. Because this seems to summarize what was said by the other authorities cited in this chapter, his ideas will be presented in some detail.

According to Fraleigh, physical education is a discipline which "attempts to investigate exercise, games, sports, athletics, aquatics, gymnastics, and dance in order to understand their uses and meanings to and for individuals and groups" (1967, p. 34). The investigation of these various movement forms serves as the central core of our interest. Each of these movement forms relates to five key areas in the body of knowledge. These five areas are: 1) biological development; 2) psychomotor learning; 3) personal expression; 4) applied mechanics; and 5) political, social, and economic influences. In turn, each of the areas can be more fully explained by listing their knowledge and understandings (which he calls the substantive content). Figure 5-2 shows these relationships.

It is now possible to combine the earlier discussion of the three domains which compose the body of knowledge with Fraleigh's five areas in the body of knowledge. Figure 5-3 depicts this relationship.

PREVIEW OF THE NEXT CHAPTERS

The substantive content of physical education will be examined in greater detail in the next five chapters. The concepts will be presented, along with the facts necessary to

FIGURE 5-2. Fraleigh's concepts and substantive content related to the discipline of physical education.

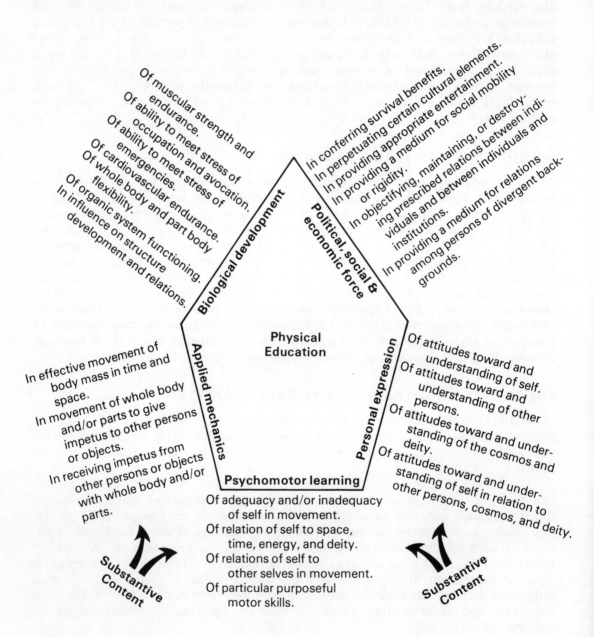

Of muscular strength and endurance.
Of ability to meet stress of occupation and avocation.
Of ability to meet stress of emergencies.
Of cardiovascular endurance.
Of whole body and part body flexibility.
Of organic system functioning.
In influence on structure development and relations.

Biological development

In conferring survival benefits.
In perpetuating certain cultural elements.
In providing appropriate entertainment.
In providing a medium for social mobility or rigidity.
In objectifying, maintaining, or destroying prescribed relations between individuals and between individuals and institutions.
In providing a medium for relations among persons of divergent backgrounds.

Political, social & economic force

Applied mechanics

In effective movement of body mass in time and space.
In movement of whole body and/or parts to give impetus to other persons or objects.
In receiving impetus from other persons or objects with whole body and/or parts.

Physical Education

Personal expression

Of attitudes toward and understanding of self.
Of attitudes toward and understanding of other persons.
Of attitudes toward and understanding of the cosmos and deity.
Of attitudes toward and understanding of self in relation to other persons, cosmos, and deity.

Psychomotor learning

Of adequacy and/or inadequacy of self in movement.
Of relation of self to space, time, energy, and deity.
Of relations of self to other selves in movement.
Of particular purposeful motor skills.

Substantive Content

Substantive Content

Adapted from Warren P. Fraleigh, Toward a conceptual model of the academic subject matter of physical education as a discipline, *NCPEAM Proceedings* (1967):36. Used by permission.

FIGURE 5-3. Body of knowledge in physical education.

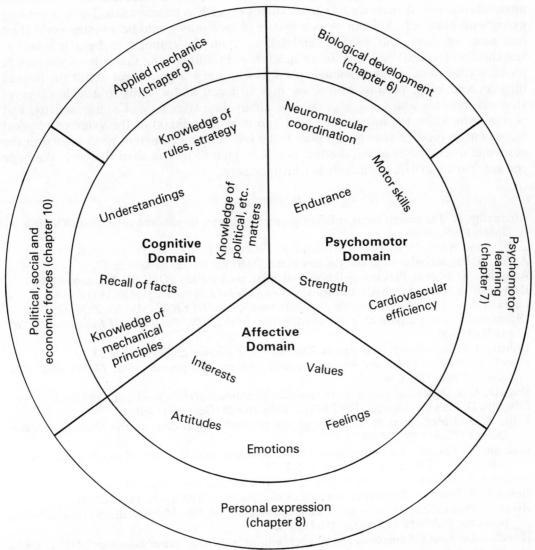

understand the concepts. A description of those courses which are designed to teach these concepts is given. Finally, in most chapters some type of evaluation device is presented. Hopefully, your instructor will find it possible to use them; comparing your results with other prospective physical education majors will enable you and your adviser to more effectively evaluate your present status.

YOUR AIM

What is your aim for this course — and for your career? Hopefully, it is to become a competent professional in the field for which you are best suited. A professional worker is one who knows how to perform a technique (teaching an activity, operating a mechanical device), but is also one who understands the concepts behind a discipline and who can tell *why* things should be done. In short, just because you already teach swimming, or have been a successful team captain or camp counselor, or were a student leader in physical education class in high school, you still are not a professional physical educator. A person who can *do* things expertly is a technician. There is nothing wrong with being a technician — as a matter of fact, ours would be a better world if we had more of them. But you are embarking upon the training to be a scholar/researcher/professional educator in an academic discipline. The majority of workers in physical education are professional: persons who know a great deal about the human intellect and body, persons who know how to teach motor skills to a wide range of students, persons who know a great deal about the psychology of motor activity, and persons who know the importance (and can convince others) of the value of physical movement in modern society. To plan to be less than a competent professional in the academic discipline of physical education is to plan to be less than the best. We hope you are striving to win, not merely to finish the race.

Bibliography

Abernathy, R. The search for significant persistent themes in physical education. *JOHPER* 36 (Mar. 1965):26-28.

———, and Waltz, M. A. Toward a discipline: First steps first. *Quest* 2 (Apr. 1964):1-7.

Angell, G. Physical education and the new breed. *JOHPER* 40 (June 1969):25-27.

Annarino, A. A., et al. Personal philosophy of physical education. *JOHPER* 27 (June 1970):24.

Benveniste, S. A case for physical education. *The Physical Educator* 28 (Mar. 1971):43-45.

Caldwell, S. F. Toward a humanistic physical education. *JOHPER* 43 (May 1972):31-32.

Digennaro, J. The purpose of physical education in the 70's. *The Physical Educator* 28 (Oct. 1971):125-26.

Doherty, J. P. Let's stop playing games. *The Physical Educator* 22 (Mar. 1965):23.

Dowell, L. Physical education: Practice, public opinion, and presumption. *The Physical Educator* 24 (May 1967):79-80.

Duggan, A. S. Dance and sports — An essential dichotomy? *JOHPER* 43 (June 1972):63.

Edwards, D. Let's be — sports. *The Physical Educator* 28 (Dec. 1971):181.

Falls, H., and McKinney, W. A philosophy of research preparation for the physical educator. *Quest* 14 (June 1970):44-49.

Fraleigh, W. Toward a conceptual model of the academic subject matter of physical education as a discipline. *NCPEAM Proceedings* (1967):31-39.

Frederich, J. Our concern as a profession. *The Physical Educator* 23 (Mar. 1966):9-10.

Green, E. R. Dance — An activity or a serious discipline? *JOHPER* 43 (Jan. 1972):91.

Henry, F. Physical education — An academic discipline. *NCPEAM Proceedings* (1964):6-9. Also published in *JOHPER* 35 (Sept. 1964):32-33.

Howell, J. Let's not kid ourselves and physical education. *The Physical Educator* 22 (Dec. 1965):147-48.

Huelster, L. The body of knowledge in physical education. *The Physical Educator* 22 (Mar. 1965):6-8.

Jensen, J. Perspectives unlimited: A new undergraduate physical education major. *JOHPER* 41 (Sept. 1970):83.

Kenricks, L. Rationale for physical education in twentieth century democratic society. *The Physical Educator* 26 (Mar. 1969):36.

Koehler, R. W. Philosophy of physical education and contemporary literature. *The Physical Educator* 27 (Oct. 1970):133.

Kovich, M. Sport as an art form. *JOHPER* 42 (Oct. 1971):42.

Laughlin, N. Physical education — 2000 A.D. *The Physical Educator* 29 (Oct. 1972):115.

Lowe, B. The aesthetics of sport: The statement of a problem. *Quest* 16 (June 1971):5.

Metheny, E., et al. Physical education as an area of study and research. *Quest* 9 (Dec. 1967):73-78.

Morford, W. R. Toward a profession, not a craft. *Quest* 18 (June 1972):88-93.

Nixon, J. E. The criteria of a discipline. *Quest* 9 (Dec. 1967):42-48.

Parker, F. Play and education. *The Physical Educator* 26 (Mar. 1969):3.

Polidoro, J. R. The affective domain: Forgotten objective in physical education. *The Physical Educator* 30 (Oct. 1973):136.

Rarick, G. L. The domain of physical education as a discipline. *Quest* 9 (Dec. 1967):49-52.

Rigan, D. Why physical education? *The Physical Educator* 13 (Mar. 1956):56.

Robbins, R., and Hughes, H. Measurement of the attitudes of teachers toward teaching as a profession. *Journal of Educational Research* 49 (Feb. 1967):243.

Schmidt, C. Education for a humane physically interacting society. *JOHPER* 43 (Jan. 1972):33.

Sheehan, T. Sport: The focal point of physical education. *Quest* 10 (May 1968):59-67.

Shelton, J. W. Physical education in perspective. *The Physical Educator* 28 (May 1971):67-69.

Siedentop, D. On tilting at windmills while Rome burns. *Quest* 18 (May 1972):94-97.

Thomas, J. C. What are the characteristics of a true profession? *The Physical Educator* 26 (Mar. 1969):9.

Ulrich, C., and Nixon, J. 1972. *Tones of theory*. Washington, D.C.: AAHPER.

Vanderzwaag, H. Sport: Existential or essential? *Quest* 12 (May 1969):47-58.

Whited, C. Sport science. *JOHPER* 42 (May 1971):21-25.

Wagner, A. A basic concept of physical education. *The Physical Educator* 21 (Dec. 1964):169-70.

Zeigler, E. F. Vigorous physical education and sport as essential ingredients in America's patterns of physical education. *The Physical Educator* 26 (Mar. 1969):14.

Student Activities

1. Survey a group in your dormitory or home town. Ask their opinions of these questions:
   a. What is physical education?
   b. What should it be?
2. Read at least two articles on one of these topics:
   a. Movement education (or human movement)
   b. Sport science (or sports education)
   c. Fitness: our primary aim

Statements for Class Discussion

1. The public is sometimes confused over the values of physical education; thus, we should not let them tell us what to do, or how to do it.
2. Learning to move (running, jumping, etc.) is more important than learning how to play a game.
3. Regardless of the title given to physical education — subject, profession, academic discipline — you learn how to play and coach sports when you major in it.
4. The better athlete you are, the more logical it is that you major in physical education.
5. The better the technician, the better the teacher.

CONCEPTS

CHAPTER **6**

BIOLOGICAL DEVELOPMENT IN PHYSICAL EDUCATION

INTRODUCTION

In Chapter 5, Fraleigh's model for the body of knowledge in physical education was presented. One of the segments outlined is "biological development." More specifically, Figure 5-2 indicates that physical educators should know a great deal about muscular and cardiovascular strength and endurance, flexibility, functioning of organic systems, the influence of structural development, and meeting various stresses which occur in life.

In the cognitive domain, this chapter presents a definition of biological development, and briefly traces its history as it has waxed and waned in importance through the years. An attempt will be made to convince you of the importance of biological development to individuals and to the discipline of physical education. Finally, you will hopefully be made aware of certain psychomotor skills if you take the Youth Fitness Test and/or a distance run and compare yourself with appropriate peer groups.

CONCEPTS TO BE GAINED FROM THIS CHAPTER

When you have mastered the material in this chapter, you will be able to demonstrate comprehension of these concepts:

1. Biological development was and is an essential segment of the body of knowledge in physical education.
2. Because biological development is based in large part on the physical sciences, it

43

is appropriate that the medical profession was and is closely related to physical education.

3. The President's Council on Physical Fitness and Sports is a unifying force in the effort to promote participation in fitness and sport activities for persons of all ages.
4. Physical fitness is a vague concept which is highly individualized.
5. Physical educators must have knowledge about the structure and function of various body parts.
6. Physical educators must have the attitude that personal fitness is a desirable attribute for themselves, now and throughout life.

DEFINITION OF BIOLOGICAL DEVELOPMENT

By its usual definition, biological development means the process of growth and expansion of a living organism. As used in physical education, the term means the process whereby the human body gains in any or all of such physical aspects as size, strength, coordination, and endurance. Biological development occurs as a result of maturation, nutrition, and exercise. Even ineffective professional physical educators can expect increased biological development in their students. The laws of nature will see to that!

HISTORICAL OUTLINE OF BIOLOGICAL DEVELOPMENT IN PHYSICAL EDUCATION

It is sometimes forgotten that ancient civilizations stressed physical activities in their scheme of education. Early "physical education" taught children to hunt, to fish, and to prepare food. In Grecian times, the sons of noblemen and upper-class citizens spent their early years learning to move gracefully and efficiently (run, jump, throw javelin, swim, etc.). Only after some years of physical training did a person begin to "train" the mind.

During the Middle Ages, the church deliberately tried to subject the physical body to the control of the soul. *Asceticism* meant that the body was deliberately punished through fasting, self-inflicted wounds, and lack of sleep so that the mind might control it. (Some say asceticism is still with us, in the form of overeating to the point of obesity, smoking or drinking to excess, and lack of exercise.) The result was the feeling that the mind and body, while obviously part of the same person, could be separated. The mind and soul became the master of the body, and thus mental training was supreme.

Educators, especially those concerned with younger children, became convinced that biological development could *not* be separated from mental development. Chapter 4 has indicated how physical education was introduced in American schools. The importance of biological development to physical education in the 1800s can be judged by the sometime use of the term "physical culture." *Anthropometry* (measurement of various body segments) was a direct result of considering biological development as a key objective in physical education.

Various terms, such as *organic vigor* and *physical fitness*, were used to describe this objective of physical education. Draft statistics of the U.S. in World War I showed that about one-third of all men were rejected for physical reasons. Even though many of these draft rejections were for reasons not remedied by physical education, the public supported increased school requirements because they were told that physical development would be enhanced.

During the 1930s emphasis was shifted from biological development toward the development of desirable personal-social traits gained through participation in physical activities. In other words, it was said that education should be *through* the physical, not *of* the physical. There was a greater stress on participation as the goal, and not so much on physical development. To some extent, this was caused by the Depression, which forced many people to have more leisure time than they were prepared to cope with. "Carryover activities" (e.g., recreational activities that could be used in later life) were stressed much more than physical development. Even during these years, however, such diverse persons as Charles Atlas (of the "97-lb. weakling" advertisements), Frederick Rand Rogers (Physical Fitness Index), and Charles McCloy (education *of* the physical) stressed the biological objective, each in his own way. (Is it a measure of the low status of professional physical education to guess that most readers of this text will have heard of Charles Atlas, but not of Rogers or McCloy?)

In 1941 the U.S. again called up many men for service in the Armed Forces, and with approximately the same rejection rate of about 30%. As is typical during wartime, physical fitness became a prized goal, and physical education programs shifted in emphasis. When the war was over, fitness faded (both literally and figuratively!), and did not become a national concern again until 1956 when the President's Council on Youth Fitness was activated.

THE PRESIDENT'S COUNCIL ON PHYSICAL FITNESS AND SPORTS

In June of 1955 President Eisenhower hosted a luncheon of 30 sports personalities, government officials, and medical researchers (no physical educators were invited) to discuss the dismal showing of American youth in the Kraus-Weber muscular strength and flexibility test. (The test was called a physical fitness test, but the poor showing of American youth in comparison with European youth was in the flexibility item.) After subsequent meetings, Eisenhower established in July of 1956 the President's Council on Youth Fitness. Its role was to alert the public to the physical fitness problem, and its first director was a public relations expert. In 1961 President Kennedy issued a call for a "national renewal of vigor and vitality," and appointed Bud Wilkinson, former Oklahoma football coach, as the director. The program emphasis was shifted to sponsorship of clinics for professional physical educators, development of tests and standards, and research grants to various experts and universities. The Advertising Council began, and still continues, a valuable public relations campaign on the fitness council's behalf. In 1963 Kennedy changed the council's name to the President's Council on Physical Fitness; this narrowed the focus of efforts to that of physical activity for persons of all ages and in all settings (school, community, and outdoor recreation).

President Johnson continued the council, although he was not as personally motivated as Kennedy. Different directors (Stan Musial, baseball star) and James Lovell (astronaut) were named in 1964 and 1967, respectively. In 1968 the name was again changed, this time to the present President's Council on Physical Fitness and Sports. This indicated a concern for sports participation, not just physical fitness, for all Americans.

Under Presidents Nixon and Ford, the influence of the council was continued. The professional staff, drawn primarily from AAHPER members, has been expanded. At the present time the council is regarded as *the* voice in American fitness. Undoubtedly you have taken the Youth Physical Fitness Test at least once in your school career. The council issues dozens of free or inexpensive publications each year. It sponsors such meetings as regional fitness clinics (each attended by hundreds of professional educators and medical personnel), industrial fitness conferences, and medical symposiums. It issues films, filmstrips, and audio tapes. It has a recognition program of certificates, emblems to be sewn on warm-ups, and pins for participants in virtually every sporting activity from archery, biathalon, and cycling through wrestling and yachting (sailing). In short, the President's Council has convinced a large segment of Americans that physical fitness and sport participation will lead to desirable biological development.

THE IMPORTANCE OF BIOLOGICAL DEVELOPMENT

"People are physical beings." This statement is trite because it is so obvious. Since the dawn of recorded history, people have devoted a great deal of time and energy to the development of mental capacity, while the physical body has undergone much less change.

Body evolution has been gradual, but our style of living has seen drastic change. Once the body was the mechanism by which people survived. They had to be cunning and strong enough to trap and kill animals for food; they had to know what, when, and how to plant; they had to learn how to construct dwellings for shelter from the elements. The body was the key to accomplishing these things. If the strength or endurance were not there, the task was not accomplished. Today, on the whole, it is the emerging and "less civilized" nations who use their physical prowess for survival. The rest of us devise new ways to do less physical work. An eminent cardiologist once said, "Golf is a stupid way to interrupt a walk." He obviously hadn't reckoned with the electric golf carts which permit us to play golf without even walking!

The concept, "What we don't use, we lose," is perhaps the chief reason why biological development remains a key objective in physical education. In primitive societies, biological development was taken care of by the process of survival. In our society, we must remain physically active to maintain strength, muscle tone, endurance, flexibility. Thus, the development of the physical body becomes even more important as we become more automated and attain higher standards of living, because a higher standard of living usually means less physical work.

Physical activity and its benefits to humans have long been important to physical educators. More recently, physicians and physiologists have become concerned with exercise as preventive medicine. Fred Hein, Ph.D., and Allan Ryan, M.D., summarized volumes of research up until 1960 by reporting:

> In the last decade, a growing body of evidence derived from clinical observations and experimental studies points to definite values for exercise in a) maintaining desirable weight; b) preserving the health of the cardiovascular system; c) aiding the individual to meet emergencies, and d) prolonging life" (Hein and Ryan 1960, p. 264).

One of the problems physical educators have had is convincing the public of the values of physical fitness. The research is so vast and scattered that it is exceedingly difficult for an individual to keep informed. The President's Council on Physical Fitness and Sports has attempted to educate physical educators, who in turn will help inform the public concerning such beliefs as:

1. A person's general learning potential for a given level of intelligence is increased or decreased in accordance with his degree of physical fitness. For example, in a California high school noted for its physical fitness program, boys in the top fitness groups obtained higher school grades by a 20:1 ratio, while the boys in the bottom 25% of fitness scores had a lower grade average than the average of all boys. High physical fitness is not a guarantee of superior mental achievement, but the evidence is overwhelming that it relates to general learning potential (Clarke 1971, pp. 9-11).

2. Positive (that is, favorable) relationships are shown between higher fitness levels and personality and social characteristics. For example, boys high on physical-motor tests tend to be popular with peers, are extroverts and leaders, are more tolerant of others, etc. Boys low on physical-motor tests tend to feel inferior, insecure, and defensive, and possess other negative characteristics. Thus, in enhancing self-concepts and acceptance by peers, higher fitness levels are of value to boys (Clarke 1972, pp. 11-12).

Whether or not the material cited by Clarke is important is a controversial point among physical educators. Though the facts are valid and reliable, we really have not ascertained the cause-effect relationship. Are superior mental achievement and positive personality and social characteristics a result of higher fitness levels, or do persons already possessed of these attributes seek physical prowess, too? Do these same facts (regardless of their implications) hold true for females? These questions must be answered by scholars and researchers in physical education.

STATUS AND IMPLICATIONS OF CURRENT FITNESS PROGRAMS

In earlier parts of this chapter, we used *biological development*, *organic vigor*, and *physical fitness* somewhat interchangeably. Broadly speaking, these are the same terms. What do we know about the current status of Americans relative to fitness and what implications does this have for physical education?

We have mentioned the dismal 1956 showing of American youth in the Kraus-Weber Test. The AAHPER Youth Fitness Test, first used in 1956, produced similar results. In the years 1958-65, substantial gains were made. The test standards were revised upward in both 1965 and 1975 as millions of youth practiced and re-took the test. Originally, European girls were slightly better than same-age American boys in 6 items of the AAHPER test, but by 1965 this was not true. Hundreds of schools in the U.S. earned Presidential Citations for their participation in the testing program and thousands of students have earned emblems rewarding superior scores. However, the years 1965-75 saw no substantial gain in scores for boys, and girls showed improvement in only 7 out of 40 scores. (Reiff 1976). The physical fitness level of American youth has improved since 1956, but it might be that the present levels are going to become the norm.

Reasons for the boom in adult fitness have been many. The need of Presidents Eisenhower and Kennedy for a personal exercise program certainly was important. The increased emphasis by physicians on preventive medicine, and the extensive public relations campaign conducted by the President's Council were equally important. A 1973 survey (President's Council 1973) showed:

1. 55% of adult Americans regularly exercised, but a great percentage of these did not meet the minimum standards of frequency or effort recommended by the Council.
2. Walking was the most popular form of exercise, followed in order by bicycle riding, swimming, calisthenics, and jogging.
3. Half the people who exercised did so for health reasons.
4. In sports participation, bowling was the leading activity (20% of Americans participating). Others were swimming (18%), golf (9%), softball (8½%), tennis (6%), volleyball (5%).

All the percentages cited above are probably higher now than in 1973, with tennis undoubtedly showing the highest increase. Sports participation of Americans of all ages is at an all-time high. The facts, however, show that we still have much room for improvement.

You have noted the current status concerning fitness and sports participation, but the question remains, "Why exercise?" The cause and effect relationship between good physical and mental health and physical fitness has not been established, but physical educators, physicians, and social scientists generally agree that these are the four main objectives of exercise.

TABLE 6–1. OBJECTIVES OF EXERCISE.

---

1. PHYSICAL FITNESS AND WORK CAPACITY
  To increase work output capacity
  To foster resistance to fatigue
  To aid in achieving neuromuscular relaxation
  To improve body mechanics and add to increased efficiency of movement

2. GENERAL HEALTH
  To maintain organic normality
  To retard the aging process
  To control body weight
  To serve as a prophylaxis

3. PHYSICAL APPEARANCE
  To assist the normal processes of growth
  To foster general physical development and achieve body symmetry
  To secure habitual good carriage and postural alignments
  To correct specific physical weaknesses and defects
  To aid in rehabilitation and in adaptation to handicaps

4. PHYSICAL RECREATION
  To gain enjoyment from active use of leisure
  To improve opportunities for social communication and friendship

---

Taken from *International guide to fitness and health* by Leonard A. Larson and Herbert Michelman. © 1973 by Leonard A. Larson and Herbert Michelman. Used by permission of Crown Publishers, Inc.

If the above objectives are reached, exercise has many benefits. However, it should be noted that exercise must be long enough and vigorous enough and therein lies another of our unknowns. Exactly how long and how hard should a person exercise? Do adults need more (or less) exercise than college-age or high school students? Do women need more or less exercise than men? The physical educator must remember that fitness is a vague concept which varies with each individual. Fitness is not stored, so exercise and sports participation to develop fitness must be regularly continued. In general, "The expectation is *unrealistic* that any conditioning program applied to a general population at any age level will produce uniform response" (McCammon and Sexton 1958, p. 1440).

Table 6-2 summarizes the thoughts of seven nationally known physical fitness experts (all M.D.s) as they rated 14 sports and exercises. It clearly shows that not all activities are of equal value, using physical fitness and general well-being as the criteria. A rating of 21 points indicates maximum benefit. It was assumed that exercise was at least four times per week, 30-60 minutes per session.

TABLE 6–2. RATINGS OF 14 SPORTS AS TO THEIR PHYSICAL FITNESS AND GENERAL WELL-BEING BENEFITS.

	JOGGING	BICYCLING	SWIMMING	SKATING (ICE OR ROLLING)	HANDBALL/SQUASH	SKIING—NORDIC	SKIING—ALPINE	BASKETBALL	TENNIS	CALISTHENICS	WALKING	GOLF*	SOFTBALL	BOWLING
Physical fitness														
Cardiorespiratory endurance (stamina)	21	19	21	18	19	19	16	19	16	10	13	8	6	5
Muscular endurance	20	18	20	17	18	19	18	17	16	13	14	8	8	5
Muscular strength	17	16	14	15	15	15	15	15	14	16	11	9	7	5
Flexibility	9	9	15	13	16	14	14	13	14	19	7	8	9	7
Balance	17	18	12	20	17	16	21	16	16	15	8	8	7	6
General well-being														
Weight control	21	20	15	17	19	17	15	19	16	12	13	6	7	5
Muscle definition	14	15	14	14	11	12	14	13	13	18	11	6	5	5
Digestion	13	12	13	11	13	12	9	10	12	11	11	7	8	7
Sleep	16	15	16	15	12	15	12	12	11	12	14	6	7	6
Total	148	142	140	140	140	139	134	134	128	126	102	66*	64	51

Reprinted from *Medical Times*, May 1976.

*Ratings for golf are based on the fact that many Americans use a golf cart and/or caddy.

The implications of this discussion on physical fitness are clear. Physical educators must be able to positively influence persons of all ages toward exercise. We must be able to document its benefits. Finally, we must be prepared to help persons learn psychomotor skills so they will enjoy what they are doing.

EDUCATION OF THE PHYSICAL, AND THE PENDULUM

Earlier in this chapter the phrases "education *of* the physical," and "education *through* the physical" were used. The contrast between these phrases has stemmed from the term "physical education." To many professionals, "physical" implies that the main goal of our discipline is education *of* the physical, i.e., that persons should learn how to move so that their growth and development is aided. The cognitive or affective benefits are of secondary importance. Advocates of education *of* the physical point out that physical fitness is our unique objective because no other discipline claims to improve the biological aspect of the person, and that it is the only objective we can prove that we accomplish. Though all physical educators may not agree that biological development is the most important objective, they all agree that satisfactory development and maintenance of the muscles, heart, lungs, nervous system, and organic systems are essential for personal survival.

The term *pendulum* is used to describe the swinging back and forth of interest in biological development as an objective of American physical education. The comments made in Chapter 4 and in this chapter would suggest this alternation to be common. But the future looks much brighter for those who truly believe that the development of the body is our most important objective. It is likely that the present public awareness of the values of exercise (as widely advertised on television and in the press) will continue. The medical profession seems to be more aware of the value of preventive medicine and the role of the physical educator in this regard. There is much interest in isometric and isotonic exercises, jogging, aerobics, the President's Council on Physical Fitness and Sport, and the Lifetime Sports Foundation. All these factors will continue to promote physical development at all age levels. Presently, a popular concern is ecology; it should be remembered that human ecology is as vital as environmental ecology.

LEARNING ABOUT BIOLOGICAL DEVELOPMENT

The learning experiences related to this concept in physical education include both activity and theory courses. Probably no two colleges or universities require the same courses; even if the course titles are the same, the course content may differ. Therefore, the experiences listed below are examples of those courses most commonly included in professional preparation curricula.

Activity Courses

1. *Conditioning.* Many schools require their physical education majors to take a class in which the goals are to improve the student's own physical condition, and at the same time learn the techniques of helping others do the same. Exercises and routines designed to improve strength and endurance of the muscular system and the cardiorespiratory system are featured. Whether this class is required or not, you can test your attitude toward physical education by making an honest appraisal of your current conditioning efforts. Many of you are now in the best physical condition of your life. As you get older, you will tend to become less physically active. If you look upon physical conditioning (not necessarily calisthenics, but any

type of vigorous activity) as difficult, boring, and unnecessary, you may need to reconsider your future involvement in physical education.

Theory Courses

1. *General biology or zoology.* Most colleges and universities require an introductory course in this subject, in which the student is generally exposed to the organizational structure of the animal kingdom and the facts and concepts which underlie the discipline of biology.
2. *Chemistry.* As with general biology an introductory course in chemistry is often required of physical education majors so they can more fully understand the various chemical reactions which take place in the body.
3. *Human anatomy.* This course consists of a thorough study of the various anatomical features (bones, joints, muscles, and nerves) which are found in the body. There is much memorizing and many details involved in the study of anatomy. Some may seem irrelevant, but as you become active workers in physical education, your attitude will change, because the bodies of your students or clients are the structures with which you are most concerned. If at all possible, a laboratory with human cadavers should be a part of the anatomy course.
4. *Human physiology.* The study of the workings of the body circulation, respiration, digestion, nervous control of movement, and growth are the typical areas of concentration in this course.

   Sometimes the anatomy and physiology courses are combined. This is logical in one respect, because the body itself cannot be divided and still function properly. The common problem, however, is that there is seldom enough time in one course for complete learning of the mass of details, facts and concepts needed, and thus students may not gain in-depth understanding.
5. *Physiology of exercise.* From the title, it should be obvious that this course is essential to members of our discipline. The functions of the body before, during, and after exercise must be studied by all physical educators. In addition, the prospective coach, teacher, health spa worker, and physical director must be especially knowledgeable. Topics usually studied include nervous control of muscular effort, muscle activity, energy sources, oxygen utilization, and body temperature regulation. Competent physical educators are able to intelligently apply the facts and concepts of exercise physiology to the people with whom they work.

BIOLOGICAL DEVELOPMENT AND YOU

As noted in Chapter 2, there are several schools which give screening tests to major students in the area of biological development. The most common measurement is a physical fitness test. As you might expect, physical fitness is defined differently by different experts, and thus there are numerous tests. The AAHPER Youth Fitness Test has been given to thousands of students of all ages. Chances are that you have already taken it. Since many of you will teach, Table 6-3 shows how beginning male and female majors compare with other groups. Hopefully, your instructor will give you the chance to compare yourself with them. Complete directions for the test are given, with scoring found in Tables 6-4 and 6-5.[1]

---

[1] Chapter 7 presents a number of psychomotor skill tests, with complete directions for administering and scoring each. Explanations are given concerning the use of scoring tables. Reference to pages 70-71 might be helpful if the physical fitness and aerobic tests are given before the psychomotor skill tests.

One item of the AAHPER Youth Fitness Test has been severaly criticized by experts: the 600-yd. run-walk. (Incidentally, the item was originally to be a run, but so many American children could not run the entire distance when the tests were first given in 1957-58 that walking was permitted. Foreign children invariably ran the entire distance, even in 1957-60; now, the cardiovascular condition has improved so much that Americans run, too.) The 600-yd. distance is criticized as being too short to really measure aerobic fitness (ability to use oxygen). Many schools are now giving a 6-, 9-, or 12-minute run. Data on two of these distances are presented in Table 6-6.

Your knowledge about biological development may be measured by the AAHPER Knowledge Test. This is a standardized knowledge test to be taken by students 10-18 years of age. Many of the questions are from the biological development area, but because some questions pertain to other concepts of physical education, data for this test will be presented in Chapter 9.

AAHPER YOUTH FITNESS TEST*

Basic Information

Six objectively scored items constitute this test. Each item measures but one component of physical fitness. Table 6-3 presents the mean scores of different groups of subjects on this test.

TABLE 6–3. MEAN SCORE OF VARIOUS GROUPS ON THE AAHPER YOUTH FITNESS TEST.

TEST ITEMS	17–18–YEAR–OLD STUDENTS		COLLEGE STUDENTS (NONMAJORS)		BEGINNING PE MAJORS	
	MALES	FEMALES	MALES	FEMALES	MALES	FEMALES
Pull-ups (male)	8		6		8	
Flexed-arm hang (female)		8 sec.		20 sec.		13 sec.
Sit-ups (flexed leg)	49	32	47	20	75	42
Shuttle run	9.8 sec.	11.2 sec.	9.7 sec.	11.6 sec.	9.4 sec.	10.7 sec.
Standing long jump	7 ft.3 in.	5 ft.5 in.	7 ft.3 in.	5 ft.4 in.	7 ft. 8 in.	6 ft. 1 in.
50-yd. dash	6.6 sec.	8.2 sec.	6.8 sec.	8.4 sec.	6.4 sec.	7.3 sec.
600-yd. dash	1:50 min.	2:51 min.	1:52 min.	2:58 min.	1:43 sec.	2:20 min.

Test Description

1. Pull-Up (males): The student hangs (arms and legs fully extended) so that his feet are free of the floor. The overhand grasp (back of hand facing the student) must be used. The student raises his body by his arms until his chin is placed over the bar, and then the body is lowered to the original fully extended hanging position. The pull-up is repeated as many times as possible. One trial is given. The number of pull-ups (to the nearest whole number) is recorded.

Total

*Adapted from AAHPER, *Youth fitness test manual* (Washington, D.C.: AAHPER, 1972), p. 75. Used by permission.

2. Flexed-Arm Hang (females): The overhand grasp (back of hand facing the student) is used. With the help of other students, the subject raises her body to a position where the chin is above the bar, the elbows are flexed, and the chest is close to the bar. This position is held as long as possible. One trial is given. The time to the nearest second is recorded.

Total

3. Sit-Ups: The student lies on back with legs flexed and feet on floor, heels not more than 12 in. from buttocks. The hands are placed on the back of the neck, with fingers interlaced. Elbows are flat on floor. Feet are held by partner. The student curls up, touching elbows to knees. The student returns to the starting position. The number of correctly performed sit-ups in 60 seconds is the score.

Total

4. Shuttle Run: On the signal "go" the student (X) runs 30 ft. to where two small blocks of wood are placed, picks up one of the blocks, carries it back to the starting line, and *places* (not drops) it behind this line. Return to pick up the other block, which is carried back across the starting line. Two trials are given. The best time, measured in seconds and tenths of seconds, is recorded.

Best Time

5. Standing Long Jump: The student stands with toes just behind the takeoff line. The student swings arms back and forth several times, bends knees in proper coordination, and jumps forward as far as possible. The distance between the takeoff line and the part of the body (usually the nearest heel) closest to the line is measured to the nearest inch. Three trials are given, with the best being recorded.

Best Jump

6. 50-Yd. Dash: At the signal "go" the student runs 50 yd. as fast as possible. The time, measured in seconds and tenths of seconds, is recorded. One trial is given.

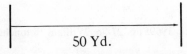

50 Yd.

Time

7. 600-Yd. Run-Walk: At the signal "go" the student walks, jogs, and/or runs 600 yd. The time is recorded to the nearest second. One trial is given. Note: Many instructors prefer to use the 6-, 9-, or 12-minute run to measure cardiorespiratory endurance, rather than the 600-yd. run-walk. For directions, see below.

Time

Evaluation

The score for each test item is recorded next to its description. These raw scores are then circled on the norm tables. The average standard score is determined by first adding all standard scores, and then dividing by the number of items. Students meeting predetermined departmental standards may be judged as physically fit.

6- OR 12-MINUTE RUN TEST*

Basic Information

Aerobics means "with oxygen"; thus, an aerobic exercise is one which forces the body to use oxygen. Oxygen can only be used when blood takes it from the lungs to the heart and then to the tissues, and the waste products are brought back to the heart and finally to the lungs. The better the cardiorespiratory (or heart-breathing) system, the more fit for aerobic work the person is.

Since running can be done almost anywhere with no special equipment, various running (or aerobic) tests have been devised. The AAHPER physical fitness test includes the 600-yd. run-walk as a cardiorespiratory measure, but most authorities say that this distance is not long enough to be either a valid or a reliable measure of maximum oxygen consumption. Cooper's 12-minute test is currently the most popular: it has been used by males and females of all age levels. Cooper tested hundreds of subjects and related their distance covered in 12 minutes to the amount of oxygen consumed per unit of body weight. The greater the oxygen consumption, the further the person could run in the time limit.

For administrative purposes, the 6-minute run and the 1½-mile run are sometimes substituted for the 12-minute run. Bolonchuk (unpublished data) showed that with beginning physical education majors, the 6-minute run was highly correlated to the 12-minute run, and could be substituted if desired. Table 6-6 summarizes mean scores for various groups on these tests.

*See Kenneth H. Cooper, *Aerobics* (New York: Bantam Books, 1969) pp. 27-36; William Bolonchuk, University of North Dakota.

TABLE 6−4. NORMS FOR AAHPER FITNESS TEST (MALE).

STANDARD SCALE	SIT−UPS	PULL−UPS	SHUTTLE− RUN	STANDING LONG JUMP
	NO.	NO.	SEC.	FT. IN.
100		23.	5.7	
95		22.	6.0	
90		20.	6.4	9.10
85		19.	6.8	9.07
80		17.	7.1	9.03
75		16.	7.5	9.00
70		14.	7.9	8.09
65	104.	12.	8.2	8.06
60	94.	11.	8.6	8.03
55	84.	9.	9.0	7.11
50	75.	8.	9.4	7.08
45	65.	6.	9.7	7.05
40	56.	5.	10.1	7.02
35	46.	3.	10.5	6.11
30	36.	2.	10.8	6.07
25	26.		11.2	6.04
20	16.		11.6	6.01
15			12.0	5.10
10			12.3	
5			12.7	
0			13.1	
MEAN*	74.630	7.876	9.359	7.083
SD	24.227	3.837	.925	.080
N	284.0	283.0	285.0	285.0
H. S.	100.0	24.0	17.8	9.07
L. S.	20.0	0.0	5.7	5.11
RANGE	80.0	24.0	12.1	3.08
8SC	1.938	.307	.074	.006
MAX. SCORE	100.0	******	******	******
NO. TRLS	1.0	1.0	2.0	3.0

*MEAN   =   arithmetic average of a set of raw scores
 SD   =   standard deviation; measure of variability of a set of raw scores
 N   =   number taking test
 HS   =   high score on test
 LS   =   low score on test
 RANGE   =   difference between HS and LS
 8SC   =   8 sigma score; description of statistical grouping used
 MAX. SCORE   =   maximum score possible in this test
 NO. TRLS   =   number of trials given on this item

TABLE 6–4 CONT. (MALE).

STANDARD SCALE	50–YD. DASH	600–YD. RUN–WALK
	SEC.	MIN. SEC.
100		
95	5.0	
90	5.1	
85	5.3	1:15
80	5.5	1:19
75	5.6	1:23
70	5.8	1:27
65	5.9	1:31
60	6.1	1:35
55	6.2	1:39
50	6.4	1:43
45	6.6	1:47
40	6.7	1:51
35	6.9	1:55
30	7.0	1:59
25	7.2	2:03
20	7.3	2:07
15	7.5	2:11
10	7.7	2:15
5		2:19
0		2:23
MEAN	6.396	1:43
SD	.393	.101
N	284.0	266.0
H. S.	7.6	2:21
L. S.	5.0	1:15
RANGE	2.6	1:06
8SC	.031	.008
MAX. SCORE	******	******
NO. TRLS	1.0	1.0

TABLE 6–5. NORMS FOR AAHPER FITNESS TEST (FEMALE).

STANDARD SCALE	SIT–UPS	FLEXED–ARM HANG	SHUTTLE RUN	STANDING LONG JUMP
	NO.	SEC.	SEC.	FT. IN.
100		52.		
95		48.		
90		44.		
85		40.		
80		36.		7.08
75		32.	8.8	7.05
70		28.	9.2	7.02
65		24.	9.6	6.11
60	51.	21.	9.9	6.07
55	47.	17.	10.3	6.04
50	42.	13.	10.7	6.01
45	38.	9.	11.1	5.10
40	34.	5.	11.5	5.06
35	30.	1.	11.9	5.03
30	25.		12.3	5.00
25	21.		12.6	4.09
20	17.		13.0	4.05
15	12.		13.4	4.02
10	8.		13.8	
5			14.2	
0				
MEAN	42.384	12.757	10.717	6.01
SD	10.688	9.698	.966	.081
N	151.0	144.0	149.0	149.0
H. S.	50.0	56.0	17.8	7.07
L. S.	10.0	0.0	9.0	4.05
RANGE	40.0	56.0	8.8	3.02
8SC	.855	.776	.077	.006
MAX. SCORE	50.0	******	******	******
NO. TRLS	1.0	1.0	2.0	3.0

TABLE 6—5 CONT. (FEMALE).

STANDARD SCALE	50—YD. DASH SEC.	600—YD. RUN—WALK MIN. SEC.
100		
95		
90		1:16
85	5.5	1:24
80	5.8	1:32
75	6.0	1:40
70	6.3	1:48
65	6.5	1:56
60	6.8	2:04
55	7.1	2:12
50	7.3	2:20
45	7.6	2:28
40	7.8	2:36
35	8.1	2:44
30	8.3	2:52
25	8.6	3:00
20	8.9	3:08
15	9.1	3:16
10		3:24
5		3:32
0		3:39
MEAN	7.308	2.199
SD	.644	.199
N	130.0	123.0
H. S.	9.0	3.37
L. S.	5.7	1.18
RANGE	3.3	2.19
8SC	.051	.016
MAX. SCORE	******	******
NO. TRLS	1.0	1.0

TABLE 6–6. DISTANCES OF VARIOUS GROUPS ON THE 6- AND 12-MINUTE RUN AND 1½-MILE RUN TESTS.

	HIGH SCHOOL STUDENTS		BEGINNING PE MAJORS	
	MALE	FEMALE	MALE	FEMALE
6-minute run			1662 yd.	1324 yd.
12-minute run	2592 yd.	1861 yd.	3073 yd.	
1½-mile run	11:29 min.	16:57 min.	10:24 min.	13:30 min.

TABLE 6–7. NORMS FOR 6- AND 12-MINUTE RUNS, 1½-MILE RUN (MALE AND FEMALE).

STANDARD SCALE	6–MINUTE RUN		12–MINUTE RUN	1½–MILE RUN	
	MALE	FEMALE	MALE	MALE	FEMALE
	YD.	YD.	YD.	MIN. SEC.	MIN. SEC.
100					
95					
90	2148.		4171.		
85	2088.	1771.	4034.		
80	2027.	1707.	3897.		
75	1967.	1643.	3760.		9:42
70	1906.	1579.	3622.		10:30
65	1845.	1516.	3485.	8:54	11:12
60	1784.	1452.	3348.	9:24	12:00
55	1723.	1388.	3210.	9:54	12:42
50	1662.	1324.	3073.	10:24	13:30
45	1601.	1260.	2936.	10:48	14:12
40	1540.	1196.	2798.	11:24	15:00
35	1479.	1132.	2661.	11:54	15:42
30	1418.	1068.	2524.	12:24	16:30
25		1004.	2387.	12:48	17:12
20		940.		13:18	18:00
15		876.			18:42
10		812.			19:30
5		748.			20:12
0					
MEAN	1662.14	1324.05	3073.38	10:24	13:30
SD	152.52	160.30	343.32	1:13	1:56
N	166.0	54.0	119.0	17.0	32.0
H. S.	2090.0	1723.0	4098.0	9:18	10:12
L. S.	1173.0	807.0	2426.0	12:48	19:48
RANGE	917.0	916.0	1672.0	3:30	9:36
8SC	12.17	12.76	27.46	.098	.15
MAX. SCORE	******	******	******	******	******
NO. TRLS	1.0	1.0	1.0	1.0	1.0

Bibliography

Anitel, J., and Cumming, G. Effect of emotions on the heart rate. *Research Quarterly* 40 (Mar. 1969):6-10.

Arthur, R. Psychological and psychotherapeutic aspects of swim coaching. *Journal of Sports Medicine and Physical Fitness* 7 (Dec. 1967):185-91.

Beck, M. R. Weight loss in high school wrestling: Beneficial or harmful? *The Physical Educator* 30 (Dec. 1973):188.

Berger, R. Isometric training in sports. *The Physical Educator* 22 (Oct. 1965):126-28.

Bigbee, R., and Doolittle, T. L. The twelve-minute run-walk: A test of cardiorespiratory fitness of adolescent boys. *Research Quarterly* 39 (Oct. 1968):491-95.

Blair, S., and Vincent, M. Variability of heart rate and blood pressure measurements on consecutive days. *Research Quarterly* 42 (Mar. 1971):7-13.

Bobb, A.; Pringle, D.; and Ryan, A. J. A brief study of the diet of athletes. *Journal of Sports Medicine and Physical Fitness* 9 (Dec. 1969):255.

Bucher, C. A. Athletic competition and the development growth pattern. *The Physical Educator* 28 (Mar. 1971):3.

Burt, J. J. Cardiovascular health. In Fact and fancy, ed. P. B. Johnson, *JOHPER* 39 (Nov.-Dec. 1968):36.

Carlson, R., and McCraw, L. Isometric strength and relative isometric endurance. *Research Quarterly* 42 (Oct. 1971):244-51.

Chu, D. Review of research concerning the hypothesis that strenuous physical activity develops masculine traits in women, and therefore should not be encouraged by physical educators. *The Physical Educator* 29 (Dec. 1972):195.

Clarke, D. H. Neuromuscular considerations. In Fact and fancy, ed. P. B. Johnson. *JOHPER* 39 (Nov.-Dec. 1968):34.

Clarke, H. H., ed. The totality of man. *Physical Fitness Research Digest*. Washington: President's Council on Physical Fitness and Sports, vol. 1, no. 3 (Oct. 1971) and vol. 2, no. 1 (Jan. 1972).

Cooper, K. H. The role of exercise in our contemporary society. *JOHPER* 40 (May 1969):22-25.

Cox, B., and Toohey, J. Anabolic steroids and athletes. *Scholastic Coach* 40 (Jan. 1971):50.

Dowell, L. J., et al. A twenty-year study of the physical fitness of entering freshmen at Texas A & M University. *Research Quarterly* 42 (May 1971):220.

Drinkwater, B. L. Research studies on the female athlete; aerobic power in females. *JOHPER* 46 (Jan. 1975):36-38.

Falls, H., and Humphrey, D. Cold water application effects on response to heat stress during exercise. *Research Quarterly* 42 (Mar. 1971):21-29.

Fitzhenry, B. Work until you are best. *JOHPER* 40 (Apr. 1969):61-62.

Fowler, W. The facts about ergogenic aids and sports performance. *JOHPER* 40 (Nov.-Dec. 1969):36-41.

Gendel, E. S. Fitness and fatigue in the female. *JOHPER* 42 (Oct. 1971):53.

Hanson, D. Cardiac response to participation in little league baseball competition as determined by telemetry. *Research Quarterly* 38 (Oct. 1967):384-87.

Hein, F., and Ryan, A. The contributions of physical activity to physical health. *Research Quarterly* 31 (May 1960, Part 2):263-85.

Herbert, W. G., and Ribisl, P. M. Effects of dehydration upon physical working capacity of wrestlers under competitive conditions. *Research Quarterly* 43 (Dec. 1972):416-22.

Hilsendager, D. Comparison of a calisthenic and a non-calisthenic physical education program. *Research Quarterly* 37 (Mar. 1966):148.

Johnston, R. W. The men and the myth. *Sports Illustrated* 41 (Nov. 14, 1974):106-20. (Body Building)

Kennedy, J. F. The soft American. *Sports Illustrated* 15 (Dec. 26, 1960):15-17.

Kusenity, I. Strength training in the varsity athletic program. *The Physical Educator* 26 (Dec. 1969):176-77.

Larson, L. A., and Michelman, H. 1973. *International guide to fitness and health*. New York: Crown.

Levitt, S. The limitations of training: Some implications for physical educators. *The Physical Educator* 30 (May 1973):89-90.

McCammon, R. W., and Sexton, A. W. Implications of longitudinal research in fitness programs. *Journal of the American Medical Association* 168 (Nov. 15, 1958):1440-45.

McCardle, W. D., et al. Aerobic capacity, heart rate, and estimated energy cost during women's competitive basketball. *Research Quarterly* 42 (May 1971):178.

McDermott, B. Exercise you later, alligator. *Sports Illustrated* 42 (April 21, 1975):36-42.

Maksud, M. G., and Coutts, K. D. Applications of the Cooper 12-minute run-walk test to young males. *Research Quarterly* 42 (Mar. 1971):54.

Manfredi, D. What makes a great athlete? *Journal of Sports Medicine and Physical Fitness* 37 (Sept. 1967):165-67.

Mood, D. Where do physical education majors learn about fitness *The Physical Educator* 28 (May 1971):75.

Moore, B. C. A fever running through the streets. *Sports Illustrated* 43 (Aug. 4, 1975):26-32. (Jogging Craze)

Penny, G. Prevention of heat injuries. *Scholastic Coach* 40 (Sept. 1970):62-64.

Pierson, W. The effects of amphetamine on motor performance. *The Physical Educator* 19 (Mar. 1962):21-22.

President's Council on Physical Fitness and Sport. National adult physical fitness survey. *Newsletter* special edition (May 1973):1-3.

Reiff, G. G., and Hunsicker, P. A. Youth fitness: 1975. *Update* (June 1976):5.

Ryan, A. J. Research studies on the female athlete: Gynecological considerations. *JOHPER* 46 (Jan. 1975):40-44.

Rarick, G. L. Exercise and the growing years. In Fact and fancy, ed. P. B. Johnson *JOHPER* 39 (Nov.-Dec. 1968):37.

Ricci, B. For a moratorium on physical fitness testing. *JOHPER* 41 (Mar. 1970):28-30.

Roby, F. B. Physical activity — Its relation to the prevention and control of obesity. *The Physical Educator* 26 (Dec. 1969):158.

Roche, A. Do women achieve their athletic potential? *Sportswoman* 1 (Sept.-Oct. 1973):18.

Ryan, A. J. Yoga and physical fitness. *JOHPER* 42 (Feb. 1971):26-27.

Sadlier, P. Jogging for emotional fitness. *Scholastic Coach* 41 (Sept. 1971):73.

Sciacchetano, L. Wrestling for younger boys. *The Physical Educator* 23 (May 1966):56.

Sharkey, B. J. Strength and endurance — Distant relations? *The Physical Educator* 28 (Mar. 1971):5.

Steinhaus, A. Fitness beyond muscle. *The Physical Educator* 23 (Oct. 1966):103-7.

Stewart, J. C. Growing weak by degrees. *Sports Illustrated* 42 (Mar. 10, 1975):58-59. (Hypothermia)

Tobey, C. Does physical fitness belong in the schools? *The Physical Educator* 26 (Oct. 1969):2.

Tompkins, R. N. The swing of the pendulum — How wide? *The Physical Educator* 27 (Oct. 1970):124.

Torg, J. S., and Quedenfeld, T. Effect of shoe type and cleat length on incidence and severity of knee injuries among high school football players. *Research Quarterly* 42 (May 1971):203.

Wetzel, M. E. Progressive weight training for girls? Yes! *JOHPER* 41 (Oct. 1970):26.

Wilmore, J. L. Research studies on the female athlete: Body composition and strength development. *JOHPER* 46 (Jan. 1975):38-40.

Student Activities

1. Interview three or four physical educators. Ask their opinion as to whether we should be most concerned with education *of* the physical, or education *through* the physical.
2. Interview at least one coach. Ask him or her to briefly explain the principles used to get athletes in shape for that sport.
3. Observe and/or assist in physical fitness testing. Especially watch the students for signs of fatigue, excitement, boredom.
4. If you are not now in reasonably good shape, begin slowly with some mild exercises and easy running. Gradually (at least 2 weeks) condition yourself and then take the 12-minute run.

5. Note the extreme difference in growth and development by observing a group of children who are the same chronological age. Measure height, weight, length of arms, etc., if possible.

Statements for Class Discussion

1. Because some psychomotor elements (endurance, strength, etc.) fade away, and cognitive elements (knowledge, concepts, etc.) do not, the school should only be concerned with intellectual subjects.
2. Professional physical educators who are obese, out of shape, or smokers should lose their jobs.
3. Departments should allow majors to remain in the program *only* if they exhibit:
    a. satisfactory scores in physical fitness
    b. normal or above normal physical growth and development
    c. no visible physical defects
    d. no grade lower than "C" in anatomy, physiology, or physiology of exercise
4. Departments should make every major pass a physical fitness test just before he or she graduates.
5. Everybody is for physical fitness, as long as they don't have to sweat and strain themselves.
6. When I get the urge to exercise, I lie down until it passes.

CONCEPTS

CHAPTER 7

PSYCHOMOTOR LEARNING IN PHYSICAL EDUCATION

INTRODUCTION

This chapter will discuss another one of the segments in Fraleigh's model for the physical education discipline, that having to do with motor learning. Fraleigh indicated that physical educators should know what motor skills they possess, how these skills can be performed in various types of activity situations, and how their movement interacts with the movement of others. More specifically, the physical educator should learn about:

1. the adequacy and/or inadequacy of self in movement
2. the relation of self to space, time, energy, and deity
3. the relation of self to others in movement
4. particular, purposeful motor skills

The concepts presented in this chapter will hopefully make you aware that physical educators must know more than just how to play a variety of games and sports. Five concepts are presented and discussed through the use of definitions, examples, historical background, and specific courses which physical education majors take. Finally, a series of psychomotor skills is presented, in the hopes that you will be able to assess your standing in comparison with other majors.

CONCEPTS TO BE GAINED FROM THE CHAPTER

When you have mastered the material in this chapter, you will be able to demonstrate comprehension of these concepts:

63

1. Psychomotor learning is a segment of physical education which can best be discussed when such terms as *learning and teaching, psychomotor learning, psychomotor skills, activity class,* and *movement education* are used.
2. Psychomotor learning involves both the entire nervous system and the muscular system: both are essential. Physical educators must understand how psychomotor skills are acquired.
3. The current psychomotor skills program in U.S. schools encompasses games, sports, and activities in five major categories. Hopefully, learners will participate in at least some of them throughout life.
4. Physical educators must possess a wide base of psychomotor skills. In addition, expertise in some activities is desirable.
5. There are valid reasons for testing the psychomotor skills of prospective physical education majors. These skills can be measured either by batteries of psychomotor tests, by activity performance, or both.

DEFINITIONS RELATED TO PSYCHOMOTOR LEARNING

The terms *learning* and *teaching* should be briefly defined. Learning refers to acquisition of knowledge or skill. We judge whether a person has learned by changes in performance or behavior. Learning most often occurs in relation to study directed by another person. That is, a teacher directs the student so that learning occurs. Thus teaching implies a process done by one person to others; learning implies that the individual has gained knowledge or skill. Remember, however, that learning can be self-directed, whereas teaching requires at least two people in the process.

In this chapter, the most important term for a physical educator is *psychomotor learning*. This is one of the keys to our discipline, because it means acquiring knowledge about our own physical movements and how they relate to others. Psychomotor learning is more than just learning patterns of movement (a dance step, or triple jump). It includes an awareness of how movement of others influences us, and involves both the physical and mental processes.

Psychomotor skills refers to those skills and abilities related to human movement. These can be basic skills (running or jumping), or combinations and refinements of these basics (high jumping or basketball). Physical educators may be referred to as psychomotor-skill specialists, because of their knowledge about skills and abilities of human movement.

Students ordinarily learn psychomotor skills in a class, but it must be realized that a great amount of learning occurs out of class also. A psychomotor skills class is ordinarily called an *activity* class to distinguish it from a *theory* class (one conducted in a classroom). These really are not appropriate terms, because they imply there is no physical activity in the classroom and that there is no mental learning in an activity class. The terms *gym* or *physical education* customarily used in school refer to an activity class which usually is taught in the gymnasium or on a playing field. Sometimes these are called *service* classes, because the physical education department offers them as a service to the entire student body.

Professional physical educators are very much concerned about how to teach psychomotor skills. The term *movement education* has been used since the late 1940s to indicate that allowing learners to discover their own ways to move might be just as beneficial as telling or showing them how to move. Indeed, many physical educators believe that movement exploration is better because it encourages individual problem-solving and leads to creativity. However, most physical educators (and especially coaches) prefer to tell students precisely how to move. Chapter 9, "Applied Mechanics," will deal at greater length with this topic.

Psychomotor skills may be evaluated by various means — actual playing performance, judgment by a qualified person, and/or by performance in a number of test items. Three terms will be used when discussing the skills tests presented at the end of the chapter. The first of these, *test battery*, means a test composed of a number of test items. For example, a volleyball test battery could be composed of such test items as volleying, serving, passing, setting and spiking. *Validity* refers to the extent to which a test measures what it is supposed to measure. A valid softball skills test, for example, would accurately measure how well a student plays softball. A valid tennis knowledge test would include questions on what a tennis student should know. Finally, *reliability* measures the extent to which a test is consistent in measuring whatever it does measure. For example, a basketball skills or knowledge test is reliable when students make consistently similar scores when the same test is given twice over a short period of time.

IMPORTANCE OF LEARNING

In a limited sense, learning may be defined as gaining knowledge about something. To a physical educator, this means knowledge concerning physical movements of self and of others. Many persons are still inclined to assume that physical movements are done "from the neck down," that they do not require any mental effort. The idea that the mind and body can be separated has long been discarded by scientists, but the thought still lingers.

Bell (1970) succinctly points out that sensorimotor learning begins with a neurological basis and includes the central nervous system (brain and spinal cord), the pyramidal and extrapyramidal nervous systems, and the sensory receptors. All of these are essential to physical movement. Even the simple reflex actions which are done without thinking (such as jerking your finger away from a hot stove) involve the lower parts of the central nervous system.

How do we learn physical skills? After observing, reading, or being helped by another, a movement is made. The result of the movement is observed through the eyes, ears, or the touch systems. This information is compared to the desired movement and any necessary adjustment is made. The movement is repeated, with the same feedback process used to improve the movement. The *feedback system* (observation, comparison with desired result, and subsequent adjustment) is the same principle that is used to build the modern "thinking machine," the computer. Finally, sufficient practice is done so that movement becomes automatic. Table 7-1 summarizes the phases of the psychomotor learning process. Remember, however, that teaching and coaching are not as simple as this chart might lead you to believe.

The values of successful physical movement are well known. We must move to survive, to work, to play. We gain status by being a good performer, either on the athletic field, on the dance floor, on the musical stage, or in the artist's studio. Our health, both physical and mental, is enhanced through movement. There is no doubt that psychomotor skill learning results from some kind of physical activity (Mohr 1960, p. 340). In short, we live to move, and we move to live.

LEARNING AS A FORCE IN PHYSICAL EDUCATION

From the beginning of formal physical education as a school subject, the movement of the individual was of supreme importance. Originally, students were taught calisthenics and formal drills in an effort to improve their health. These were done in a

TABLE 7–1. PHASES OF PSYCHOMOTOR SKILL ACQUISITION.

PHASE	PURPOSE	COMMENTS
Cognitive	Learner must understand what is to be done.	Learner usually observes live demonstration or watches film. Learner can only think about few things at one time. Learner must concentrate on sequence of movements, not "correct form" shown in demonstration.
Fixation	Practice often to reduce conscious thought as to sequence, etc.	Usually requires more time than other two phases. Sometimes learner practices whole movement, sometimes works on the parts. Practice must be meaningful to produce results. Feedback is essential. Self-analysis is usually inaccurate, so a qualified teacher is most desirable. The length of practice periods varies with the task and the learner.
Automatic	Make psychomotor skills easier so movements become almost "unconscious."	Learner much less anxious or stressful over performance. Requires less "thinking," thus freeing learner to concentrate on strategy, etc. Difficult to change movement patterns once they reach automatic stage; qualified teacher most desirable.

Adapted from Margaret Robb, Man and sports — The acquisition of skill, *Quest* 14 (June 1970): 50-56.

rather rigid pattern, with the teacher serving as a combination demonstrator and director. It was only logical to assume that the teacher should know how to do the calisthenics and drills, and this type of training is what the early American physical education teacher-training schools provided. As American physical education progressed, there developed a strong feeling against this formal program. Games, leading to athletic contests, began to be popular, and the role of the teacher changed somewhat. Students were taught to perform the physical skills of the particular game, and then spent part of the class period playing. The teacher's role became that of a coach.

In the 1930s, another dimension was added to physical education in the U.S. Games and activities useful in later life (called *carryover* activities) were taught, in addition to the team games which were useful primarily in school. Thus the physical education teacher was asked to become proficient in golf, tennis, badminton, swimming, etc. so that he or she might teach them. In the late 1940s the role of the teacher in elementary school physical education was expanded as movement education became popular. There was no set method of performing a skill; rather, the teacher became concerned with time, space, energy, and mass relationships — not "form."

The result of these changing emphases has given the physical education teacher many different activities to include in a program. Most schools have curriculum guides (written plans which tell teachers what activities should be taught with suggestions on how to teach them effectively). A good physical education program will consist of activities from each of these categories:

1. team games (volleyball, softball, field hockey, etc.)
2. individual and dual games (golf, tennis, etc.)
3. rhythms (modern dance, social dance, folk and square dance, etc.)
4. self-testing or conditioning (gymnastics, weight training, fitness, etc.)
5. aquatics (swimming, SCUBA, etc.)

The physical education teacher is expected to know several specific activities in each category and how to teach them. In most good physical education programs, students are taught 12 to 15 different activities during their 12 years of public school. (Some physical educators make the mistake of trying to teach 12 to 15 activities each year. Students can play the activities, but learning how to do them requires more than four or five days of instruction. The difference between physical education and recreational playing will be emphasized in later chapters.)

Countries with national physical education programs have established standards of performance which indicate to teachers and parents exactly how well similarly aged students should perform. AAHPER has made a start in this direction with the publication of sport skills tests in archery, basketball, football, volleyball, softball, and physical fitness. Now it is possible to compare test scores with a nationwide group. More recently, two special interest groups in AAHPER (dance and aquatics) have formulated standards for the physical education teacher — that is, they have listed what the physical educator should know in order to be a competent teacher.

Thus physical educators, whether teachers or not, must know how to perform a wide range of physical movements. They must understand not only the physical skills, but also the applied mechanical principles underlying their performance. Most physical educators are well skilled in a few areas but may be relatively unskilled in several others. This might be acceptable if these persons assume a job in which they could specialize in their strengths. Unfortunately, most K-12 teaching positions call for broad knowledge and ability in many activities. When teachers feel incompetent in an activity, they quite often do not teach it; their students may learn only a few of the physical activities deemed necessary. Your college will undoubtedly have specialists in many areas because physical educators need expert instruction. People who teach in public schools are often expected to teach such a variety of activities that they become generalists rather than specialists.

It is discouraging to observe that our best psychomotor expert — the coach — works with those who already possess skill or aptitude for movement, and that our least-trained psychomotor person — the classroom teacher — is given the job of guiding the young child during development. There is a trend, however, toward the earlier teaching of motor skills by specialists. The study of the learning problems of retarded and brain-damaged children shows rather conclusively that the ability to perform coordinated physical movements is a necessary prerequisite for normal physical and mental development.

LEARNING ABOUT MOVEMENT

Courses which will help prospective physical educators know about their own and others' movement patterns are discussed below.

Activity Courses

1. *Team games.* Usually, the skills, rules, and strategies in these activities are covered: field hockey, touch football, soccer, speedball, speedaway, basketball, volleyball, and softball.

2. *Individual and dual sports.* Usually, the skills, rules, and strategies in these activities are covered: archery, bowling, badminton, golf, track and field, tennis, and wrestling (boys).
3. *Rhythms.* Usually, the skills and history of modern dance, folk dance, square dance, ballet, and social dance are covered.
4. *Self-testing and conditioning.* Usually the skills and basic principles of human movement, gymnastics (including tumbling and apparatus), track and field, weight training, "slimnastics," and physical fitness are covered.
5. *Aquatics.* Usually the skills equivalent to an intermediate swimming course must be mastered, along with knowledge related to aquatics (principles of movement in water, small craft safety, and safety in swimming and diving).

Theory Courses

1. *Psychomotor learning.* One of the most recent developments in the preparation of physical educators is the inclusion of a motor-learning course on the undergraduate level. This is a direct result of the effort to make the physical education body of knowledge more directly applied to the teaching-learning process. Typical concepts studied include the relationship of motor performance to maturation, to age and sex, to motivation, to practice patterns, to emotions, and to speed and accuracy.
2. *Teaching methods.* For those planning to teach, at least one methods course (such as Teaching Techniques, or Methods and Materials) is required. These courses contain information about how to teach a category of activities (e.g., Methods and Materials of Tennis). Quite often they are taught by a specialist, and include detailed discussions of all the techniques of teaching the activity or activities. Lesson plans, psychomotor learning, techniques, evaluation, and motivation are usually discussed.
3. Related courses, discussed in other chapters, include kinesiology and physiology of exercise.

ASSESSING YOUR CURRENT STATUS

According to most physical educators, the ability to perform the skills of an activity is highly desirable if one wishes to teach well. All physical educators will not be teachers, but the consensus is that those who can perform a minimum of skills in a variety of activities will tend to be more successful in whatever phase of physical education they work.

A current popular belief in education circles is that instruction is most beneficial when it is specifically geared to the needs of each student. To individualize instruction requires a great deal of information about each person. This is usually gained by some combination of testing (such as entrance exams, advanced placement exams, or aptitude tests), by observation of the student's performance in an activity, and/or by personal interviews. It is ironic that there are hundreds of research studies in physical education which concern the testing of physical skills, yet Chapter 2 showed that only a few colleges or universities use any test (with the possible exception of a physical fitness test) to ascertain anything about the physical abilities of their beginning physical education majors. Even fewer schools give competency tests at the end of their students' training.

The problem is most acute when it concerns the beginning physical education major. Invariably, the majority of these students are well skilled in a few activities, yet unskilled in others. Wilson points out:

Frequently, all major students upon entrance to an institution are placed in the same skills courses, regardless of previous experience. Once universal, today this pattern is questioned widely, since it frequently necessitates teaching geared near the beginning level. Such required instruction wastes the time of the highly skilled student (Wilson 1964, p. 65).

The material at the end of this chapter is designed to give you and your department a chance to evaluate your sports skills. The purposes of the tests are given, the tests are described, and norms are presented.

Bibliography

Bell, V. L. 1970. *Sensorimotor learning.* Pacific Palisades, Calif.: Goodyear Publishing Co.

Bowers, L., and Klesius, S. Interdisciplinary approach to perceptual-motor understanding. *JOHPER* 41 (June 1970):23.

Buckellew, W. The role of perceptual organization, feedback and communication in the development of physical skill. *The Physical Educator* 28 (Oct. 1971):29.

Curtis, D. M. Young child: The significance of motor development. *JOHPER* 42 (May 1971):29.

Lockhart, A. Communicating with the learner. *Quest* 6 (May 1966):57-66.

———, and Singer, R. What do we mean by the expert in motor learning? *JOHPER* 42 (Feb. 1971):34-37.

Martens, R., et al. Money and praise: Do they improve motor learning and performance? *Research Quarterly* 43 (Dec. 1972):429-42.

Mohr, D. R. The contributions of physical activity to skill learning. *Research Quarterly* 31 (May 1960, Part 2):321-50.

Richardson, A. Mental practice: A review and discussion. Part 1, *Research Quarterly* 38 (Mar. 1967):95-107; Part 2, 38:263-73.

Robb, M. Man and sports — The acquisition of skill. *Quest* 14 (June 1970):50-56.

Smith, P. Perceptual-motor skills and reading readiness of kindergarten children. *JOHPER* 41 (Apr. 1970):43.

Stafford, E. G. Professional activity courses, mainstay of the physical education curriculum. *The Physical Educator* 29 (Mar. 1972):17.

Tharp, R. G., and Gallimore, R. What a coach can teach a teacher. *Psychology Today* 9 (Jan. 1976):75.

Torpey, J. E. Motor-perceptual development and physical education. *The Physical Educator* 28 (Mar. 1971):11.

Wasserman, B. New directions in physical education skill acquisition. *The Physical Educator* 29 (Oct. 1972):135.

Whiting, H. T. A. Overview of the skill learning process. *Research Quarterly* 43 (Oct. 1972):266.

Williams, H. G. Learning. *JOHPER* 39 (Nov.-Dec. 1968):28-31.

Williams, I. Effects of practice and prior learning on motor memory. *Journal of Motor Behavior* 3 (Sept. 1971):205-11.

Wilson, R. M. Competency testing. *JOHPER* 35 (Feb. 1964):64-66.

Student Activities

1. Using the card catalogue or periodical indexes in your school library, list four or five titles of books or articles on any one of these topics:
   a. Psychomotor learning
   b. Sensorimotor learning
   c. Mental practice in physical education
   d. Perceptual-motor skill acquisition
   e. Learning of physical skills by mentally and/or emotionally handicapped persons
   f. Teaching psychomotor skills
2. Observe a class in which mentally, emotionally, and/or physical handicapped persons are being taught a motor skill. Compare the procedures with those used for normal students.

3. Interview senior physical education majors. What do they think about the skills test used at your school?

Statements for Class Discussion

1. Playing the game is the best way to determine how good a person is in physical skills.
2. Since it is possible to learn how to play basketball from a fellow student, it is a waste of money to hire a physical education teacher to do the same thing.
3. Some coaches may be excellent teachers of psychomotor skills, yet the same persons may be terrible physical education teachers. Why?

SKILLS TESTS

Purposes

As stated above, skilled students may waste time taking classes in which they already know the material. It is equally obvious that an unskilled student is unsuited for advanced activity classes. The first purpose of the screening tests described in this chapter is to ascertain the score of each student in as many skills tests as can be given. The number of tests given will vary from institution to institution, and perhaps from term to term. It is logical to assume that the more tests that are given and evaluated, the greater knowledge both you and the department will have of your competence.

The second purpose of this program is to indicate how the score achieved compares to those scores recorded by a similar group of students. (Because each school differs in its philosophy, facilities and staff, the evaluation of these test results will vary. Each department will decide for itself the standards which its students must meet.) After evaluation according to departmental standards, the department can then devise an appropriate series of experiences or courses for the student.

Thirdly, skills testing should help encourage the attitude that physical skills can be accurately measured and evaluated. Development of this attitude will be hastened if the tests in this text are administered by other physical education majors enrolled in the tests and measurements course. If this is possible, beginning majors should become aware that the administration of these tests is part of their future professional training. Students using this text might be asked to keep a record of their performance (see Figure 7-1, p. 72), and to compare the results with the new majors some three or four years later.

Selection of Test Batteries

1. *Physical skills tests.* AAHPER has published a battery of sports skills tests designed for males and females between the ages of 10 and 18. Even though these tests were not specifically designed for college-age students, they were selected as screening tests for the following reasons:

    a. The AAHPER tests were constructed by leading physical educators in the United States. Though designed for youth, the assumption is made that they can serve as screening tests for older students. (Unfortunately, the AAHPER test booklets do not present specific validity and reliability statistics; this aspect of their testing program needs to be completed.)

    b. Each of the published AAHPER tests has national norms. Thus, if a department wishes, the beginning major in physical education can be compared to high school students. (For an example, see Table 7-2 in this chapter.)

    c. Those who teach physical education customarily test and evaluate their students. The public and the school administration expect it. It seems logical to use those tests specifically developed for the age group taught. Being exposed to these tests as participants will familiarize students with the tests they probably will be using when they themselves are teachers.

In some instances, an AAHPER test in a particular skill has yet not been published. In such cases, previously published tests or a locally constructed test are presented.

Thirteen specific tests are described on the following pages. These are:

Archery	Football (touch)	Soccer	Track and field
Badminton	Golf	Softball	Volleyball
Basketball	Bowling	Swimming	Wrestling
		Tennis	

2. *Playing ability tests.* There are many teachers and students who feel that a skills test does not fairly rate the ability of a person to perform a particular activity. In theory, a valid and reliable skills test should give the same results as a subjective rating by expert judges, but this is a very controversial issue. If a department wishes to, it may administer the playing ability test as described for most of the activities presented here.

General Procedures for Taking Skills Test

While it is impossible for each department of physical education to establish exactly the same procedures for taking and evaluating these tests, the following general directions would seem logical:

1. You will receive notice of the forthcoming test.
2. You may become familiar with the items by reading the direction sheet for that particular test. If you wish to do so, practice on the items.
3. After taking the test, record in this text the results of each item.

Note carefully the explanations given with the Archery test. This will be the pattern to use on all tests, and will enable you to more accurately record and interpret the results.

ARCHERY SKILLS TEST*

Basic Information

Students will shoot arrows at a target from two different distances. The results at each distance will be compared to previously established norms. Table 7-2 presents the mean scores for three different groups of subjects on these test items.

**TABLE 7–2. MEAN SCORES OF VARIOUS GROUPS
ON SELECTED ITEMS OF THE AAHPER ARCHERY TEST.**

EVENT	17– 18–YEAR–OLD GIRLS	17– 18–YEAR–OLD BOYS	BEGINNING MAJORS
20 yd.	26 pts.[a]	43 pts.[a]	42 pts.[b]
30 yd.	Not given	26 pts.[a]	26 pts.[b]

[a] 48-in. target, 12 arrows   [b] 48-in. target, 6 arrows x 2

*Adapted from AAHPER, *Archery for boys and girls (skills test manual)* (Washington, D.C.: AAHPER, 1967). David K. Brace, test consultant. Used by permission.

FIGURE 7-1. Skills tests profile sheet.

Standard score	Archery	Badminton	Basketball	Bowling	Football	Golf	Physical fitness	Run	Soccer	Softball	Swimming	Tennis	Track & field	Volleyball	Wrestling
100															
95															
90															
85															
80															
75															
70															
65															
60															
55															
50															
45															
40															
35															
30															
25															
20															
15															
10															
5															
0															
Take class															
Exempt from class															

Sample (at right):

	Track & field	Volley-ball	Wrestling
60			
55		59	
50	53		
45			45
40			

Directions: Indicate your rating by inserting the average standard score for each skills test in the proper space, and then outlining the space. Example: an average standard score of 53 is placed next to 50, an average score of 59 is placed by 55, an average of 45 is placed by 45. (Sample at right)

NAME _____ DATE _____

TABLE 7–3. NORMS FOR AAHPER ARCHERY SKILLS TEST.

| STANDARD SCALE | 36 IN. TARGET | | | | 48 IN. TARGET | |
| | MALES | | FEMALES | | MALES AND FEMALES | |
	20 YD.	30 YD.	20 YD.	30 YD.	20 YD.	30 YD.
100						
95						
90						47
85						43
80					50	39
75					45	34
70			39	24	40	30
65		24	32	20	36	26
60	31	19	26	16	31	21
55	23	15	20	12	26	17
50	15	10	14	8	21	13
45	8	5	7	4	16	9
40	1	1	1		12	4
35					7	
30					2	
25						
20						
15						
10						
5						
0						
MEAN	15.41	9.82	13.65	8.03	21.2	12.8
SD	19.36	11.8	15.70	10.08	11.99	10.74
N	17.0	17.0	43.0	33.0	133.0	133.0
H. S.	23.0	23.0	33.0	22.0	48.0	45.0
L. S.	0.0	0.0	0.0	0.	0.	0.0
RANGE	23.0	23.0	33.0	22.0	48.0	45.0
8SC	1.54	.94	1.25	.80	.96	.86
MAX. SCORE	54.0	54.0	54.0	54.0	54.0	54.0
NO. TRLS	6.0	6.0	6.0	6.0	6.0	6.0

Test Description

1. Standing 20 yd. from a target, students will shoot six arrows. Scoring will be on a 9, 7, 5, 3, 1 point basis. The total of all six arrows is the score, 54 being maximum.

20 yd.

2. Standing 30 yd. from the same target, six more arrows are shot, with the score of all six being totaled and recorded as before.

30 yd.

Evaluation

The score for each objective test item is recorded next to its description above. These raw scores are then circled on the norm tables (Table 7-3). The average standard score is determined by first adding all standard scores, and then dividing by the number of items. Students meeting predetermined departmental standards may be examined further, or be excused from instruction in archery.

BADMINTON SKILLS TEST*

Basic Information

The objective three-item test measures the ability to perform selected skills which are basic to the game. Each test measures one skill. The number of trials for each item are reduced from the original test, so a group may complete the entire test in the allotted time. If the department wishes, a playing ability test will be given. Table 7-4 gives the mean scores for a group of beginning majors on these test items.

TABLE 7–4. MEAN SCORES OF VARIOUS GROUPS ON ITEMS OF
THE SCOTT, FOX, AND FRENCH BADMINTON TEST.

ITEM	*BEGINNING FEMALE MAJORS*	*BEGINNING MALE MAJORS*
Short serve	8 pts.	14 pts.
Long serve	5 pts.	8 pts.
High clear	17 pts.	27 pts.

Test Description

1. Short Serve: While standing at X, the player will attempt to serve into the marked area. A serve which passes between the net and a string 20 in. above it will count 5, 4, 3, 2, or 1 points, depending upon where it lands. No points are given if the serve goes above the string or lands outside the marked area. Two groups of five serves each are given.

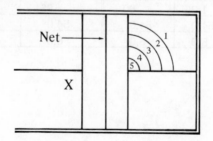

Total

---

*Items 1-3 adapted from M. Gladys Scott and Esther French, *Measurement and evaluation in physical education* (Dubuque, Iowa: Wm. C. Brown Publishing Co., 1959), pp. 65-74. Used by permission.

2. Long Serve: While standing anywhere in the left service court, the player will attempt a long, high serve into the marked area. A serve which passes over a rope 8 ft. above the floor 14 ft. back from the net will count 5, 4, 3, 2, or 1 points, depending upon where it lands. No points are awarded if the serve does not pass over the rope or lands outside the marked area. Two groups of five serves each are given.

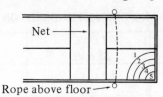

3. High Clear: While standing in prescribed area, the player (X) will attempt to return a high serve with a high clear. A high clear which passes over a rope 8 ft. above the floor 14 ft. back from the net will count 2, 3, 4, or 5 points, depending upon where it lands. No points are given if the clear does not pass over the rope or lands outside the marked area. Two groups of five high clear shots are given.

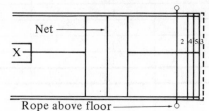

4. Playing Ability Test: [1] The class will be divided into small groups. A tournament will be conducted, in which each player plays all others in his group (or as many of the players as time permits). The object is to score as many points as possible in each five-minute game. At the conclusion of each game, each player will report the number of points he served. In theory, players who score more points in these abbreviated games are better skilled in the game of badminton than those who scored fewer points.

Evaluation

The score for each objective test item is recorded next to its description. These raw scores are then circled on the norm tables (Tables 7-5 and 7-6). The average standard score is determined by first adding all standard scores, and then dividing by the number of items. Students meeting predetermined departmental standards may be examined further, or be excused from instruction in badminton.

BASKETBALL SKILLS TEST*

Basic Information

Nine tests covering the fundamental skills of basketball are presented. Certain adaptations will be made in order that the entire test can be given in the allotted time. These involve reducing the number of trials in some of the shooting tests. Table 7-7 presents the mean (average) scores for the test items for two different groups.

---

[1] Idea gained from Kenneth A. Penman, Dual sport evaluation, *The Physical Educator* 24 (Dec. 1967): 175-76.

*Adapted from AAHPER, *Basketball skills test manual (boys)* (Washington, D.C.: AAHPER, 1966). David K. Brace, test consultant. Used by permission.

TABLE 7—5. NORMS FOR SCOTT, FOX, AND FRENCH BADMINTON TEST (MALES).

STANDARD SCALE	SHORT SERVE	LONG SERVE	HIGH CLEAR
	NO.	NO.	NO.
100			
95			
90	42.		
85	39.	22.	
80	35.	20.	52.
75	32.	18.	48.
70	28.	16.	44.
65	25.	14.	40.
60	21.	12.	36.
55	18.	10.	31.
50	14.	8.	27.
45	10.	6.	23.
40	7.	5.	19.
35	3.	3.	15.
30		1.	11.
25			7.
20			3.
15			
10			
5			
0			
MEAN	13.961	8.370	27.292
SD	8.878	4.813	10.277
N	154.0	154.0	154.0
H. S.	39.0	21.0	48.0
L. S.	0.0	0.0	0.0
RANGE	39.0	21.0	48.0
8SC	.710	.385	.822
MAX. SCORE	50.0	50.0	50.0
NO. TRLS	10.0	10.0	10.0

TABLE 7—6. NORMS FOR SCOTT, FOX, AND FRENCH BADMINTON TEST (FEMALE).

STANDARD SCALE	SHORT SERVE NO.	LONG SERVE NO.	HIGH CLEAR NO.
100		23.	
95		21.	
90		19.	
85	28.	17.	
80	25.	16.	43.
75	22.	14.	38.
70	19.	12.	34.
65	16.	10.	30.
60	13.	8.	26.
55	11.	7.	21.
50	8.	5.	17.
45	5.	3.	13.
40	2.	1.	9.
35			4.
30			
25			
20			
15			
10			
5			
0			
MEAN	7.613	4.782	17.183
SD	7.330	4.507	10.628
N	142.0	142.0	142.0
H. S.	26.0	24.0	41.0
L. S.	0.0	0.0	0.0
RANGE	26.0	24.0	41.0
8SC	.586	.361	.850
MAX. SCORE	50.0	50.0	50.000
NO. TRLS	10.0	10.0	10.000

TABLE 7–7. MEAN SCORES OF VARIOUS GROUPS ON AAHPER BASKETBALL SKILLS TEST.

TEST	17–18–YEAR OLD		BEGINNING MAJORS	
	MALES	*FEMALES*	*MALES*	*FEMALES*
Front shot	16 pts. [a]	11 pts. [a]	12 pts. [c]	8 pts. [c]
Side shot	18 pts. [b]	12 pts. [b]	10 pts. [c]	9 pts. [c]
Foul shot	8 pts. [b]	4 pts. [b]	4 pts. [c]	2 pts. [c]
Under basket shot	13 pts.	6 pts.	14 pts.	8 pts.
Speed pass	9.0 sec.	12.5 sec.	7.9 sec.	11.5 sec.
Jump and pass	20 in.	13 in.	21 in.	16 in.
Overarm pass	16 pts.	19 pts.	18 pts.	22 pts.
Push pass	24 pts.	24 pts.	23 pts.	26 pts.
Dribble	11.7 sec.	14.0 sec.	10.7 sec.	13.5 sec.

[a] 15 shots   [b] 20 shots   [c] 10 shots

Test Description

1. **Front Shot:** While standing at a spot just outside the free throw circle, the player (X) will try to make a basket, using any method of shooting. After one practice shot, two groups of five shots each are taken. Two points are awarded for each shot made, one point is awarded for a shot that hits the rim first, but then fails to go in. No points are awarded for a shot which hits the backboard first and does not go in.

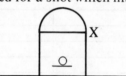

Total Points

2. **Side Shot:** While standing near the corner of the court, the player (X) will shoot five shots. He then moves to the other side of the basket (XX) and attempts five more shots. One practice shot is allowed. Two points are awarded for each shot made and one point for balls that hit the rim of the basket even though they may have hit the backboard also.

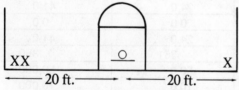

— 20 ft. —   — 20 ft. —

Total Points

3. **Foul Shot:** While standing at the free throw line, the player (X) will attempt five free throws using any style of shooting he prefers. He then takes another group of five free throws. One practice shot is allowed. One point is awarded for each shot that goes in, regardless of how the ball goes in.

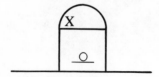

Total Points

4. Under Basket Shot: The player stands under the basket (X). At the signal "Go" he attempts to make as many one- or two-handed lay-up shots as possible, recovering the ball and shooting again rapidly to make as many goals as possible in 30 seconds. One practice shot is allowed. If the player loses the ball entirely, he may start over again, but only once. Two trials are given, with the best one being the final score.

Best Score

5. Speed Pass: While standing 9 ft. from the wall, the player (X) passes the ball (any method) as fast as he can to the wall, catches the rebound, and passes again. The time that it takes the ball to hit the wall 10 times is recorded. One practice throw is allowed. Two trials are given, with the best being the final time.

Best Score

6. Jump and Reach: The player, holding a small piece of chalk in his fingers, stands with his side to the wall with his knees straight and feet flat on the floor. He reaches up as far as possible and makes a mark. He then crouches, swings his arms, jumps as high as possible, and makes a second mark on the wall. The distance between the first and second marks is recorded to the nearest inch. One practice jump is allowed. Two trials are given, with the best being the final mark.

Best Score

7. Overarm Pass for Accuracy: The player, standing 35 ft. from the wall, makes a one-handed overarm throw toward a target. After one practice throw, 10 throws are made. Depending upon where the ball hits, 3, 2, or 1 points are given. Balls hitting on a line count the higher score.

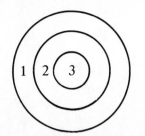

Total Points

TABLE 7–8. NORMS FOR AAHPER BASKETBALL TEST (MALE).

STANDARD SCALE	FRONT SHOT	SIDE SHOT	FOUL SHOT	UNDER BASKET SHOT	SPEED PASS
	NO.	NO.	NO.	NO./30 SEC.	SEC.
100					
95					
90		20.			4.9
85		18.	10.		5.3
80	20.	17.	9.	23.	5.7
75	18.	16.	8.	22.	6.0
70	17.	15.	7.	20.	6.4
65	16.	13.	6.	19.	6.8
60	14.	12.		17.	7.2
55	13.	11.	5.	16.	7.6
50	12.	10.	4.	14.	7.9
45	10.	8.	3.	13.	8.3
40	9.	7.	2.	11.	8.7
35	7.	6.	1.	10.	9.1
30	6.	5.		9.	9.4
25	5.	3.		7.	9.8
20	3.	2.		6.	10.2
15	2.	1.		4.	10.6
10	1.			3.	11.0
5					11.3
0					
MEAN	11.573	9.659	3.902	14.397	7.934
SD	3.401	3.105	2.013	3.682	.945
N	267.0	267.0	266.0	267.0	228.0
H. S.	19.0	19.0	9.0	22.0	11.1
L. S.	2.0	1.0	0.0	4.0	5.2
RANGE	17.0	18.0	9.0	18.0	5.9
8SC	.272	.248	.161	.295	.076
MAX. SCORE	20.0	20.0	10.0	******	10.0
NO. TRLS	10.0	10.0	10.0	2.0	2.0

TABLE 7—8 CONT. (MALE).

STANDARD SCALE	JUMP & REACH	OVERARM PASS FOR ACCURACY	PUSH PASS FOR ACCURACY	DRIBBLE
	IN.	NO.	NO.	SEC.
100				
95	32.			
90	30.			6.4
85	29.	29.		6.9
80	28.	28.		7.5
75	27.	26.	31.	8.0
70	26.	24.	29.	8.5
65	25.	23.	27.	9.1
60	23.	21.	26.	9.6
55	22.	19.	24.	10.2
50	21.	18.	23.	10.7
45	20.	16.	21.	11.2
40	19.	14.	20.	11.8
35	18.	13.	18.	12.3
30	16.	11.	17.	12.9
25	15.	9.	15.	13.4
20	14.	8.	14.	13.9
15	13.	6.	12.	14.5
10		4.	11.	15.0
5		3.	9.	15.5
0				
MEAN	21.060	17.721	22.865	10.698
SD	2.915	4.204	3.850	1.346
N	266.0	244.0	266.0	248.0
H. S.	31.0	28.0	30.0	15.2
L. S.	13.0	4.0	10.0	6.9
RANGE	18.0	24.0	20.0	8.3
8SC	.233	.336	.308	.108
MAX. SCORE	******	30.0	30.0	******
NO. TRLS	2.0	10.0	10.0	2.0

TABLE 7-9. NORMS FOR AAHPER BASKETBALL TEST (FEMALE).

STANDARD SCALE	FRONT SHOT	SIDE SHOT	FOUL SHOT	UNDER BASKET SHOT	SPEED PASS
	NO.	NO.	NO.	NO./30 SEC.	SEC.
100					
95					
90					
85	17.	19.	7.	18.	
80	16.	18.		16.	
75	15.	16.	6.	15.	8.4
70	14.	15.	5.	14.	9.0
65	12.	13.		12.	9.6
60	11.	12.	4.	11.	10.3
55	10.	11.	3.	10.	10.9
50	8.	9.	2.	8.	11.5
45	7.	8.		7.	12.1
40	5.	7.	1.	6.	12.8
35	4.	5.		4.	13.4
30	3.	4.		3.	14.0
25	1.	2.		2.	14.7
20		1.			15.3
15					15.9
10					16.5
5					17.2
0					
MEAN	8.133	9.333	2.434	8.450	11.522
SD	3.433	3.465	1.754	3.331	1.569
N	128.0	129.0	129.0	129.0	129.0
H. S.	16.0	18.0	7.0	17.0	17.0
L. S.	0.0	1.0	0.0	2.0	9.0
RANGE	16.0	17.0	7.0	15.0	8.0
8SC	.275	.277	.140	.266	.125
MAX. SCORE	20.0	20.0	10.0	******	10.0
NO. TRLS	10.0	10.0	10.0	2.0	2.0

TABLE 7–9 CONT. (FEMALE).

STANDARD SCALE	JUMP AND REACH	OVERARM PASS FOR ACCURACY	PUSH PASS FOR ACCURACY	DRIBBLE
	IN.	NO.	NO.	SEC.
100	28.			
95	27.			
90	26.			
85	25.			
80	23.			
75	22.	31.		10.2
70	21.	29.	31.	10.9
65	20.	27.	29.	11.6
60	18.	25.	28.	12.2
55	17.	24.	27.	12.9
50	16.	22.	26.	13.5
45	14.	20.	24.	14.2
40	13.	18.	23.	14.8
35	12.	16.	22.	15.5
30	11.	14.	21.	16.2
25	9.	13.	19.	16.8
20	8.	11.	18.	17.5
15		9.	17.	18.1
10		7.	16.	18.8
5			14.	19.4
0			13.	20.1
MEAN	15.754	21.692	25.703	13.526
SD	3.146	4.559	3.121	1.642
N	125.0	117.0	128.0	119.0
H. S.	27.0	30.0	30.0	19.7
L. S.	9.0	8.000	14.0	10.4
RANGE	18.0	22.000	16.0	9.3
8SC	.252	.365	.250	.131
MAX. SCORE	******	30.0	30.0	******
NO. TRLS	2.0	10.0	10.0	2.0

8. Push Pass for Accuracy: The player, standing 25 ft. from the same target used for the overarm pass for accuracy, makes a two-handed pass. After one practice pass, 10 more passes are made. Depending upon where the ball hits, 3, 2, or 1 points are given. Balls hitting on a line count the higher score.

Total Points

9. Dribble: The player stands behind the starting line. At the signal "Go" he starts to dribble to the right of a chair 5 ft. away, and then continues weaving in and around five other chairs placed 8 ft. apart. He continues this until he returns to the starting line. One practice trial is allowed. The ball may be dribbled with either hand, so long as a legal dribble is used. Two trials are given, with the time recorded in seconds and tenths of seconds. The best time is the final score.

Best Time

10. Playing Ability Test:[2] Each player will be assigned a partner of supposedly equal ability. This team will then participate in a series of half-court games. In theory, the better players will be shown by the number of points they score against their opponents. If a foul occurs, the offended player will take one or two free throws as the regular rules apply. The games will be five minutes in length. At the whistle, the number of points each team has scored are reported. (If desired, games of one-on-one may be substituted for the two-man teams.)

Evaluation

The score for each objective test item is recorded next to its description. These raw scores are then circled on the norm tables. The average standard score is determined by first adding all standard scores, and then dividing by the number of items. Students meeting predetermined departmental standards may be examined further, or be excused from instruction in basketball.

BOWLING SKILLS TEST*

Basic Information

The ability to bowl effectively is usually measured by rolling several lines, and then comparing the average with a comparable group. Sometimes this is combined with a subjective test in order that form may be judged.

---

[2] Idea gained from Penman. Dual sport evaluation, pp. 175-76; and Arne L. Olson, Two man volleyball. *The Physical Educator* 16 (Dec. 1959): 157.

*Unpublished test. Used by permission of John B. Hodapp, Mankato (Minnesota) State University, test consultant.

Test Description

As you roll for score, an expert will evaluate your form as follows:

1.

Stance	Deficient	Satisfactory
Approach		
Pendulum swing		
Delivery		
Follow through		

2. A practical bowling test is to roll 15 balls in the following sequence.
   a. First 5 balls rolled for the pocket (1-3 for right-handed bowlers, 1-2 for left-handed bowlers). If the pocket is hit, score 10 points; if head pin hit full or a Brooklyn, score 5 points. If head pin is missed, 0 points. Total the points for all 5 balls rolled.

Total

   b. Second 5 balls rolled at 7 pin. If 7 pin is covered by the ball, score 5 points. If 7 pin not covered, 0 points. Total the points for all 5 balls rolled.

Total

   c. Third 5 balls rolled at 10 pin. If 10 pin is covered, score 5 points. If 10 pin not covered, 0 points. Total the points for all 5 balls rolled.

Total

3. Bowling Ability Test: You will bowl three lines on approved lanes, with at least one opponent. At the completion of the lines, have an opponent verify your score, and then turn it in to the instructor.

Game 1	Game 2	Game 3	Average

Evaluation

None of the above tests have been given to enough majors to compute accurate norms. Departmental standard must be used to determine whether students should be examined further, or excused from instruction in this activity.

AAHPER FOOTBALL SKILLS TEST*

Basic Information

Nine skills common to touch football will be evaluated by objective test items. Each item measures but one skill. If time permits, a playing ability test will be given. Certain adaptations will be made in order that the group may finish the entire test in the allotted time. These include eliminating one item from the original test, and reducing the number of trials in five other items. Table 7-10 presents the mean scores for two different groups of subjects on these test items.

TABLE 7–10. MEAN SCORES OF VARIOUS GROUPS ON AAHPER FOOTBALL SKILLS TEST.

EVENT	17–18–YEAR–OLDS [a]	BEGINNING MAJORS	
		MALE	FEMALE
Forward pass (distance)	38 yd.	42 yd.	20 yd.
50-yd. dash with football	6.7 sec.	6.5 sec.	7.7 sec.
Blocking	7.2 sec.	6.8 sec.	8.5 sec.
Forward pass (accuracy)	14 pt. [b]	14 pt. [c]	4 pt. [c]
Punt for distance	33 yd.	36 yd.	20 yd.
Catching forward pass	15 pts. [d]	18 pts. [e]	12 pts. [e]
Pull-out	3.1 sec.	2.9 sec.	3.4 sec.
Kick-off	32 yd.	37 yd.	20 yd.
Dodging run	20.6 sec.	25.2 sec.	27.2 sec.

[a] Apparently males (test manual is unclear)   [b] 10 trials   [c] 5 trials x 2
[d] 20 catches   [e] 10 catches x 2

Test Description

1. Forward Pass for Distance: The player (X) stands within two lines 6 ft. apart. He takes one or more running steps inside this zone and throws a football as far as possible. One practice pass is allowed, and then two passes are made. The longest pass, recorded to the nearest yard, is the recorded score.

Best Distance

2. 50-Yd. Dash with Football: The player (X) stands behind the starting line holding a football. On the signal "Go" the player runs directly to the finish line 50 yd. away. The player must warm up before making his two trials, and must carry the ball the

*Adapted from AAHPER, *Football for boys (skills test manual)* (Washington, D.C.: AAHPER, 1965). David K. Brace, test consultant. Used by permission.

full distance. The time is recorded in seconds and tenths, with the best time of the two trials being recorded.

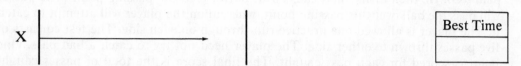

3. Blocking: Blocking (O) bags are arranged as shown. Bag 1 is about 15 ft. from the starting line. At the signal "Go" the player (X) charges from the starting line and crossbody blocks bag 1 clear to the ground. He then blocks bags 2 and 3 in a similar fashion. After one practice run-through, the player is given two trials. The fastest time for the circuit (recorded in seconds and tenths) is the final time.

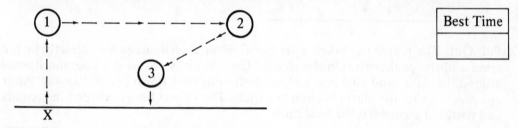

4. Forward Pass for Accuracy: The player stands 15 yd. from the target. He takes two or three small running steps (either right or left) parallel to the line, hesitates, and then throws to the target. Depending upon where the ball hits, the player is awarded 3, 2, 1, or 0 points. One practice pass is allowed, then five passes are given.

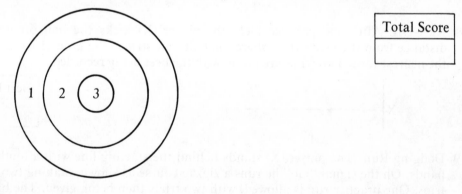

5. Football Punt for Distance: The player (X) after taking one practice punt, is allowed two punts for distance. He must remain in the punting zone during his kicks. The longest kick, recorded to the nearest yard, is given as the best kick.

6. Catching the Forward Pass: The player (X) is lined up 9 ft. away from the center. When the ball is snapped to the passer, the player runs straight ahead to the turning point (O). He then turns and heads 30 ft. outward to the passing point. The passer will pass the ball over this passing point, whereupon the player will attempt to catch it. The player is allowed one practice run-through on each side. The test consists of five passes thrown to either side. The player need not try to catch a bad pass. One point is scored for each pass caught. The final score is the total of passes caught from each side.

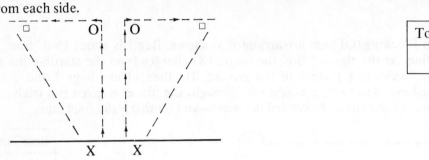

Total Points

7. Pull-Out: The player (X) takes a set position on a scrimmage line directly in the middle of the goal posts. On the signal "Go" he pulls out of the line and dashes around the right hand goal post and heads directly for a finish line 30 ft. away. After one practice run, the player is given two trials. The fastest time (recorded in seconds and tenths of seconds) is the final time.

Best Time

8. Kick-Off: After one practice kick, the player (X) kicks the ball off a tee. The distance from the kick-off to where the ball first strikes the ground is measured to the nearest yard. Two trials are given, with the best being recorded.

Best Distance

9. Dodging Run: The player (X) stands behind the starting line with a football in his hands. On the signal "Go" he runs a zigzag course as shown, making two complete trips. One practice run is allowed, with two trials then being given. The ball can be carried in any way and need not be shifted from side to side. If it is dropped the run does not count. The best of the two trials is recorded.

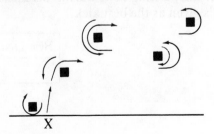

Best Time

TABLE 7–11. NORMS FOR AAHPER FOOTBALL TEST (MALE).

STANDARD SCALE	FORWARD PASS FOR DISTANCE	50–YD. DASH WITH FOOTBALL	BLOCKING	FORWARD PASS FOR ACCURACY	FOOTBALL PUNT FOR DISTANCE
	YD.	SEC.	SEC.	NO.	YD.
100					66.
95					63.
90	63.				60.
85	61.				57.
80	58.			14.	54.
75	55.		4.9	12.	51.
70	53.	5.8	5.3	11.	48.
65	50.	5.9	5.7	10.	45.
60	47.	6.1	6.1	9.	42.
55	45.	6.3	6.5	8.	39.
50	42.	6.5	6.8	7.	36.
45	39.	6.7	7.2	5.	33.
40	37.	6.9	7.6	4.	30.
35	34.	7.0	8.0	3.	27.
30	31.	7.2	8.4	2.	24.
25	29.	7.4	8.7	1.	21.
20	26.	7.6	9.1		18.
15	23.	7.8	9.5		16.
10	21.	7.9	9.9		13.
5	18.	8.1	10.3		10.
0	15.	8.3			7.
MEAN	41.983	6.492	6.833	6.519	36.363
SD	6.704	.453	.953	2.984	7.447
N	233.0	232.0	183.0	233.0	234.0
H. S.	61.0	10.0	10.0	13.0	63.0
L. S.	15.0	5.8	5.2	0.0	5.0
RANGE	46.0	4.2	4.8	13.0	58.0
8SC	.536	.036	.076	.239	.596
MAX. SCORE	******	******	******	15.0	******
NO. TRLS	2.0	2.0	2.0	5.0	2.0

TABLE 7-11 CONT. (MALE).

STANDARD SCALE	CATCHING FORWARD PASS NO. (5 TO EACH SIDE)	PULL-OUT SEC.	KICK-OFF YD.	DODGING RUN SEC.
100			74.	
95			70.	
90			66.	
85		2.0	63.	17.8
80		2.1	59.	18.8
75		2.2	55.	19.9
70		2.4	52.	21.0
65		2.5	48.	22.0
60	10.	2.6	44.	23.1
55		2.8	41.	24.2
50	9.	2.9	37.	25.2
45	8.	3.1	33.	26.3
40		3.2	30.	27.3
35	7.	3.3	26.	28.4
30		3.5	22.	29.5
25	6.	3.6	19.	30.5
20		3.8	15.	31.6
15	5.	3.9	11.	
10		4.0		
5	4.			
0	3.			
MEAN	9.035	2.920	37.005	25.218
SD	1.401	.343	9.164	2.658
N	173.0	217.0	217.0	158.0
H. S.	10.0	4.0	72.0	31.2
L. S.	1.0	2.1	13.0	18.0
RANGE	9.0	1.9	59.0	13.2
8SC	.112	.028	.733	.213
MAX. SCORE	10.0	******	******	******
NO. TRLS	10.0	2.0	2.0	2.0

TABLE 7–12. NORMS FOR AAHPER FOOTBALL TEST (FEMALE).

STANDARD SCALE	FORWARD PASS FOR DISTANCE	50–YD DASH WITH FOOTBALL	BLOCKING	FORWARD PASS FOR ACCURACY	FOOTBALL PUNT FOR DISTANCE
	YD.	SEC.	SEC.	NO.	YD.
100					
95					
90	36.			10.	
85	34.		.8	9.	
80	32.		1.9	8.	
75	30.		3.0	7.	36.
70	28.		4.1	6.	33.
65	26.		5.2	5.	29.
60	24.	6.8	6.3	4.	26.
55	22.	7.3	7.4	3.	23.
50	20.	7.7	8.5	2.	20.
45	18.	8.2	9.6	1.	17.
40	16.	8.7	10.7		14.
35	14.	9.2	11.8		11.
30	12.	9.7	12.9		8.
25	10.	10.2	14.0		5.
20	8.	10.6	15.1		2.
15		11.1	16.2		
10		11.6			
5		12.1			
0					
MEAN	19.747	7.748	8.502	2.458	20.229
SD	4.941	1.209	2.743	2.510	7.691
N	83.0	82.0	60.0	83.0	83.0
H. S.	34.0	13.5	15.4	10.0	35.0
L. S.	9.0	7.0	1.0	0.0	1.0
RANGE	25.0	12.8	14.4	10.0	34.0
8SC	.395	.097	.219	.201	.615
MAX. SCORE	******	******	******	15.0	******
NO. TRLS	2.0	2.0	2.0	5.0	2.0

TABLE 7-12 CONT. (FEMALE).

STANDARD SCALE	CATCHING FORWARD PASS NO. (5 TO EACH SIDE)	PULL-OUT SEC.	KICK-OFF YD.	DODGING RUN SEC.
100				
95				
90				18.5
85				19.6
80		2.7	38.	20.7
75		2.8	35.	21.8
70	11.	2.9	32.	22.9
65	10.	3.1	29.	23.9
60	9.	3.2	26.	25.0
55	7.	3.3	23.	26.1
50	6.	3.4	20.	27.2
45	5.	3.6	17.	28.3
40	4.	3.7	14.	29.4
35	3.	3.8	11.	30.5
30	2.	3.9	8.	31.6
25	1.	4.1	5.	32.7
20		4.2		
15		4.3		
10				
5				
0				
MEAN	6.373	3.439	19.8	27.227
SD	2.695	.306	7.521	2.733
N	83.0	75.0	75.0	82.0
H. S.	10.0	4.2	36.0	32.0
L. S.	0.0	2.8	6.0	19.5
RANGE	10.0	1.4	30.0	12.5
8SC	.216	.026	.602	.219
MAX. SCORE	10.0	******	******	******
NO. TRLS	10.0	2.0	2.0	2.0

10. Playing Ability Test: Teams with an equal number of players are formed. A touch football game is played, with each player playing a different position each time the ball changes possession (alternate between the line and the backfield if possible). The quarterback (offense) and deep safety (defense) direct their respective teams for that particular series of downs. An expert observer attempts to evaluate the running, passing, blocking, and defensive skills of each player as the game progresses.

Evaluation

The score for each objective test item is recorded next to its description. These raw scores are then circled on the norm tables. The average standard score is determined by first adding all standard scores, and then dividing by the number of items. Students meeting predetermined departmental standards may be examined further, or be excused from instruction in football.

GOLF SKILLS TEST*

Basic Information

The ability to hit effectively with different clubs is best measured by actually playing golf, but in some instances this cannot be done. Both types of tests are described here.

Test Description

1. Test on Form: Each student will be asked to demonstrate his or her golf swing while hitting real or plastic balls. An expert golf instructor will evaluate golf skill, as follows:

	Deficient	Average	Superior
Full swing a. Wood			
b. 5 iron			
Half swing c. 9 iron			

2. Playing Ability Test: Each student will go to a golf course designated by the instructor and shoot nine holes of golf. At the conclusion of the round the official scorecard will be submitted. If the instructor permits, the player may play more than once, with the best score being recorded.

Evaluation

Students meeting predetermined departmental standards may be examined further, or be excused from instruction in golf.

---

*Used by permission of Jack Amann, golf coach at Mankato (Minnesota) State University, test consultant.

TABLE 7–13. NORMS ON GOLF-PLAYING ABILITY TEST (MALE).

STANDARD SCALE	STROKES
100	
95	
90	
85	
80	
75	
70	
65	38.
60	43.
55	48.
50	53.
45	57.
40	63.
35	68.
30	73.
25	78.
20	83.
15	88.
10	93.
5	98.
0	103.
MEAN	53.279
SD	9.865
N	86.0
HIGH	115.0
LOW	41.0
RANGE	74.0
8SC	0.789
MAX. SCORE	******
NO. TRLS	1.0

General description of the course on which these norms are based: slightly rolling, moderately difficult, narrow fairways, 3400 yd.

SOCCER SKILLS TEST*

Basic Information

Five objectively scored items (three from the Warner test) are given. Each test item measures but one skill. If time permits, a playing ability test is given. Table 7-14 presents the mean scores for two different groups of subjects on these items.

TABLE 7–14. MEAN SCORES OF VARIOUS GROUPS ON WARNER SOCCER SKILLS TEST.

EVENT	MALES	FEMALES
Right foot kick	33 yd.	20 yd.
Left foot kick	28 yd.	16 yd.
Dribbling	20.6 sec.	29.0 sec.
Throw-in	19 yd.	9 yd.
Corner kick	9 pts.	4 pts.

Test Description

1. Kick for Distance, Right Foot: Taking a running start (5 or 6 yd.), the student (X) attempts to kick the ball in the air as far as it will go. The ball must land within the kicking zone (25 yd. wide). Three trials are given, with the best being recorded. A ball which lands outside the kicking area counts zero.

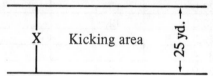

Best Score

2. Kick for Distance, Left Foot: This is the same as the test described above for the right foot.

Best Score

3. Dribbling: On the signal, the subject (X) dribbles the ball between the chairs in a figure eight fashion. The chairs are 15 ft. apart, with 15 ft. to the first chair. If a chair is missed, or if the hands are used, the trial does not count. If control of the ball is lost, it must be returned and started again at the point where control was lost. Two trials are given, with the fastest time (in seconds) being recorded. The watch is stopped when the subject, not the ball, recrosses the starting line.

Best Time

*Adapted from Glen Warner of the National Soccer Coaches Association of America, and William Bolonchuk, University of North Dakota.

TABLE 7–15. NORMS FOR WARNER SOCCER TEST (MALE).

STANDARD SCALE	RT. FOOT KICK	LT. FOOT KICK	DRIBBLING	THROW–IN	CORNER KICK FOR ACCURACY
	YD.	YD.	SEC.	YD.	PTS.
100				34.	
95				33.	
90		58.		31.	23.
85		54.		30.	21.
80		50.	11.3	28.	20.
75	56.	47.	12.9	27.	18.
70	52.	43.	14.4	25.	16.
65	47.	39.	16.0	24.	14.
60	42.	36.	17.5	22.	12.
55	37.	32.	19.1	21.	10.
50	33.	28.	20.6	19.	9.
45	28.	25.	22.1	18.	7.
40	23.	21.	23.7	16.	5.
35	18.	18.	25.2	15.	3.
30	13.	14.	26.8	13.	1.
25	9.	10.	28.3	12.	
20	4.	7.	29.9		
15		3.	31.4		
10			32.9		
5			34.5		
0					
MEAN	32.563	28.488	20.599	19.184	8.625
SD	11.923	9.134	3.858	3.765	4.586
N	215.0	215.0	214.0	103.0	104.0
H. S.	55.0	55.0	33.6	41.0	23.0
L. S.	0.0	0.0	12.9	13.0	0.0
RANGE	55.0	55.0	20.7	28.0	23.0
8SC	.954	.731	.309	.301	.367
MAX. SCORE	******	******	******	******	25.0
NO. TRLS	3.0	3.0	2.0	2.0	5.0

TABLE 7–16. NORMS FOR WARNER SOCCER TEST (FEMALE).

STANDARD SCALE	RT. FOOT KICK	LT. FOOT KICK	DRIBBLING	THROW-IN	CORNER KICK FOR ACCURACY
	YD.	YD.	SEC.	YD.	PTS.
100					23.
95					21.
90		40.			19.
85	39.	37.			17.
80	36.	34.			15.
75	33.	31.		21.	14.
70	31.	28.		19.	12.
65	28.	25.	18.2	16.	10.
60	25.	22.	21.8	14.	8.
55	23.	19.	25.4	11.	6.
50	20.	16.	29.0	9.	4.
45	17.	13.	32.6	6.	2.
40	15.	10.	36.2	4.	
35	12.	7.	39.8	1.	
30	9.	4.	43.5		
25	6.	1.	47.1		
20	4.		50.7		
15	1.		54.3		
10			57.9		
5			61.5		
0			65.1		
MEAN	19.927	15.598	29.019	8.705	3.837
SD	6.779	7.543	9.021	6.253	4.836
N	123.0	122.0	123.0	122.0	123.0
H. S.	37.0	39.0	65.2	20.0	23.0
L. S.	0.0	0.0	18.8	0.0	0.0
RANGE	37.0	39.0	46.4	20.0	23.0
8SC	.542	.603	.722	.500	.387
MAX. SCORE	******	******	******	******	25.
NO. TRLS	3.	3.	3.	3.	5.

4. Throw-In: The subject (X) throws the ball overhead with two hands while having any part of both feet in contact with the ground. Two trials are given, with the best score (to the nearest yard) being recorded.

Best Score

5. Corner Kick: The subject (X) stands in the corner area of a soccer field, and attempts to kick a ball so that it lands (first bounce) in the zone with the highest point value. The points for five kicks are added together, and become the final score.

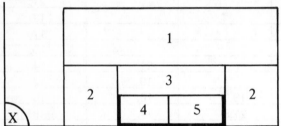

Total Points

Evaluation

The score for each objective test item is recorded next to its description. These raw scores are then circled on the norm tables. The average standard score is determined by first adding all standard scores, and then dividing by the number of items. Students meeting predetermined departmental standards may be examined further, or be excused from instruction in soccer.

AAHPER SOFTBALL SKILLS TEST*

Basic Information

Seven fundamental skills of softball will be measured by objective tests. Each test measures but one skill. Certain adaptations will be made so that a group may finish the test in the allotted time. These involve reducing the number of trials in three items and eliminating at least one and maybe two items from the original test. If the department desires, a regulation softball game will be played, thus permitting a subjective evaluation of skill. Table 7-17 presents mean scores for various groups on this test.

Test Description

1. Throw for Distance: While remaining within a 6 ft. restraining distance, the student (X) throws a softball as far as he can. The distance from the starting line to where the ball touches the ground is measured to the nearest foot. Three trials are given, the best recorded.

Best Distance

*Adapted from AAHPER, *Softball for boys and girls (skills test manual)* (Washington, D.C.: AAHPER, 1966). David K. Brace, test consultant. Used by permission.

TABLE 7–17. MEAN SCORES FOR VARIOUS GROUPS ON AAHPER SOFTBALL SKILLS TEST.

EVENT	17– 18–YEAR–OLD		BEGINNING MAJORS	
	MALES	FEMALES	MALES	FEMALES
Throw for distance	188 ft.	80 ft.	198 ft.	99 ft.
Overhead throw	13 pts.	10 pts.	12 pts.	11 pts.
Underhand pitch	10 pts. [a]	9 pts. [a]	11 pts. [b]	11 pts. [b]
Speed throw	19.8 sec.	19.8 sec.	15.0 sec.	19.5 sec.
Fungo hitting	28 pts. [c]	17 pts. [c]	34 pts. [d]	22 pts. [d]
Base running	15.7 sec.	15.7 sec.	12.7 sec.	15.2 sec.
Fielding balls	17 pts. [e]	17 pts. [e]	16 pts. [f]	15 pts. [f]

[a] 15 pitches   [b] 10 pitches x 1.5   [c] 20 hits   [d] 10 hits x 2   [e] 20 balls   [f] 15 balls x 1.25

2. Overhead Throw for Accuracy: After one or two practice throws, the player makes an overhead throw at a target 65 ft. away. Depending upon where the ball hits, 3, 2, 1, or 0 points are awarded. Ten throws are taken; final score is total of the 10 throws.

Total Points

3. Underhand Pitching: After one practice pitch, the player makes an underhand pitch toward a target 45 ft. away. Depending upon where the ball hits, 2, 1, or 0 points are awarded. Ten trials are given, with the total points being the final score.

Total Points

4. Speed Throw: After one practice trial, the player (X) makes an overhead throw to a wall 9 ft. away. He catches the rebound, and continues throwing and catching as rapidly as he can until he has completed 15 hits on the wall. Time, measured in seconds and tenths of seconds, begins when the first hit is made and ceases with the last hit. Two trials are given; the better score is recorded.

Best Time

5. Fungo Hitting: The player (X) stands behind home plate with a bat and ball. He tosses the ball up and attempts to hit a fly ball into right field. The next attempt should be into left field. After one practice hit to each field, he then hits 10 balls, alternating from one field to the other. Fly balls which land beyond the baseline on the intended side count 2 points; ground balls hit across the baseline on the intended side count 1 point.

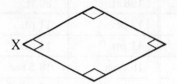

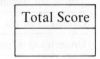

Total Score

6. Base Running: The Player (X), holding an imaginary bat, stands in the right-hand batter's box as if ready for a pitch. On the signal "hit," he swings at an imaginary ball, drops the bat (must not be thrown) and runs around all four bases, touching each one. One practice run is allowed. Two trials, measured in seconds and tenths of seconds, are given. The better trial is the final score.

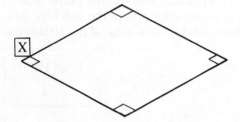

Best Score

7. Fielding Ground Balls: The player (X) stands within an area which is 50 ft. away from the thrower (T). Midway between them (25 ft.) is another line. The thrower starts throwing grounders toward the player, making the ball hit at least once before it crosses the 25-ft. line. The player must field each ball cleanly, hold it momentarily, and then toss it aside and be ready for the next ball. Balls are thrown every five seconds. The player starts back of the 50-ft. line but may move forward once the ball is thrown. Balls will be thrown at various speeds and directions (although they must remain inside the sidelines). Each ball correctly fielded counts 1 point. One practice trial is allowed, after which 15 balls are fielded.

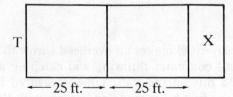

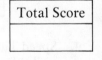

Total Score

8. Playing Ability Test: Teams will be formed with an equal number of players on each side. A modified softball game will be played, with each player playing a different position each inning (alternating between the infield and outfield if possible). In order that hitting, baserunning, fielding, and throwing will be at a maximum, the pitcher for each team will pitch to his teammates. An expert observer will attempt to evaluate players as they hit, run, field, and throw.

TABLE 7–18. NORMS FOR AAHPER SOFTBALL TEST (MALE).

STANDARD SCALE	THROW FOR DISTANCE	OVERHEAD THROW	UNDERHAND PITCH	SPEED THROW
	FT.	NO.	NO.	SEC.
100				
95			21.	
90			19.	
85	296.	26.	18.	
80	282.	24.	16.	
75	268.	22.	15.	
70	254.	20.	13.	11.8
65	240.	18.	12.	12.6
60	226.	16.	10.	13.4
55	212.	14.	9.	14.2
50	198.	12.	7.	15.0
45	184.	10.	6.	15.8
40	170.	8.	5.	16.6
35	156.	6.	3.	17.4
30	142.	4.	2.	18.1
25	128.	2.		18.9
20	114.			19.7
15	100.			20.5
10	86.			21.3
5	72.			22.1
0				22.9
MEAN	198.329	12.042	7.477	14.968
SD	34.982	4.850	3.686	1.987
N	228.0	239.0	216.0	239.0
H. S.	287.0	25.0	20.0	33.4
L. S.	75.0	0.0	0.0	12.0
RANGE	212.0	25.0	20.0	21.4
8SC	2.799	.388	.295	.159
MAX. SCORE	******	30.0	20.0	15.0
NO. TRLS	3.0	10.0	10.0	2.0

TABLE 7–18 CONT. (MALE).

STANDARD SCALE	FUNGO HITTING	BASE RUNNING	FIELDING BALLS
	NO.	SEC.	NO.
100			
95			
90			
85			
80		10.8	
75		11.1	
70		11.5	
65	21.	11.8	
60	19.	12.1	15.
55	18.	12.4	14.
50	17.	12.7	13.
45	15.	13.0	
40	14.	13.3	12.
35	13.	13.7	11.
30	11.	14.0	
25	10.	14.3	10.
20	9.	14.6	9.
15	8.	14.9	
10	6.	15.2	8.
5	5.	15.5	7.
0	4.	15.9	
MEAN	16.667	12.718	13.468
SD	3.230	.786	1.695
N	144.0	227.0	216.0
H.S.	20.0	18.1	15.0
L.S.	4.0	11.1	6.0
RANGE	16.0	7.0	9.0
8SC	.258	.063	.136
MAX. SCORE	20.0	******	15.0
NO. TRLS	10.0	2.0	15.0

TABLE 7–19. NORMS FOR AAHPER SOFTBALL TEST (FEMALE).

STANDARD SCALE	THROW FOR DISTANCE	OVERHEAD THROW	UNDERHAND PITCH	SPEED THROW
	FT.	NO.	NO.	SEC.
100			26.	
95			24.	
90			22.	
85	186.		20.	
80	174.	23.	18.	
75	161.	21.	16.	
70	149.	19.	15.	13.4
65	136.	17.	13.	14.9
60	124.	15.	11.	16.4
55	112.	13.	9.	18.0
50	99.	11.	7.	19.5
45	87.	9.	5.	21.0
40	74.	7.	3.	22.5
35	62.	5.	1.	24.0
30	50.	3.		25.5
25	37.	1.		27.0
20	25.			28.5
15				30.1
10				31.6
5				33.1
0				34.6
MEAN	99.252	10.992	6.870	19.467
SD	30.979	5.155	4.790	3.781
N	123.0	131.0	131.0	131.0
H. S.	180.0	22.0	28.0	44.8
L. S.	32.0	0.0	0.0	14.5
RANGE	148.0	22.0	28.0	30.3
8SC	2.478	.412	.383	.303
MAX. SCORE	******	30.0	20.0	15.0
NO. TRLS	3.0	10.0	10.0	2.0

TABLE 7–19 CONT. (FEMALE).

STANDARD SCALE	FUNGO HITTING	BASE RUNNING	FIELDING BALLS
	NO.	SEC.	NO.
100			
95			
90			
85			
80			
75		12.4	
70	22.	13.0	16.
65	19.	13.5	15.
60	17.	14.1	14.
55	14.	14.6	13.
50	11.	15.2	12.
45	8.	15.7	11.
40	5.	16.3	10.
35	2.	16.8	9.
30		17.4	8.
25		17.9	7.
20		18.5	
15		19.0	6.
10		19.6	
5		20.1	
0		20.7	
MEAN	10.916	15.198	11.991
SD	7.084	1.374	2.253
N	95.0	122.0	108.0
H. S.	17.0	21.0	15.0
L. S.	0.0	12.7	6.0
RANGE	17.0	8.3	9.0
8SC	.567	.110	.180
MAX. SCORE	20.0	******	15.0
NO. TRLS	10.0	2.0	15.0

Evaluation

The score for each objective test item is recorded next to its description. These raw scores are then circled on the norm tables. The average standard score is determined by first adding all standard scores, and then dividing by the number of items. Students meeting predetermined departmental standards may be examined further, or be excused from instruction in softball.

SWIMMING CLASSIFICATION TEST*

Basic Information

Up to nine different aquatic skills will be evaluated by the subjective judgment of an expert. All students will take the Level One Test; those who score 12 or more points should then take the Level Two Test. If the student scores 19 or more points on this latter test, he or she then should take the Level Three Test.

Test Description

Description of subjective test items: After watching an expert demonstrate each skill, the student will attempt to perform each one. Skills are:

1. Level One

    SWIMMING ON BACK 10 YD. (Elem. or Finning)

Kick	2	1	0
Arms	2	1	0
Distance	2	1	0

    CRAWL STROKE

Kick	2	1	0
Arms	2	1	0
Coordination	2	1	0
Breathing	2	1	0

    COMBINED TEST

Jump into deep water	2	1	0
Swim 15 yd.	2	1	0
Turn around	2	1	0
Float 30 sec.	2	1	0
Return 15 yd.	2	1	0

    Total Points _____

2. Level Two

    BREAST STROKE (10 yd.)

Kick	4	3	2	1	0
Arms	4	3	2	1	0
Coordination	4	3	2	1	0
Breathing	4	3	2	1	0

    TREADING WATER

Arms alone — 15 sec.			2	1	0
Legs alone — 30 sec.		3	2	1	0

    Total Points _____

*Unpublished test. Used by permission of Robert Clayton, swimming instructor at Colorado State University, test consultant.

TABLE 7–20. NORMS FOR CLAYTON SWIMMING CLASSIFICATION TEST.

STANDARD SCORE	BEGINNING	INTERMEDIATE	ADVANCED
100			
95			
90			
85			
80			
75			
70			45.
65		21.	42.
60	24.	18.	39.
55	22.	15.	36.
50	20.	12.	33.
45	18.	9.	30.
40	16.	6.	27.
35	14.	3.	24.
30	12.		21.
25	10.		18.
20	8.		16.
15	6.		
10	4.		
5	2.		
0	1.		
MEAN	19.663	11.747	33.087
SD	4.788	7.269	7.329
N	98.0	75.0	23.0
H. S.	24.0	20.0	44.0
L. S.	0.0	1.0	17.0
RANGE	24.0	20.0	27.0
8SC	0.383	0.582	0.586
MAX. SCORE	24.0	21.0	43.0
NO. TRLS	1.0	1.0	1.0

3. Level Three
   SIDESTROKE

Kick	3	2	1	0
Arms	3	2	1	0
Coordination		2	1	0
Breathing		2	1	0

   BACK CRAWL

Kick		2	1	0
Arms		2	1	0
Coordination		2	1	0
Breathing		2	1	0

   TRUDGEN (Single, Double, or Crawl)

Kick	4	3	2	1	0
Arms	4	3	2	1	0
Coordination	4	3	2	1	0
Breathing	4	3	2	1	0

   RUNNING DIVE

Hurdle	3	2	1	0
Flight	3	2	1	0
Entry	3	2	1	0

Total Points _____

Evaluation

Because all students will not take all the tests, the norm sheets will not be used in the usual manner. Data presented on page 106 are for general information only. A suggested evaluation scheme is as follows:

1. A score of 0-11 points on the Level One Test indicates that the student is very deficient in aquatic skills, and probably would be classified as a beginner.
2. After taking the Level One Test, a score of 0-18 points on the Level Two Test means that the student is probably an intermediate swimmer.
3. After taking the Levels One and Two Tests, a score of 0-41 on the Level Three Test implies that the student might be classified in the advanced swimmer category.
4. A score of 42 or more points on the Level Three Test indicates that the student is probably proficient in aquatic skills and can successfully challenge an advanced swimming course.

AAHPER TENNIS SKILLS TEST*

Basic Information

Four objectively scored tennis skills will be evaluated. Each test measures but one skill. If time permits, abbreviated tennis matches will be held. Table 7-21 presents the mean scores for beginning majors on this test.

Test Description

1. Serve: After taking two practice serves, the player (X) attempts to serve into the right service court. Depending upon where the ball lands, 6, 4, 2, or 0 points are earned. The serve must go between the net and a rope 7 ft. above the ground. After 10 serves are taken into the right service court, the player moves so that he serves into a

*Adapted from AAHPER, *Tennis skills project*, mimeographed (Washington, D.C.: AAHPER, 1966). Used by permission.

**TABLE 7–21. MEAN SCORES FOR VARIOUS GROUPS ON
AAHPER TENNIS SKILLS TEST.**

	BEGINNING MAJORS	
TEST	*MALE*	*FEMALE*
Serve	33 pts.	21 pts.
Forehand drive	35 pts.	20 pts.
Backhand drive	30 pts.	12 pts.
Backboard test	70 hits	31 hits

similarly marked left service court. The score on the 20 serves is recorded. A let serve is replayed. Balls hit over the rope count 0.

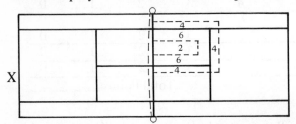

2. Forehand Drive: The player (X) stands near a circle drawn behind the right baseline. He attempts to hit a ball, dropped by his partner, over the net (and under a rope 7 ft. above the ground) into the opposite side of the net. Depending upon where the ball lands, 8, 6, 4, 2 or 0 points are scored. Two practice trials are given, and then seven forehand drives are hit. After these drives, the player moves behind the left baseline and repeats the process. The total score on all drives is recorded. Balls hit over the rope count 0.

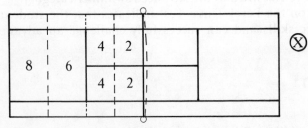

3. Backhand Drive: This is the same test as described above, except that the drives are made with the backhand.

4. Backboard Test: The player (X) stands behind a line 5 ft. from the wall. The player has a racket and two balls in his hands. At the signal "Go," he drops one ball, lets it bounce and then strikes it so that it hits the wall above a line 3 ft. from the floor.

TABLE 7–22. NORMS FOR AAHPER TENNIS TEST (MALE).

STANDARD SCALE	SERVE TEST	FOREHAND DRIVE	BACKHAND DRIVE	BACKBOARD TEST NO./30 SEC.
100			84.	
95		92.	78.	
90		86.	73.	145.
85	71.	80.	67.	135.
80	66.	73.	62.	126.
75	60.	67.	57.	116.
70	55.	61.	51.	107.
65	49.	54.	46.	98.
60	44.	48.	40.	88.
55	39.	42.	35.	79.
50	33.	35.	30.	70.
45	28.	29.	24.	60.
40	22.	23.	19.	51.
35	17.	16.	13.	41.
30	11.	10.	8.	32.
25	6.	3.	3.	23.
20				13.
15				
10				
5				
0				
MEAN	33.059	35.222	29.624	69.583
SD	13.603	15.867	13.497	23.427
N	219.0	216.0	218.0	218.0
H. S.	68.0	86.0	78.0	138.0
L. S.	2.0	6.0	2.0	15.0
RANGE	66.0	80.0	76.0	123.0
8SC	1.088	1.269	1.080	1.874
MAX. SCORE	120.0	112.0	112.0	******
NO. TRLS	20.0	14.0	14.0	3.0

TABLE 7–23. NORMS FOR AAHPER TENNIS TEST (FEMALE).

STANDARD SCALE	SERVE TEST	FOREHAND DRIVE	BACKHAND DRIVE	BACKBOARD TEST NO./30 SEC.
100	76.		56.	
95	71.		52.	84.
90	65.	63.	47.	78.
85	60.	58.	43.	72.
80	54.	52.	39.	66.
75	49.	47.	34.	60.
70	43.	42.	30.	54.
65	38.	36.	25.	48.
60	32.	31.	21.	42.
55	27.	25.	17.	37.
50	21.	20.	12.	31.
45	16.	15.	8.	25.
40	10.	9.	3.	19.
35	5.	4.		13.
30				7.
25				1.
20				
15				
10				
5				
0				
MEAN	21.264	20.093	12.243	30.598
SD	13.702	13.493	10.995	14.841
N	106.0	107.0	107.0	107.0
H. S.	72.0	58.0	60.0	81.0
L. S.	0.0	0.0	0.0	3.0
RANGE	72.0	58.0	60.0	78.0
8SC	1.096	1.079	.880	1.187
MAX. SCORE	120.0	112.0	112.0	******
NO. TRLS	20.0	14.0	14.0	3.0

After the ball rebounds, the player hits it again, and keeps repeating the process. The ball can be hit either on the fly or after bouncing on the floor. The object is to have the ball hit the wall as many times as possible in 30 seconds. The player can cross the restraining line to hit a ball, but the hit that results does not count. Any number of balls may be used in each trial. Each ball hitting the wall in accordance with the above rules counts 1 point. Three trials are given, with the total score on all trials being recorded.

Trial 1	Trial 2	Trial 3	Total Score

5. Playing Ability Test:[3] The class will be divided into small groups. Regulation games, except for three items, will be played on a round-robin basis within each of these small groups. The changes are: each game will last only six minutes; one player will serve (regardless of the score) for three minutes and then the other will serve; the scoring will be 1, 2, 3, etc. rather than the usual 0-15-30-40-game basis. At the end of the six-minute period, each player's score is recorded. In theory, players who score many points are better than those who score fewer.

Evaluation

The score for each objective test item is recorded next to its description. These raw scores are then circled on the norm tables. The average standard score is determined by first adding all standard scores, and then dividing by the number of items. Students meeting predetermined departmental standards may be examined further, or be excused from instruction in tennis.

TRACK AND FIELD TEST*

Basic Information

Different track skills will be evaluated by objective means. Each test measures one skill. The skills are representative of those normally found in a comprehensive track and field examination. Table 7-24 presents the mean scores for beginning majors on this test.

Test Description

1. Dash: Three different distances may be run, depending upon the facilities available. Beginning in a crouch start (starting blocks, tennis shoes) the runner runs as fast as he or she can on a regulation track. Two trials are given, with the faster time (in seconds and tenths) being recorded.

---

[3] Idea gained from Penman, Dual sport evaluation, pp. 175-76.

*Unpublished test. Used by permission of Charles Petersen, track coach, Mankato (Minnesota) State University, test consultant.

**TABLE 7–24. MEAN SCORES FOR BEGINNING MAJORS
ON THE PETERSEN TRACK AND FIELD SKILLS TEST.**

| EVENT | BEGINNING MAJORS | |
	MALE	FEMALE
30-yd. dash	3.9 sec.	4.8 sec.
50-yd. dash		7.9 sec.
100-yd. dash	12.3 sec.	14.8 sec.
Running long jump	14 ft. 7 in.	10 ft. 7 in.
60-yd. low hurdles	10.0 sec.	13.0 sec.
Shot put	31 ft. 4 in. (12 lb.)	22 ft. (8 lb.)
High jump	4 ft. 7 in.	3 ft. 10 in.
880-yd. dash	2 min. 48 sec.	3 min. 42 sec.

2. Running Long Jump: Competing with a regulation pit and usual rules, each jumper will be allowed three trials in the running long jump. Illegal jump counts as a trial but is not measured. The longest jump (to the nearest foot and inch) will be recorded.

3. 60-Yd. Low Hurdles: Beginning with a crouch start (starting blocks, regular tennis shoes) the hurdler will run 15 yd., pass over a hurdle, run another 10 yd., pass over a hurdle, etc. There are five hurdles in all, followed by a 5-yd. dash to the finish line. Two trials are given, with the best (measured in seconds and tenths) being recorded.

4. Shot Put: Using an 8- or 12-lb. shot and a regulation hard-surfaced throwing circle, each student will throw the shot three times. Any legal throw counts, with illegal throws (by the usual rules) counting as a trial. The best put (measured to the nearest foot and inch) will be recorded.

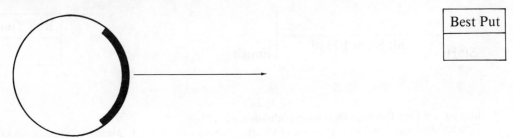

TABLE 7−25. NORMS FOR PETERSEN TRACK AND FIELD TEST (MALE).

STANDARD SCALE	30−YD. DASH	100−YD. DASH	LONG JUMP	60−YD. LOW HURDLES
	SEC.	SEC.	FT. IN.	SEC.
100				
95	3.4			
90	3.5			
85				
80	3.6	10.3	18.06	8.1
75		10.6	17.10	8.4
70	3.7	10.9	17.02	8.8
65		11.3	16.06	9.1
60	3.8	11.6	15.10	9.4
55		11.9	15.03	9.7
50	3.9	12.3	14.07	10.0
45		12.6	13.11	10.3
40	4.0	12.9	13.03	10.7
35		13.3	12.07	11.0
30	4.1	13.6	11.11	11.3
25		13.9	11.03	11.6
20	4.2	14.2	10.07	11.9
15		14.6	9.11	12.3
10		14.9	9.03	12.6
5		15.2	8.07	12.9
0				13.2
MEAN	3.860	12.262	14.066	10.03
SD	.161	.825	1.079	.794
N	36.0	192.0	187.0	246.0
H. S.	3.5	15.1	18.01	13.4
L. S.	4.1	10.4	9.00	8.2
RANGE	0.7	4.7	9.01	5.2
8SC	.050	.066	.016	.063
MAX. SCORE	******	******	******	******
NO. TRLS	2.0	2.0	3.0	2.0

TABLE 7—25 CONT. (MALE).

STANDARD SCALE	SHOT PUT (12 LB.)	HIGH JUMP	880
	FT. IN.	FT. IN.	MIN. SEC.
100	48.08		
95	46.11		
90	45.02		
85	43.06	5.09	
80	41.09	5.07	2:07
75	40.00	5.05	2:14
70	38.03	5.03	2:20
65	36.07	5.01	2:27
60	34.10	4.11	2:34
55	33.01	4.09	2:41
50	31.04	4.07	2:48
45	29.08	4.05	2:54
40	27.11	4.03	3:01
35	26.02	4.01	3:08
30	24.05	3.11	3:15
25	22.09		3:21
20	21.00		3:28
15			3:35
10			3:42
5			
0			
MEAN	31.045	4.07	2.475
SD	4.039	5.691	.169
N	249.0	27.00	224.0
H. S.	49.03	5.08	3.39
L. S.	21.03	4.00	2.08
RANGE	28.0	1.08	1.31
8SC	.041	2.270	.014
MAX. SCORE	******	******	******
NO. TRLS	3.0	******	1.0

TABLE 7–26. NORMS FOR PETERSEN TRACK AND FIELD SKILLS TEST (FEMALE).

STANDARD SCALE	30—YD. DASH	50—YD. DASH	100—YD. DASH	LONG JUMP	60—YD. LOW HURDLES
	SEC.	SEC.	SEC.	FT. IN.	SEC.
100					
95					
90					
85				15.06	
80				14.10	
75	4.3			14.01	
70	4.4		12.9	13.05	9.3
65	4.5		13.4	12.08	10.2
60	4.6	6.6	13.9	12.00	11.2
55	4.7	7.3	14.3	11.03	12.1
50	4.8	7.9	14.8	10.07	13.0
45	4.9	8.6	15.3	9.10	14.0
40	5.0	9.2	15.8	9.02	14.9
35	5.1	9.9	16.2	8.05	15.8
30	5.2	10.5	16.7	7.09	16.8
25	5.3	11.2	17.2	7.00	17.7
20	5.4	11.8	17.6	6.04	18.6
15		12.5	18.1	5.07	19.6
10		13.1			20.5
5		13.8			21.4
0		14.5			22.4
MEAN	4.790	7.905	14.816	10.065	13.044
SD	.261	1.637	1.176	1.092	2.330
N	18.0	98.0	25.0	135.0	78.0
H. S.	5.3	15.2	17.9	15.0	24.90
L. S.	4.4	6.8	13.0	5.09	9.70
RANGE	.9	8.9	4.9	9.03	15.20
8SC	.340	0.131	.094	.017	.186
MAX. SCORE	******	******	******	******	******
NO. TRLS	2.0	2.0	2.0	3.0	2.0

TABLE 7–26 CONT. (FEMALE).

STANDARD SCALE	SHOT PUT (8 LB.) FT. IN.	HIGH JUMP FT. IN.	880 MIN. SEC.
100			
95	35.03		
90	33.09		
85	32.04		
80	30.10		
75	29.04	4.05	2:27
70	27.11	4.03	2:42
65	26.05	4.02	2:57
60	25.00	4.01	3:12
55	23.06	3.11	3:27
50	22.00	3.10	3:42
45	20.06	3.09	3:57
40	19.01	3.07	4:13
35	17.07	3.06	4:28
30	16.01		4:43
25	14.08		4:58
20			5:13
15			5:23
10			5:43
5			5:58
0			6:13
MEAN	21.119	3.099	3.425
SD	3.082	3.360	.375
N	134.0	13.0	76.0
H. S.	35.0	4.04	6.0
L. S.	14.1	3.07	2.310
RANGE	20.02	.07	3:29
8SC	.035	1.30	.030
MAX. SCORE	******	******	******
NO. TRLS	3.0	******	1.0

5. High Jump: With the starting height of 3 ft. 6 in., each student will attempt to clear the bar. Three trials at a height are given. The bar is raised 1 in. for subsequent jumps. A jumper can pass at any height. The best jump (measured in feet and inches) will be recorded.

Best Jump

6. 880-Yd. Dash: Beginning with any kind of start the student wishes, he or she runs 880 yd. as fast as possible. One trial is given, with the time being recorded to the minute and nearest second.

Time

Evaluation

The score for each objective test item is recorded next to its description. These raw scores are then circled on the norm tables. The average standard score is determined by first adding all standard scores, and then dividing by the number of items. Students meeting predetermined departmental standards may be examined further, or be excused from instruction in track and field.

VOLLEYBALL TEST*

Basic Information

Four tests covering the fundamental skills of volleyball are presented. Each test measures one skill and is designed so that players of all abilities will be able to score. If time permits, a playing ability test will be given. Table 7-27 presents the mean score for different groups.

TABLE 7–27. MEAN SCORES FOR VARIOUS GROUPS ON AAHPER VOLLEYBALL SKILLS TEST.

TEST	17– 18–YEAR–OLD		BEGINNING MAJORS	
	MALES	FEMALES	MALES	FEMALES
Volleying	32 volleys	12 volleys	31 volleys	16 volleys
Serving	24 pts.	16 pts.	22 pts.	16 pts.
Passing	11 pts.	6 pts.	8 pts.	5 pts.
Setting-up	9 pts.	6 pts.	8 pts.	6 pts.

*Adapted from AAHPER, *Volleyball for boys and girls (skills test manual)* (Washington, D.C.: AAHPER, 1969). Clayton Shaw, test consultant. Used by permission.

Test Description

1. Volleying: The player, volleyball in hand, stands facing the wall. On the signal "Go" the ball is tossed against the wall into the marked area. On the rebound the ball is volleyed (legally) into the marked area and is continued to be volleyed consecutively for one minute. The number of legal volleys (maximum of 50) is the score. Only one trial is given.

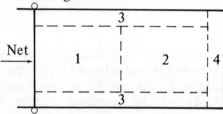

No. of Legal Volleys

2. Serving: The player stands opposite the marked court in the proper serving position. Ten serves are made (any legal serve) with the score being dependent upon where the ball lands. Any ball hitting the net counts as a serve. Any ball that strikes a line counts the higher score.

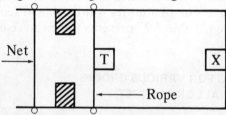

Total Points

3. Passing: The player (X) stands in a marked area. He receives a throw from tester (T) and executes a pass so that it goes over a rope 8 ft. high and lands into another marked area (▨). Twenty passes are made, alternating between the right and left marked areas. The trial counts (but no points are awarded) if the ball hits the rope or net, or does not fall in the target area. One point is awarded for each pass going over the rope and landing on the target area.

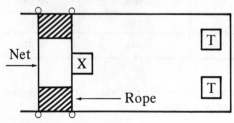

Total Points

4. Set-Up: Player (X) stands in his area and receives a high throw from tester (T), and then executes a set-up so that it goes over a rope 10 ft. high and onto the target area (▨). Twenty set-ups are made, ten to the right target and ten to the left. The trial counts (but no points are awarded) if the ball hits the rope or net, or does not fall in the target area. One point is awarded for each pass going over the rope and landing in the target area.

Total Points

TABLE 7—28. NORMS FOR AAHPER VOLLEYBALL TEST (MALE).

STANDARD SCALE	REPEATED VOLLEYS NO./60 SEC.	SERVING NO.	PASSING NO.	SET—UP NO.
100				
95				20.
90		40.		18.
85	58.	37.	18.	17.
80	54.	35.	16.	16.
75	50.	33.	15.	14.
70	46.	31.	13.	13.
65	42.	29.	12.	12.
60	38.	26.	11.	10.
55	34.	24.	9.	9.
50	31.	22.	8.	8.
45	27.	20.	7.	6.
40	23.	18.	5.	5.
35	19.	15.	4.	4.
30	15.	13.	3.	2.
25	11.	11.	1.	1.
20	7.	9.		
15	3.	7.		
10		4.		
5				
0				
MEAN	30.592	21.966	8.069	7.760
SD	9.679	5.509	3.333	3.292
N	233.0	232.0	232.0	233.0
H. S.	54.0	38.0	16.0	18.0
L. S.	7.0	6.0	0.0	1.0
RANGE	47.0	32.0	16.0	17.0
8SC	.774	.441	.267	.263
MAX. SCORE	50.0	40.0	20.0	20.0
NO. TRLS	1.0	10.0	20.0	20.0

TABLE 7–29. NORMS FOR AAHPER VOLLEYBALL TEST (FEMALE).

STANDARD SCALE	REPEATED VOLLEYS NO./60 SEC.	SERVING NO.	PASSING NO.	SET–UP NO.
100				
95				17.
90				15.
85	45.	34.	15.	14.
80	41.	31.	14.	13.
75	37.	29.	12.	12.
70	33.	26.	11.	11.
65	29.	24.	9.	9.
60	24.	21.	8.	8.
55	20.	18.	7.	7.
50	16.	16.	5.	6.
45	12.	13.	4.	5.
40	8.	11.	2.	3.
35	4.	8.	1.	2.
30		6.		1.
25		3.		
20		1.		
15				
10				
5				
0				
MEAN	16.170	15.948	5.163	5.837
SD	10.361	6.312	3.480	2.958
N	135.0	135.0	135.0	135.0
H. S.	41.0	31.0	14.0	15.0
L. S.	0.0	0.0	0.0	0.0
RANGE	41.0	31.0	14.0	15.0
8SC	.829	.505	.278	.237
MAX. SCORE	50.0	40.0	20.0	20.0
NO. TRLS	1.0	10.0	20.0	20.0

5. Playing Ability Test:[4] In an attempt to make a subjective rating of total playing ability in volleyball, each player will be assigned a partner who appears to be of equal skill. The partners will then become a team, and participate in a round-robin series of two-man volleyball games. In theory, the better players will be shown by the number of points they score against their opponents. The court will be divided longitudinally, so the partners will be able to play "one man up, one man back." Begin the game with one team serving; score points as in a regular game. Use regular boundaries, except for the one sideline (which will have to be estimated). Rotate up and back when changing servers. Games will last five minutes. If needed, two games can be played at once, players making certain they stay on their quarter of the regulation court.

Evaluation

The score for each objective test item is recorded next to its description. These raw scores are then circled on the norm tables. The average standard score is determined by first adding all standard scores, and then dividing by the number of items. Students meeting predetermined departmental standards may be examined further, or be excused from instruction in volleyball.

WRESTLING SKILLS TEST*

Basic Information

Eight different wresling skills will be evaluated by the subjective judgment of an expert. Each test measures one skill. If the department desires, a wrestling match (with three shortened rounds) will be held between students of approximately equal weight in addition to or instead of the test battery.

Test Description

1. Each student will be paired with a partner of approximately equal weight. After watching an expert demonstrate the following test items once only, the student will attempt to perform each one. The partner will attempt to remain in his original position. As the skills are performed, the expert will rate each performance from 0 (failed) through 5 (excellent).
Score
   _____ a. Double leg takedown (partner standing)
   _____ b. Single leg takedown (partner standing)
   _____ c. Duck under takedown (partner standing)
   _____ d. Stand up escape or reversal (partner in riding position)
   _____ e. Switch escape or reversal (partner in riding position)
   _____ f. Side roll escape or reversal (partner in riding position)
   _____ g. Half Nelson and crotch pinning combination (partner in riding position)
   _____ h. Reverse Nelson and crotch pinning combination (partner in riding position)

2. Wrestling Ability Test: Each pair of students will wrestle a regulation match (except that the rounds are shortened to one minute each). After the match is over,

---

[4] Idea gained from Olson, Two man volleyball, p. 157.

*Unpublished test. Used by permission of Percy Morrison, former wrestling coach, University of North Dakota.

TABLE 7-30. NORMS FOR MORRISON WRESTLING SKILLS TEST (MALE).

STANDARD SCALE	SUM OF EIGHT-ITEM WRESTLING TEST
100	
95	
90	
85	
80	
75	41.
70	38.
65	34.
60	31.
55	27.
50	24.
45	20.
40	16.
35	13.
30	9.
25	
20	
15	
10	
5	
0	
MEAN	23.500
SD	8.846
N	28.000
H. S.	40.000
L. S.	10.000
RANGE	30.000
8SC	0.708
MAX. SCORE	40.0
NO. TRLS	1.0

each competitor will be rated according to the following scale:

0-1-2	Extremely Poor (no evidence of having wrestled before)
3-4-5	Poor (very little evidence of having wrestled before)
6-7-8	Below Average (probably has wrestled, but is below average)
9-10-11	Average (has wrestled, but is no better than average boy in a high school class)
12-13-14	Above Average (probably has turned out for wrestling in high school or else had a good unit in high school)
15-16-17	Good (evidence of knowing the moves and holds expected of a high school varsity wrestler)
18-19-20	Excellent (evidence of superior moves and holds, could be a candidate for the varsity)

Evaluation

The score for each objective test item is recorded next to its description. These raw scores are then circled on the norm tables. The average standard score is determined by first adding all standard scores, and then dividing by the number of items. Students meeting predetermined departmental standards may be examined further, or be excused from instruction in wrestling.

CHAPTER **8**

PERSONAL EXPRESSION IN PHYSICAL EDUCATION

INTRODUCTION

Fraleigh indicates that one area of study by physical educators is concerned with personal expression. Specifically, he calls upon physical educators to be knowledgeable about:

1. attitudes toward understanding of self, or other persons, of the cosmos and deity
2. attitudes toward understanding of self in relation to other persons, cosmos and deity

This chapter presents concepts to be understood, followed by needed definitions. The historical importance of this segment is then described. The current feeling of physical educators and coaches as to the significance of personal expression is discussed, including a table which shows the existing state of confusion. To close the chapter, specific courses taken by physical educators are mentioned, along with a superficial means of assessing your status in this area.

CONCEPTS TO BE GAINED FROM THIS CHAPTER

When you have mastered the material in this chapter, you will be able to demonstrate comprehension of these concepts:

1. The personal expression objective ("education *of* the physical") has been a major goal of physical educators and coaches for many years.

2. Whether or not participation in athletics causes beneficial effects in competitors is an unsettled issue, and much research is needed in this area.
3. Regardless of what the evidence "proves," most physical educators and coaches are convinced that athletic participation is beneficial.

DEFINITIONS RELATED TO PERSONAL EXPRESSION

In a general way, *personal expression* refers to the outward appearance of the inner makeup of a person. The concept has been used for many years in physical education in relation to such terms as personality, character, emotional control, and personal-social values. All those terms refer to a person's psychological and social development.

Most people go through certain developmental paths as they progress from infantile to adult behavior. *Psychological development* refers to the state of mental and emotional maturity, while *social development* refers to the person's maturity level in his ability to relate to others. Neither can be separated from the other.

Personality and *character* are well-known terms which refer to abstract inner qualities a person possesses. However, until they are outwardly exhibited (either by actions, word, or a written test) these qualities are not recognized by others, and cannot be called expression. Personality and character are thus qualities which are basic to expression.

The ability to outwardly control the inner feelings is called *emotional control.* We all can cite numerous examples of sportsmanlike actions, of remaining cool under pressure — and at the same time cite many deviations from such desirable behavior. The possession of emotional control is a desirable aspect of personal expression.

The question is, "Can physical education (which includes the competitive phase which we call athletics) alter personality, character, sociability, expression?" For many years we have claimed that students gain these personal-social values from our program. The personal-social objective is a part of almost all lists of objectives. Unfortunately, it is easier to define personal-social than it is to show that our program accomplishes it.

HISTORICAL IMPORTANCE OF PERSONAL EXPRESSION

Chapter 4 indicates that American physical education became a school subject in the 1850s as a means of improving the physical health of students. Up through the anthropometric measurement era of the 1880s this remained true. But the influence of the "new" physical education in the early 1900s caused a shift in program emphasis to that of featuring athletic games. The justifications of this program were that American youth were much more interested in a games-type approach and, at the same time, that these games could be educational in nature. The vigorous competitive play found in physical education (and especially athletics) was thought to be highly effective in teaching various desirable character traits. The term *educational athletics* was used to signify this thought. An example of what was done is the following. For one year, coaches in New York City were not permitted to actively coach during the game itself. They had to sit in the stands, their only power being to remove an injured player. The team captain was responsible for all strategy and decisions during the actual contest. The newspapers seemed to be filled with more reports of immature decisions, poor strategy, and breakdown in team play than they were of situations where teams did well. Physical educators felt that if the games were truly educational, students should be taught during the week, and then "tested" in games without help from the coach. The newspapers and public, however, felt that the quality of play was decidedly inferior to what they were used to. And so, after one year, the responsibility for game control was put back into the hands of the coaches, where it has remained to this day.

The phrase "education through the physical" (as opposed to "education of the physical" — see Chapter 6) was used to describe a main objective of physical education beginning in the 1920s. For many, this became the only objective. Much was claimed for it, although the research was scanty in comparison to that done in physiology and in motor learning. There were a few persons, however, who used sociometric instruments (sociograms, sportsmanship tests, attitude inventories, group opinionnaires) and personality tests in an attempt to ascertain to what degree this goal was attained.

Athletics for boys continued to expand, and received a strong emphasis during World War II. Junior high and grade school teams were formed. At the college level, a greater variety of sports (bowling, volleyball, tennis, etc.) was sponsored. Some critics contended that we had gone too far in one emphasis because we permitted substitution of athletics for physical education, letting a few athletes use the facilities during prime after-school time, and publicizing young persons so much they became unduly impressed by their own importance. Women physical educators especially were quite strong in their criticisms, and were very firm in their support of intramural and play-day activities instead of interscholastic competition. But people began to ask, "If athletics is so good for boys, why not for girls?" And so, even though there is no clear-cut evidence that athletics is entirely good, we are now seeing a boom in women's athletics.

CURRENT THOUGHT RELATING TO PERSONAL EXPRESSION

As cited above, we have a long history of believing in the positive personal-social values of physical activity. However, our beliefs seem grounded more in opinions than facts. For example, Scott (1960) concluded that proof was lacking that physical activity caused beneficial psychological effects in persons, and Cowell (1960, p. 287) made the same conclusion in regard to social dividends due to physical activity. A closer look at each of these assertions should be enlightening to you.

Only in the past 20 years have physical educators begun systematic research into the whole area of personal expression, using psychology, physiology, and sociology as the foundational sciences. Although it is much too early to say that physical activity definitely does (or does not) cause personality and social changes, we do know much more about the many parts which make up these broad terms. For example, Chapter 7 has already indicated how physical activity is essential in learning motor skills, and the role that psychological development plays in that learning. In turn, we know that motor skills are used as the basis of play activity for persons of all ages, and psychiatrists and physical educators agree that serious play (as opposed to aimless play) favorably influences the personality of persons (Menninger 1948, p. 343). However, it is wise to remember that while play and sports have potentialities of contributing positively to the attainment of emotional health, there are indications that for some groups and for some individuals, under some circumstances, this might not be true. Layman (1972, p. 181) writes:

> Sports are conducive to emotional health if they promote physical fitness [but not not all sports do]. They encourage healthy emotional development if the participant has enough skill to merit the approval and admiration of his peers, and

enough so that he can have a feeling of success [but not all participants have enough skill]. They encourage healthy emotional development if the participant can use them for spontaneous expression of positive feelings and discharge of aggressive tensions [but not all can do this].

What have we learned about the effect of physical activity on psychological development? Usually we study groups of athletes, either by themselves or in comparison to nonathletic groups. A sample of various findings by researchers shows the wide variety of conclusions.

1. Male and female athletes basically are emotionally healthy, self-confident, able to cope with stress, leaders, tough-minded. Numerous other "desirable" personality traits are attributed to them. But as they continue to compete, they also become less interested in personal concerns of others, and more dominant (Ogilvie 1967, p. 48).

2. Male athletes tend to be extroverted and possess greater general emotional control than do unathletic males. Women athletes are likewise extroverted, but show a lower level of emotional control than men athletes. (Kane 1972, p. 118).

3. Kistler (1957) showed that adult and college males who had varsity experience had a poorer attitude about sportsmanship than did those who had no varsity experience.

4. Lakie surveyed 228 athletes at three different colleges, and concluded that "outcomes in sportsmanlike behavior may vary under different leadership and environment." (Lakie 1964, p. 497).

5. Pearson (1972) showed that grade-12 male athletes had greater mean scores than did nonparticipant grade-12 males on nine personal traits and three academic achievement measures.

6. Thomas (1973) felt that high school football players of high ability may undergo subtle personality modification during a season, but that the low ability players are unaffected.

7. Collis (1975) developed a written aggression test, and found that as male hockey, swimming, gymnastics, and soccer players got older (into high school) they became more aggressive. They had more disregard for sporting laws. The soccer and ice hockey players, especially, favored extralegal aggression.

8. Peterson, Weber, and Trousdale (1967) found that there were personality trait differences between women team sport participants when compared to women who competed in individual sports. Individual sport women rated higher on dominance, adventurousness, sensitivity, introversion, radicalism and self-sufficiency, and were lower on the sophistication trait.

9. O'Connor and Webb (1976) compared female college athletes (swimmers, gymnasts, basketball players, tennis players) with a nonathletic group of college females, using the Cattell 16 PF test. They reported some disagreement with earlier studies in that various groups scored significantly higher on such traits as intelligence, radicalism, group dependence, and self-control than other investigators had found.

10. Snyder and Kivlin (1975) compared college women athletes versus college women nonathletes to see if the "girl jock" image was of concern to the athletes. They found that on measures of psychological well-being and body image, the athletes were more positive; that is, they felt that sports participation was psychologically satisfying and rewarding. Female basketball players were as pleased with their body image as female gymnasts.

What effect does physical activity have on the socialization of individuals? Kenyon (1968, p. 33) reported that persons might learn particular roles in order to be involved with sport (e.g., sportsmanlike conduct), but these are not necessarily the ones needed in later life (e.g., high moral character). Very little evidence is found which suggests that physical education programs facilitate socialization in either the specific or diffuse roles which we assume. Finally, Kenyon suggests that when planned for, physical education could contribute to the socialization process. Stevenson (1975, p. 287) concluded that there is no valid evidence that participation in sport causes any verifiable socialization effects.

Some would claim that athletics, because it calls for greater personal dedication and effort on the part of the individual, would contribute more toward socialization than does physical education. However, racial problems between teammates offer proof that merely playing together will not cause mutual respect and friendship. Fights occur between teams and/or spectators. As mentioned earlier, Cowell has referred to many individual studies that relate physical activities to social development, antisocial behavior, personal-social adjustments, social mobility, social integration, aggression, and cooperation. The majority of these studies do show positive changes when comparing athletic or physical education groups to nonathletic or nonphysical education groups, yet a cause-and-effect relationship is not indicated. Actually, two authorities have stated that athletics might *not* be the way to develop character, cooperation, etc. (Ogilvie and Tutko 1971, p. 60).

What about the overall benefits of athletic competition? Earlier, mention was made that some physical educators have been highly critical. Yet most of us would agree with Alley when he said, "High school (male) athletics, if directed by coaches of resolute integrity dedicated to optimum development of their players as individuals, can be an exceedingly potent tool for developing desirable behavior patterns. . ." (Alley 1974, p. 102).

We are sure that you have been convinced that competition "does something good" for participants. Study Table 8-1. It summarizes the assumed values of school and college athletics, together with comments from critics which point out inconsistencies. There is no attempt to "prove" one side or the other; rather, we are indicating to you that it is not easy to show a cause-and-effect relationship.

The relationship of expression to personality development has long intrigued researchers. The most prominent American researchers in this regard are not physical educators, but psychologists. Bruce Ogilvie and Thomas Tutko of San Jose State University have studied thousands of athletes of either sex, all age levels, and all skill levels. Their reports have appeared in medical journals, physical education literature, and popular magazines such as *Sports Illustrated* and *Psychology Today*. They have served as consultants to thousands of athletes, and dozens of coaches and/or teams who are interested in using paper and pencil tests as possible aids to improved athletic performance (Ogilvie and Tutko 1972, pp. 209-12).

A recent trend is to include professional psychiatrists as part of the coaching staff of teams, especially professional football, baseball, basketball, and hockey. They observe, talk to players, give advice to coaches as to how players can be handled. Many of the psychiatrists use Ogilvie and Tutko's Athletic Motivational Inventory, which measures 11 personality traits. (Bruns 1973, pp. 8-15). It is interesting to note that most successful foreign Olympic teams have a psychologist who travels with them; perhaps that day will come in the United States.

One other aspect of this concept bears mention here. Successful teaching is considered by most people to be an "art," and therefore not reducible to objective measurement. One of the invariable reasons given for successful teaching is that the person seems to have a "suitable personality" — able to communicate well, gain the respect of students, etc. Because of this, many persons feel that the personality traits

TABLE 8–1. VALUE OF INTERSCHOLASTIC-INTERCOLLEGIATE ATHLETICS—AN ENIGMA!

	ASSUMED VALUES	INCONSISTENCIES
Control	Participation helps develop self-control, self-discipline, etc.	Training rules, dress codes, conformity are dehumanizing. Teamwork doesn't breed individuality.
	Coaches, schools, and community, who know best, exert much control over athletes.	Who knows what is best? Title IX passed to force desirable changes.
	Athletics builds character.	Better to say, athletics reveals character. No proof it builds it.
	Society benefits from athletics. Entertainment occupies students' leisure time, athletes must stay in school to compete.	Is entertainment or education the reason for school athletics? No evidence that delinquency is reduced due to sports participation.
	Studies show athletes are superior to nonathletes in desirable personality traits.	No evidence that athletics causes desirable personal characteristics. "Ruthless selection" perhaps weeds out those lacking in such traits.
Competition	Life is competitive, and athletics is preparation for life.	"Win at all costs" is certainly not preparation for life in a democracy.
	Healthy competition (e.g., fair and vigorous) is valuable to all.	
	Those with success in competition are associated with desirable personality traits.	Studies show coaches want to win more than athletes; who is benefitting? "Ruthless weeding out" of unfit?
Social security	Athletes show increased social status.	
	Success in athletics increases chances to escape the ghetto.	Edwards, black sociologist, says no.
	One may increase one's social standing.	
	Good athletic program is of economic value to community or school.	Cost of scholarships, etc., means most college programs are not self-supporting. Cost of Title IX implementation will not help finances. Relatively few students in any college get athletic scholarship aid.

TABLE 8–1 CONT.

	ASSUMED VALUES	*INCONSISTENCIES*
Physical well-being	Athletes are in better physical condition than nonathletes.	Great variation between sports, and between individuals in same sport. Study shows IM athletes are as well conditioned.
	Injury rate may be increased but not appreciably.	In Germany, 10% of all hospitalized accidents due to sports; don't know about US.
Spirit value	Athletics promotes team-work, cooperation, school spirit.	Can't show that participation in athletics voluntarily promotes teamwork cooperation.
	Students and alums are vitally interested in athletic prowess of school teams.	In some U. S. cities, fans so riotous that they are barred from watching.
Summary	Arguments used in supporting or attacking athletics are same ones used 50 years ago.	
	Physical education teachers and coaches have different philosophies and goals concerning athletics. When the same person has both roles, internal conflict often results.	
	Research in area is sparse and inconclusive.	
	Not able to support one side or other with valid research.	

Adapted from Charles R. Kniker, The values of athletics in schools: A continuing debate, *Phi Delta Kappan* 56 (Oct. 1974):116-20. Used by permission.

of successful workers in a given discipline should be studied so that future workers may be assessed beforehand to estimate their effectiveness. Several studies have been done on physical education teachers. Typical findings are that physical educators tend to be more conservative, traditional, and rigid in their thinking than other teachers.

In summary, it must be said that we have much research concerning the small parts (e.g., personality, perception, maturation, sociability, and motivation) of psychological and social development. Physical educators, psychiatrists, and sociologists strongly believe that physical education and sport does exert positive influences in skill development, mental health, personality development, and social development. As Ismail (1972) points out, the physical, intellectual, emotional, and social types of development are not independent, but are so closely related that the whole is more than the sum of its parts. Until we know more about the whole, we cannot make broad statements.

LEARNING ABOUT PERSONAL EXPRESSION

Courses which a physical educator needs to help him or her understand about the concept of personal expression are listed below.

1. *Introduction to Psychology.* This course is a student's first exposure to the scientific study of behavior. Individual and group similarities and differences are studied.

2. *Introduction to Sociology.* All schools offer this beginning course, which calls attention to the social and cultural forces which influence behavior.

3. *Psychomotor Learning.* This course, usually taught by physical educators, has been described in Chapter 7.

4. *Sport and Society.* This course, usually taught by physical educators, will be described in Chapter 10.

5. *Psychology of Coaching.* If teaching and/or coaching is your desire, this course is extremely beneficial. Typical topics discussed are motivation (just as important in teaching as it is in coaching), personality traits (of both the student and the teacher/coach), social pressures upon student athletes, and discipline. Quite often the course is taught by a physical educator who possesses successful coaching experience.

ASSESSING YOUR CURRENT STATUS

At this writing, no specific objective means are universally used to measure the personal expression of physical education majors. Some studies have been done, using such personality inventories as the Edwards Personal Preference Schedule, the Cattell 16 PF Test, the Minnesota Multiphasic Personality Inventory (MMPI), and the Guilford-Zimmerman Temperament Survey. When compared to nonmajors, physical education majors of either sex usually appear dominant and more extroverted, but in some (for example, Timmermans 1968, p. 1088) there was no difference. It may be that your instructor, in cooperation with the counseling center of your school, will afford you the chance for professional guidance in this area. Data illustrating how prospective physical education teachers score in the latter two tests will be presented as a part of Chapter 11.

There are some informal subjective ways you can assess your status in this area. Examine some of your attitudes. Is it necessary to make a contest out of every game? Are you upset when you lose a "friendly game?" Is it worth playing hard, or do you prefer just to "play around?" Can you cite specific instances where athletics has positively influenced your life? Does the end (winning) justify means (cheating)? Must there be officials when you play, or can you call your own fouls? Do you subscribe to the "Winners never quit — quitters never win" philosophy? There are no absolute right or wrong answers to these questions, but they represent the type of inquiry which is good for all physical educators.

Bibliography

Alley, L. E. Athletics in education: The double-edged sword. *Phi Delta Kappan* 56 (Oct. 1974):102-5.

Berger, R., and Littlefield, D. Comparison between football athletes and non-athletes on personality. *Research Quarterly* 40 (Oct. 1969):663-65.

Berkowitz, L. Sports, competition and aggression. *The Physical Educator* 30 (May 1973):59-61.

Brown, G. Winning one for the Ripper. *Sports Illustrated* 39 (Nov. 26, 1973):46.

Brown, R. B. Personality characteristics related to injuries in football. *Research Quarterly* 42 (May 1971):133.

Bruns, B. Psychologist in the lineup. *Human Behavior* 2 (June 1973):8-15.

Caldwell, S. F. Toward a humanistic physical education. *JOHPER* 43 (May 1972):31-32.

Check, J. F. The psychology of competition as it relates to the physical educator and the athletic coach. *The Physical Educator* 27 (Oct. 1970):110.

Collis, M. L. 1972. Collis scale of athletic aggression. In *Abstracts of Research Papers,* p. 68. Washington, D.C.:AAHPER.

Cowell, C. C. The contributions of physical activity to social development. *Research Quarterly* 31 (May 1960, Part 2):286-306.

Cronley, J. It's no way to get one's kicks. *Sports Illustrated* 38 (Apr. 30, 1973):43-50.

Curry, N. L. Self-concept and the educational experience in physical education. *The Physical Educator* 31 (Oct. 1974): 116-19.

Darden, E. Sixteen personality factor profiles of competitive bodybuilders and weightlifters. *Research Quarterly* 43 (May 1972):142.

Fisher, A. C. Sports as an agent of masculine orientations. *The Physical Educator* 29 (Oct. 1972):120.

Galloway, C. Teaching is more than words. *Quest* 15 (Jan. 1971): 67-71.

Garrison, C. A study of factors contributing to the success or failure of physical education teachers and/or coaches in selected schools of Arkansas. *The Physical Educator* 15 (Mar. 1958):18-19.

Gerber, E. W. Changing female image: A brief commentary on sport competition for women. *JOHPER* 42 (Oct. 1971):59.

Hammer, W. M. Status of sport psychology in western Europe and the Far East. *Journal of Sports Medicine and Physical Fitness* 10 (June 1970):114-22.

Hart, M. Women sit in the back of the bus. *Psychology Today* 2 (Oct. 1971):64-66.

Harris, D. V. Research studies on the female athlete: Psychological considerations. *JOHPER* 46 (Jan. 1975):32-36.

Hellison, D. Physical education and the self-attitude. *Quest* 13 (Jan. 1970):41-44.

Hoehn, R. The coach as a psychologist. *Scholastic Coach* 40 (Apr. 1971):78.

Ismail, A. H. 1972. Integrated Development. In *Psychological aspects of physical education and sport,* ed. J. E. Kane, pp. 1-37. Boston: Routledge and Kegan Paul.

Johnson, M. Construction of sportsmanship attitude scales. *Research Quarterly* 40 (May 1969):312-16.

Johnson, P. A. A comparison of personality traits of superior skilled women athletes in basketball, bowling, field hockey, and golf. *Research Quarterly* 43 (Dec. 1972):409-15.

Kane, J. E. 1972. Personality, body concept and performance. In *Psychological aspects of physical education and sport,* ed. J. E. Kane, pp. 91-127. Boston: Routledge and Kegan Paul.

Kenyon, G. Sociological considerations. *JOHPER* 39 (Nov.-Dec. 1968):31-33.

Kistler, J. Attitudes expressed about behavior demonstrated in certain specific situations occurring in Sports. *NCPEAM Proceedings* (1957):55-59.

Knicker, C. R. The values of athletics in schools: A continuing debate. *Phi Delta Kappan* 56 (Oct. 1974):116-20.

Kroll, W., and Lewis, G. America's first sport psychologist. *Quest* 13 (Jan. 1970):1-4.

Lakie, W. Expressed attitude of various groups of athletes toward athletic competition. *Research Quarterly* 35 (Dec. 1964):497-503.

Layman, E. C. 1972. The contribution of play and sports to emotional health. In *Psychological aspects of physical education and sports,* ed. J. E. Kane, pp. 163-86. Boston: Routledge and Kegan Paul.

McCleary, I., and McDonough, T. Competition and cooperation. *The Physical Educator* 20 (Mar. 1973):9-11.

Marshall, B., and Burchard, J. How to motivate athletes. *Coach and Athlete* (Dec. 1969):24-25.

Martens, R. Influences of participation and motivation in team performance. *Research Quarterly* 41 (Dec. 1970): 510-18.

Massengale, J. A certified look at sportsmanship instructions. *The Physical Educator* 26 (Oct. 1969):1.

Menninger, W. C. Recreation and mental health. *Recreation* 42 (Nov. 1948):340-46.

Neal, P. Psychological aspects of coaching women in sports. *JOHPER* 41 (Oct. 1970):75.

O'Connor, K. A., and Webb, J. L. Investigations of personality traits of college female athletes and non-athletes. *Research Quarterly* 47 (May 1976):203-10.

Ogilvie, B. What is an athlete? *JOHPER* 38 (June 1967):48.

_____, and Tutko, T. 1972. Motivation and psychometric approach to coaching. In

Psychological aspects of physical education and sport, ed. J. E. Kane, pp. 209-23. Boston: Routledge and Kegan Paul.

———. Sport: If you want to build character, try something else. *Psychology Today* 2 (Oct. 1971):60-64.

Pearson, J. M. 1972. Single year and longitudinal comparisons of personality, intelligence, and academic achievement characteristics of senior high school athletes and non-participants. In *Abstracts of Research Papers,* p. 103. Washington, D.C.: AAHPER.

Peterson, S. L.; Weber, J. C.; and Trousdale, W. W. Personality traits of women in team sports vs. women in individual sports. *Research Quarterly* 38 (Dec. 1967):686-90.

Reed, W. An ugly affair in Minneapolis. *Sports Illustrated* 36 (Feb. 7, 1972):18-21. Also see Letters to Editor, *Sports Illustrated* 36 (Feb. 21, 1972):80-82.

Ruffer, W. A. Personality traits of athletes: Part I (Bibliography). *The Physical Educator* 32 (May 1975):105. Also see Oct. 1975, p. 161 and Dec. 1975, p. 213.

Scott, J. Sport and the radical element. *Quest* 19 (Jan. 1973):71-77.

Scott, M. G. The contributions of physical activity to psychological development. *Research Quarterly* 31 (May 1960, Part 2):307-21.

Singer, R. Personality and sport. *The Physical Educator* 26 (Dec. 1969):153-54.

Snyder, E. Aspects of socialization in sports and physical education. *Quest* 14 (June 1970):1-7.

———, and Kivlin, J. E. Women athletes and aspects of psychological well-being and body image. *Research Quarterly* 46 (May 1975):191-99.

Stevenson, L. Socialization effects of participation in sport. *Research Quarterly* 46 (Oct. 1975):287-301.

Tandy, R. E., and Laflin, J. Aggression and sport: Two theories. *JOHPER* 44 (June 1973):19-20.

Thomas, T. D.; Young, R. J.; Ismail, A. H. 1973. The effects of a football season on the personality of high school athletes. In *Abstracts of Research Papers,* p. 67. Washington, D.C.: AAHPER.

Timmermans, H. A comparison between physical education majors and nonmajors in certain personality traits. *Research Quarterly* 39 (Dec. 1968):1088-93.

Todd, K. Love can be taught in dance. *JOHPER* 41 (Jan. 1970):89.

Tutko, T. Some clinical aspects of sport psychology. *Quest* 13 (Jan. 1970):12-17.

Wagman, E. Physical education and the disadvantaged. *JOHPER* 44 (Mar. 1973):29-30.

Weiner, P. The role of physical education in gender identification. *The Physical Educator* 29 (Mar. 1972):27.

Underwood, J. Golf's Jekyll and Hyde. *Sports Illustrated* 38 (June 18, 1973):71-81.

Student Activities

1. Survey one or more of the groups listed below. Ascertain what benefits, if any, they received from athletic competition. (Remember that their background should strongly influence their answers.) Report your results.
   a.   Current athletes in your school (both male and female)
   b.   Students who have never been out for athletics at college, but did so in high school
   c.   Students who have never turned out for athletics
   d.   Adults who have not competed in athletics for at least 15 years
2. Ask nonmajors to describe the typical education major.

Statements for Class Discussion

1. The best way to survive the competition of real life is to play athletics.
2. Education through the physical is more important than education of the physical.
3. Education of the mind is more important than education of the body.

CONCEPTS

CHAPTER 9

APPLIED MECHANICS IN
PHYSICAL EDUCATION

INTRODUCTION

To most people, physical education is a school subject in which students physically move while engaged in a variety of activities. Under this concept, the main job of the physical educator is to teach the student how to move correctly. Fraleigh indicates that the physical educator should know about the effective and efficient:

1. movement of body mass in relation to time and space (examples: running, swimming, jumping)
2. movement of the whole body and/or parts to give impetus to other persons or objects (examples: throwing, hitting)
3. receiving of impulses from other persons or objects with the whole body and/or parts (examples: catching, absorbing a blow from another person)

In attempting to make this more meaningful, the chapter will present definitions of three important terms, followed by material designed to show you the importance of this concept. An account of the historical background leading up to today's tremendous research and professional education emphasis on applied mechanics will be given. Courses which physical education majors customarily take to gain knowledge about this concept are listed, followed by data which permit the assessment of your current status in this segment of our body of knowledge.

CONCEPTS TO BE GAINED FROM THIS CHAPTER

When you have mastered the material in this chapter, you will be able to demonstrate comprehension of these concepts:

1. Applied mechanics is an essential segment of our body of knowledge because all physical movements must interact with certain anatomical, physiological, physical, and mathematical facts and laws.
2. Scholars and researchers have the opportunity to use the tools of the space age in discovering new facts and principles related to efficient body movement.
3. Professional educators, after study of the anatomical, physiological, physical, and mathematical foundations of applied mechanics, must be able to help individuals achieve efficient form and/or desirable results as they perform bodily movements throughout life.

DEFINITIONS RELATED TO APPLIED MECHANICS

To some, *kinesiology* is the key term when physical education is discussed. It may be defined as the science of human movement. Bodily movement, whether loosely organized as in walking or highly organized as in games, is based on interactions among body structure, anatomical and physiological principles, the physical laws of the universe, and mathematical principles. Kinesiology, then, is the application of these concepts and facts found in the sciences of anatomy, physiology, physics, and mathematics.

In our discipline, we are concerned with how humans supply the force to begin or receive motion. *Anthropomechanics* (*anthro* = man, *mechanics* = action of forces upon all bodies) might more accurately describe what we study in physical education (Alley 1966). Newton's basic laws of motion (inertia, momentum, equal reaction) govern how humans begin or receive various forces — and govern the practical limits of what we can do with our bodies.

Movement education is a term used to describe the process of learning through self-discovery how to efficiently move the body. The emphasis is on exploration of the body-space relationship, trying to discover alternate ways of achieving the same goal. The term will be discussed later in this chapter, and also when referring to one aspect of motor learning in Chapter 8.

THE IMPORTANCE OF APPLIED MECHANICS

The importance of applied mechanics should be obvious. Efficient and purposeful movement depends upon the knowledge and skill of the individual. Despite machines and other labor-saving devices, the body is still the basic human movement instrument. In addition, persons who appear skillful in their bodily movements often are at a social advantage when judged by their peers.

Earlier, we said kinesiology is the key word to some physical educators. These people would prefer that we change the name of our discipline. The feeling is that the term *physical education* does not adequately describe what we do, and implies the false concept that it is possible to separate the physical from the mental. Calling our discipline by another name — kinesiology, kinetics, movement exploration, or biokinetics — has been suggested. It is doubtful that such a change will be made within the near future, but the acceptance of physical education as a discipline could mean that you may call yourself a movement educator, or kinesiologist, before your career is over.

APPLIED MECHANICS AS A FORCE IN PHYSICAL EDUCATION

As mentioned in Chapter 4, early American physical education was marked first by athletic games played after school (coached by a playing captain) and later by formal exercises conducted in a rather strict routine. In both instances students were told how to perform — that is, what the "proper form" was. Correct form depended upon the way the champions did the skill or upon principles derived from the study of human anatomy. Since the arms, legs, and trunk of the body are moved by muscles, the body was (and still is) considered a system of levers and forces. In this way movement could be rather scientifically related to mechanical principles.

Relationship of movement to scientific principles meant that physical educators had to know more than just human anatomy. However, the kinesiology texts of the 1900-1940 era were primarily thorough reviews of anatomy and levers, with much less attention paid to the scientific principles of momentum, gravity, etc. Since the 1940s the emphasis has shifted. *The Scientific Principles of Coaching* (written by John Bunn, an engineer turned basketball coach), *Efficiency of Human Movement* by Marion Broer, and *The Mechanics of Athletics* by Geoffrey Dyson are three very significant texts which have caused physical educators to integrate physics, mathematics, and anatomy into one area of our body of knowledge.

A slightly different emphasis has been advocated by some physical educators. It is common knowledge that some athletic skills (hitting, for example) may not always be done with a universal or "proper" form. Results are more important than proper form, in these cases. In the late 1940s physical educators encouraged children to seek their own solutions to bodily movement problems rather than follow a prescribed form. Whatever worked best for the student, after experimentation, was recommended. They said students should still follow the anatomical principles and physical laws, but exploration of space and the results of that exploration were more important. For example, if a person wanted to move from one place to another, he might walk, crawl, roll on the ground, hop, or walk backward. A ball did not necessarily have to be thrown with "correct" form, if another way was more effective for a particular person. Movement education was thus deemed important for the development of coordination, skill, and problem solving. Movement exploration did not violate anthropomechanical principles; it merely sought workable alternatives to a certain problem within the limits imposed by these principles.

These two emphases have continued to this day. Movement education continues to gain advocates, especially for lower elementary school programs. There are too many instances of persons succeeding without "proper" form for us to spend hours trying to copy an expert. There are so many individual differences (height, weight, strength, visual acuity, reaction time, etc.) that one way is not the best for everyone. Finally, there is not enough known to tell us precisely what is the "best" method for any movement.

On the other hand, the great majority of champions conform to basic physical, anatomical, physiological, and mathematical principles in their important movements. Our problem has been that we have not understood the basics well enough, and have had to copy the experts. (A leading American high jumper was amazed when told that the Russians had published a several-hundred-page scientific book on that activity. "I didn't know there was that much to write about high jumping," he was reported to have said.)

What will the future bring? No doubt better athletic performances will occur; pole vault, high jump, and shot put records are being set annually. Why do these improvements occur? Alley (1966, p. 68) reports, "Most of the improvements in athletic performances that have resulted from radical changes in style have come about through trial and error or intuitive tinkering by persons with little sophistication in mechanics. These improvements are later explained *post facto* by persons with a knowledge in mechanics." An outstanding example is the influence of Perry O'Brien in the shot put. Originally, shot putters faced the direction of the put. O'Brien turned 180 degrees from the direction of the put and was able to throw further, because of the torque developed as his body untwisted. Currently, shot putters are trying to master a 360-degree turn because this should enable them to throw even further. The bent-arm pull in crawl stroke swimming is a radical departure from the straight-arm pull advocated up until the 1950s. As long as physical educators and coaches continue to expand their knowledge of anthropomechanics, and as long as competitors continue to tinker with their style, more efficient bodily movement will result.

LEARNING ABOUT APPLIED MECHANICS

Courses which most schools require of physical educators are briefly described here.
1. *Algebra* and *trigonometry*. Many colleges expect majors to have a basic knowledge of these areas. This ordinarily means a high school course in each. It is difficult to relate the physical principles of motion, angle of force, and pull of gravity to the body without at least a cursory knowledge of these two subjects. If not taken in high school, introductory college courses in these areas are often required.
2. *Physics.* A high school physics course is the bare minimum a physical educator should have, and is often required in college.
3. *Human anatomy.* This course was described in Chapter 6. It is logical to expect students to have an understanding of body structure before they can understand how the body moves.
4. *Kinesiology.* For many years, this course was an in-depth study of those anatomical features (origins and insertions of muscles, levers, etc.) used in bodily movement. "Correct" form for various activities was discussed, and students were given experience in analyzing movement. These features are still included in any good kinesiology course. Sometimes two kinesiology courses are offered, one dealing with structural matters (anatomy), and the other with applied mechanics (force, motion, and gravity.
5. *Physiology* and *physiology of exercise.* These courses were described in Chapter 6.

ASSESSING YOUR CURRENT STATUS

As you probably know, there are national standardized achievement tests for students in almost every school subject. The value of these tests is that they permit easy comparisons of achievement among groups in widely separated schools. In some cases, they provide the standards used for promotion. AAHPER was asked to develop such a test for physical education. First, a committee developed a teacher's guide, *Knowledge and Understanding in Physical Education.* This guide was to be used in helping the teacher know what concepts, facts, etc., should be taught. Then a test, the AAHPER Knowledge Test, was developed. The questions asked were mostly in the biological and kinesiological areas.

Forms 2A and 2B of the AAHPER Knowledge Test have been given to various groups, as shown in the following tables. Hopefully, your instructor will arrange for you to take one form. Note that while there is a modest increase in mean scores for

TABLE 9–1. NORMS FOR AAHPER KNOWLEDGE TEST (MALES AND FEMALES, FORM 2A).

STANDARD SCORES	FRESHMEN [1]	0 SCIENCE COURSES [2]	1 SCIENCE COURSE [3]	2 OR MORE SCIENCE COURSES [4]	GRADUATE STUDENTS [5]
100					
95					
90					
85	56.		56.		
80	54.		54.	56.	
75	51.	52.	51.	54.	57.
70	49.	50.	49.	52.	55.
65	46.	48.	47.	50.	52.
60	43.	45.	44.	47.	50.
55	41.	43.	42.	45.	48.
50	38.	41.	40.	43.	46.
45	36.	39.	37.	41.	44.
40	33.	37.	35.	39.	41.
35	31.	35.	32.	37.	39.
30	28.	32.	30.	35.	37.
25	26.	30.		32.	35.
20	23.	28.		30.	32.
15	21.	26.			
10	18.				
5					
0					
MEAN	38.320	41.049	39.512	43.101	45.694
SD	6.350	5.392	6.006	5.368	5.585
N	269.0	144.0	43.0	79.0	36.0
H. S.	56.0	51.0	55.0	54.0	57.0
L. S.	19.0	22.0	31.0	30.0	34.0
RANGE	37.0	29.0	24.0	24.0	23.0
8SC	.508	.431	.480	.429	.447
MAX. SCORE	60.	60.0	60.0	60.0	60.0
NO. TRLS	1.0	1.0	1.0	1.0	1.0

[1] These students have probably had general biology, and perhaps chemistry and/or physics in college, but no physical education science courses listed in 2 below.

[2] These sophomores, juniors, and seniors have not had any of these courses: human anatomy, human physiology, kinesiology, exercise physiology.

[3] These sophomores, juniors, and seniors have had at least one of the courses listed in 2 above.

[4] These sophomore, junior and senior students have had two or more of the courses listed in 2 above.

[5] These graduate students supposedly have had all the science courses listed in 2 above.

TABLE 9–2. NORMS FOR AAHPER KNOWLEDGE TEST
(MALES AND FEMALES, FORM 2B).

STANDARD SCORES	FRESHMAN [1]	NO SCIENCE [2]	1 SCIENCE [3]	2 SCIENCE [4]	GRADS [5]
100					
95					
90					
85					
80		54.			
75	52.	52.	53.		57.
70	50.	50.	51.	55.	55.
65	48.	49.	49.	53.	53.
60	46.	47.	47.	51.	52.
55	44.	45.	45.	49.	50.
50	42.	44.	42.	46.	48.
45	40.	42.	40.	44.	46.
40	38.	40.	38.	41.	44.
35	36.	38.	36.	39.	42.
30	33.	37.	34.	37.	40.
25	31.	35.		34.	38.
20	29.	33.			
15	27.				
10					
5					
0					
MEAN	41.724	43.512	42.417	46.091	47.737
SD	5.230	4.251	5.468	6.024	4.701
N	29.0	43.0	12.0	11.0	19.0
H. S.	52.0	52.0	51.0	53.0	56.0
L. S.	29.0	34.0	34.0	35.0	38.0
RANGE	23.0	18.0	17.0	18.0	18.0
8SC	.45	.340	.437	.482	.376
MAX. SCORE	60.0	60.0	60.0	60.0	60.0
NO. TRLS	1.0	1.0	1.0	1.0	1.0

[1] These students have probably had general biology, and perhaps chemistry and/or physics in college, but no physical education science courses listed in 2 below.

[2] These sophomores, juniors, and seniors have not had any of these courses: human anatomy, human physiology, kinesiology, exercise physiology.

[3] These sophomores, juniors, and seniors have had at least one of the courses listed in 2 above.

[4] These sophomore, junior and senior students have had two or more of the courses listed in 2 above.

[5] These graduate students supposedly have had all the science courses listed in 2 above.

each grade level, physical education majors are very little above the mean of his school students as they begin their training.

What do these scores, and yours, mean? It is hard to say. It might reflect your background in high school physical education — or your background in biology and physiology. It might also reflect the type of physical education program you had in high school — whether all you did was play, or whether your instructor helped you meet both the psychomotor and cognitive objectives.

Knowing about the kinesiological principles and performing adequately might be two different things. One way to judge your ability is to watch your performance. If you consistently throw off the wrong foot, bob up and down while swimming the crawl stroke, or cannot hit the target with a "handful of BB's," these are indications that you do not perform as most average athletes do. Chapter 7 outlined a series of skill tests which might be given to you. Low scores on test items might indicate lack of practice in this activity, but they could also indicate violation of sound anthropomechanical principles.

TABLE 9–3. MEAN SCORES OF VARIOUS GROUPS ON THE AAHPER KNOWLEDGE TEST, FORMS 2A AND 2B.

| HIGH SCHOOL STUDENTS [1] | | | PHYSICAL EDUCATION MAJORS | | |
FORM 2A	FORM 2B			FORM 2A	FORM 2B
Grade 10	33 pts.	36 pts.	Freshmen [2]	38 pts.	42 pts.
Grade 11	34 pts.	37 pts.	Sophomores, juniors, seniors— 0 science [3]	41 pts.	44 pts.
Grade 12	35 pts.	38 pts.	Sophomores, juniors, seniors— 1 science [4]	40 pts.	42 pts.
			Sophomores, juniors, seniors— 2 science [5]	43 pts.	44 pts.
			PE graduate students [6]	45 pts.	48 pts.

[1] Includes persons in an introductory physical education course, some of whom do not remain as a major or minor.
[2] These students have probably had general biology, and perhaps chemistry and/or physics in college, but no physical education science courses listed in 3 below.
[3] These sophomores, juniors, and seniors have not had any of these courses: human anatomy, human physiology, kinesiology, exercise physiology.
[4] These sophomores, juniors, and seniors have had at least one of the courses listed in 3 above.
[5] These sophomore, junior and senior students have had two or more of the courses listed in 3 above.
[6] These graduate students supposedly have had all the science courses listed in 3 above.

Bibliography

Adrian, M. Formation and organization of human motion. *JOHPER* 41 (May 1970):73.
Barrett, K. The structure of movement tasks. *Quest* 15 (Jan. 1971):22-30.
Bowen, R. Putting errors of beginning golfers using different points of aim. *Research Quarterly* 39 (Mar. 1968):31-35.
Broer, M. R. 1966. *Efficiency of human movement.* Philadelphia: W. B. Saunders Co.
Brown, G. They have wind on their sails. *Sports Illustrated* 39 (July 9, 1973):62. (Throwing the discus, aided by the wind.)
Bunn, J. W. 1955. *Scientific principles of coaching.* Englewood Cliffs, N.J.: Prentice-Hall.

Clifton, M. Developmental approach to perceptual-motor experiences. *JOHPER* 41 (Apr. 1970):34

Coccaro, A. Movement education offers an alternative to drug abuse. *JOHPER* 43 (May, 1972):48.

DeMaria, C. Movement education: An overview. *The Physical Educator* 29 (May 1972):73-76.

Dyson, G. H. 1964. *Mechanics of athletics*. London: University of London Press.

Flinchum, B., and Hanson, M. R. Who says the young child can't? *JOHPER* 43 (June 1972):16-19.

Galloway, C. Teaching is more than words. *Quest* 15 (Jan. 1971):67-71.

Gimblin, K. Tips on passing from pro quarterbacks. *Scholastic Coach* 39 (May 1970):56-57.

Hay, J. G. Experiments in the mechanics of physical education. *JOHPER* 40 (Jan. 1969):89-90.

Hays, J. Creative movement exploration. *JOHPER* 44 (Jan. 1973):95-96.

Hoffman, F. The use of electrical stimulation as a teaching aid in kinesiology. *JOHPER* 39 (Jan. 1968):79-82.

Horine, L. An investigation of the relationship of laterality groups to performance on selected motor ability tests. *Research Quarterly* 39 (Mar. 1968):90-95.

Lay, K. Knowledge and understanding in physical education: Identifying the body of knowledge. *JOHPER* 42 (Jan. 1971):21.

Lawther, J. Directing motor skill learning. *Quest* 6 (May 1966):68-76.

Pleasants, F. Kinesthesis: That uncertain feeling. *The Physical Educator* 28 (Mar. 1971):36.

Richardson, P. A., and Tandy, R. E. Kinesthesis: Its influence on movement performance and athletic skill. *The Physical Educator* 30 (Dec. 1973):206.

Rizzitiello, T. Movement education challenges an inner-city school. *JOHPER* 43 (Jan. 1972):35.

Roberton, M. A. Developmental kinesiology. *JOHPER* 43 (Oct. 1972):65.

Shornik, M. The magnificent obsession. *Sports Illustrated* 38 (Apr. 30, 1973):32.

Smith, H. M. Implications for movement education experiences drawn from perceptual-motor research. *JOHPER* 32 (Apr. 1970):30.

Sturtevant, M. Movement efficiency and the novice swimmer. *The Physical Educator* 40 (Mar. 1969):24.

Sweigard, L. Better dancing through better body balance. *JOHPER* 36 (May 1965):22.

Tanner, P. and Barrett, K. Movement education: What does it mean? *JOPER* 46 (Apr. 1975):19-20.

Torg, J., and Quedenfeld, T. Effect of shoe type and cleat length on incidence and severity of knee injuries among high school football players. *Research Quarterly* 42 (May 1971):203-11.

Verschoth, A. Her turn at a record. *Sports Illustrated* 39 (July 16, 1973):56.

Wasserman, B. Universal concepts in gymnastics. *The Physical Educator* 28 (Oct. 1971):138-39.

Whitehurst, K. E. What movement means to the young child. *JOHPER* 42 (May 1971):34.

Yessis, M. Kinesiological research in the Soviet Union. *JOHPER* 43 (Jan. 1972):93.

Student Activities

1. Observe someone performing a motor skill. Analyze the movement, listing specific actions in the proper sequence.
2. Complete this sequence of statements.
   Stranger: What do you do?
   You: I'm a kinesiologist.
   Stranger: Oh? What do you do?
   You:
3. Talk to one or more physics majors. See if they can explain, using the principle of levers, how a person walks.

Statements for Class Discussion

1. The terms physical education, coach, and kinesiologist are all synonymous.
2. From a kinesiological standpoint, answer these questions.
   a. The bigger you are, the harder you fall.
   b. Weight lifters are certainly not double-jointed.
   c. The taller you are, the faster you should run.

CONCEPTS

CHAPTER 10

POLITICAL, SOCIAL, AND ECONOMIC
INFLUENCES IN PHYSICAL EDUCATION

INTRODUCTION

One of the concepts presented in Fraleigh's model of the discipline of physical education is "political, social, and economic force." From what you know of these terms now, it may be difficult to see how they relate to physical education. Yet, unless you understand how physical education and sport have been a factor in every society since the beginning of recorded history, you may underestimate their significance. Specifically, Fraleigh said a physical educator should be knowledgeable about how physical education helps society by:

1. conferring survival benefits
2. perpetuating certain cultural elements
3. providing a medium for social mobility or rigidity
4. objectifying, maintaining, or destroying prescribed relationships between individuals and institutions
5. providing a medium for relations among persons of divergent backgrounds

This chapter begins with a statement of concepts to be mastered. Examples related to the various influences discussed in the chapter are presented, followed by a discussion which hopefully shows the importance of these forces in past and present American physical education. Specific courses taken by physical education majors are described. Finally, a superficial means of assessing your status in this area is shown.

CONCEPTS TO BE GAINED FROM THIS CHAPTER

When you have mastered the material in this chapter, you will be able to demonstrate comprehension of these concepts:

1. Political, social, and economic forces have directly and indirectly influenced sport in every known civilization. American society today is but one more example of the interrelatedness of these forces.

2. Physical education teachers, researchers, and scholars must have knowledge of the history and current status of numerous sport and game-related problems (and challenges) facing our society today. Broadly speaking, these problems and challenges intermingle within such areas of societal pressure as religion, politics, mass media, and economics.

EXAMPLES RELATING TO VARIOUS FORCES AFFECTING PHYSICAL EDUCATION

From the beginning of time, physical prowess was an economic, political and social force. The person who could provide food for self and family was able to survive. As the fittest persons survived, tribes were formed. The tribes with the strongest and most cunning members took land from weaker tribes. As more land was accumulated, greater political, social and economic pressures were felt. Societies evolved, and eventually physical recreation evolved from physical survival. Activities that were formerly utilized for protection and food gathering (e.g., running, spear throwing) became focal points for social interaction (e.g., foot races and javelin throwing). The Olympics in Greece and the knighthood contests in medieval England are prime examples of such adaptations. These contests attracted spectators, which affected societies economically as well as socially. Then, as now, sports and games affected nearly every person in some way.

DEFINITIONS RELATED TO POLITICAL, SOCIAL, AND ECONOMIC INFLUENCES

Certain terms need to be clarified before you can fully consider the implications of this chapter. *Political influence* relates to the impact of local and national governments upon the lives of the citizens. Examples are regulations which say that married high school students are ineligible to compete in athletics, or that all students must take physical education. Many of you live in or near a community which has a public swimming pool, or professional football or baseball stadium. It was a political decision to tax citizens for these and similar facilities.

Social influences are numerous because they relate to the impact of peers and society upon the lives of the citizens. Have you experienced the community spirit fostered within the squad, student body, and townspeople when a basketball team wins the state championship? What about the influence sports have on religion, and vice versa? Did you realize that "blue laws" formerly forbade the playing of athletics on Sunday? Are you familiar with the Athletes in Action teams that tour the U.S.?

Economic influences are concerned with the impact of money and business upon the lives of the citizens. Examples would be the rise in tourism because of local sporting events, the million-dollar salaries paid to professional athletes, and the school budget for athletics.

Admittedly, it is impossible to separate these influences into the three categories described above. For example, requiring student athletes to have school insurance at their own expense is both an economic and political matter. Raising money by con-stributions to finance our Olympic team is political, social, and economic in nature. Interscholastic sports for both men and women has both economic and social over-tones. The murder of Israeli athletes at Munich certainly involved all the forces men-tioned here. The fact that these terms and their implications are interrelated makes it essential that you recognize their existence and their power.

POLITICAL INFLUENCES

The earliest accounts of athletics had a political flavor; they were of contests be-tween tribes or persons, between city-states in Greece, and between nations in the Olympic contests. Early societies had to stress physical abilities to survive, but later militaristic purposes and international esteem became prime reasons for athletics. Today we see physical activity as having extreme political purposes in some countries. The ultimate in physical activity for military purposes was found in the Hitler Youth Movement of the 1930s, culminating in what Hitler thought would be a Nazi triumph in the 1936 Olympics. Currently, the countries of China, U.S.S.R., and East Germany are examples of nations where personal fitness is viewed as a duty to the state. These and many countries (not the U.S.) support national touring teams in several sports. Many persons look upon international sport triumphs as an indication that a certain political idealogy is superior to all others. This deep nationalistic flavor (seen at its highest in the opening parade and medal ceremonies at the Olympics) is deplored by some, but is a source of pride for many.

International sport has long been regarded as a means whereby athletes can com-pete in a friendly atmosphere, free of hatreds and prejudices. Even a slight knowledge of the facts will show that this simply is untrue. For example, take the question of amateurism. Americans accuse the Russians of permitting professionals to compete on their teams, because many of the Russian athletes train the year round and have a state job to support themselves and their families. But the Russians are unimpressed with the American view of granting athletic scholarships. If the scholarships are given for athletic ability, and are worth thousands of dollars in tuition, board, and room, the Russians ask, "Just what is an amateur?"

Consider another example from "friendly" international sport. Most years a track meet is held between the United States and Russia. The events are agreed upon, the site alternates between the two countries — but the scoring controversy lingers on. The U.S. wants two separate team scores kept, one for men and one for women. The Russians want a combined score. Why the difference? Under our system, the American men usually will win and the women will usually lose. Under their system, Russia will usually win because the Russian women generally win most of their events. (Before you think the Russians are changing the rules for their benefit, you should know that in Europe the men's and women's scores are always combined in meets be-tween countries.) Recently the U.S. women have done much better, so the issue may eventually be resolved.

All nations of the world, and especially the small ones, use sport as a vehicle to gain international respect and fame. The success of the Ethiopian distance runners in recent Olympics has done a great deal to focus world attention on that country. Asia is con-sidered a continent of poverty, overpopulation, and unrest. Yet every four years the Asian Games are held and the host country spends millions to build beautiful facilities to impress the visiting athletes and spectators. The Pan-American Games since 1971 have seen "little" Cuba battle "giant" U.S.A. in the quest for gold medals. The

British Empire Games and the European Championships are supposedly held for sporting reasons — but political use is made of the results.

Finally, the Olympics offer clear proof of the political problems in competition. The number of serious arguments before, during, and after the Games staggers the senses of most sportspersons. Hitler's action in the 1936 Olympics, snubbing Jesse Owens, is well known. The 1968 Summer Olympics in Mexico City gave blacks from the U.S. the opportunity to bring world attention to their feelings. In 1972 South Africa was not allowed to compete because several nations objected to its racial policies. An Austrian skiier was disqualified before the 1972 Games because he used skis that too clearly indicated the manufacturer's name. The murder of Jewish athletes in Munich was an outrage viewed by millions on television. Is it any wonder that the Olympics are losing their aura of prestige as a vehicle for good will and understanding?

SOCIAL INFLUENCES

Bearing in mind that political, social, and economic influences are intermingled, let us look at the racial problem in American sports. For years it was said that athletics was a perfect way to achieve racial tolerance because teammates would learn to respect and understand each other. One prominent basketball coach was quoted in 1968 as indicating that no athletic team would ever be involved in campus unrest because athletes know the value of teamwork and self-discipline. Just a few months later the black athletes at several major universities indicated their extreme dissatisfaction with policies and procedures. Several years ago no male athlete with long hair was tolerated by coaches; now, a crew-cut is the exception. Social influences on sport are noted in leadership levels, too. Very few blacks, for example, have risen to top positions in either business or sports. Eitzen and Yetman (1977) report that, in 1975, blacks constituted 33% of college basketball players, 60% of professional basketball players, 42% of professional football players, and 21% of professional baseball players (excluding Latins). At that time there were only approximately five black head coaches of college basketball teams, five black head coaches in professional basketball, no black head coaches in professional football, and only one black baseball manager. Sports are integrated, but leadership is not!

Religious groups abound in American society, and this force is and has been an influence on sports. Despite what you might infer from contemporary newspaper reports, the early Olympic Games were held to honor Greek gods, not to see which nation could win the most medals. Because gods were thought to help the competitors, petitors, sacrificial altars were part of these early athletic contest sites. During the golden age of Greece, the mind-body-spirit triangle was depicted as being essential to the development of the whole person. In later years, the goals of organized religion were generally incompatible with those of sports. The Roman Church eventually forbade the Olympics, and the peasants and slaves had to be more concerned with survival than with sports participation. The masses participated in recreational pursuits, but since these took time away from the study of spiritual matters, the church was not at all supportive.

In early colonial America, the Puritans were concerned with hard work and were opposed to frivolous play. In spite of these conflicts, many early American churches realized that there was more to life than just spirituality. Gyms and playgrounds built by churches were often publicly used. Turnverein halls were (and still are) sports centers supported by religious institutions. Perhaps the best known group today emphasizing the dual role of sports and spiritual needs is the YMCA. To attract young men to their religious program, the YMCA deliberately fostered sports participation. In the 1880s it became so involved in providing facilities and leadership in physical activities that it was among the first members of the AAU. Springfield College, a prominent Massachusetts institution that trains physical education teachers even today, began as a YMCA teacher-training institution. Today Ys across the country are providing both facilities and physical activities.

It is most likely that you have been exposed to a more evangelistic interrelationship of athletics and religion than the low-key YMCA. Incorporating Christianity and athletics is a primary purpose of both the Fellowship of Christian Athletes, and a traveling group — Athletes in Action. Fellowship of Christian Athletes groups are organized on both the high school and college levels. They sponsor workshops and summer camps whose purpose is to bring school athletes and professional athletes together in a Christian atmosphere. A different technique is followed by Athletes in Action. Their teams travel the land, playing local teams in regular competitive games. During halftime or intermissions, athletes give their witness to the relationship of athletics and Christianity. There is no doubt that religion will continue to make use of sports to influence American society.

A most significant piece of social legislation with important economic and political overtones was made law in June, 1972. A portion of the Education Amendment of 1972, more popularly called Title IX, relates specifically to physical education and athletics. In essence, the governing clause states that "no person in the United States shall, on the basis of sex, be excluded from part in, be denied the benefits of, or be subjected to discrimination under any educational program or act receiving Federal financial assistance." Since virtually all public and private schools receive Federal aid in varying amounts, they must comply with the provisions of Title IX or lose all Federal funds. The practical implication is that there can be no discrimination on the basis of sex in any education program or act sponsored by a school district, college, or university.

Title IX Makes specific demands in health, physical education and athletics. The following are examples of requirements.

1. Health education classes may be separated by sex only in sessions dealing with human sexuality.
2. Physical education classes may be separated by sex only for contact sports. The key requirement is that all classes must be available to both sexes, just as are classes in mathematics and English. This will cause concern to some physical education teachers, who have the attitude that only girls take dance class and that only boys take touch football class.
3. Facilities and equipment must be equally available to members of both sexes. Gone are the days when boys' teams automatically get the gym during prime time. Alternating and compromising on the scheduled use of fields, courts, and gyms will be a common practice. Equipment must be comparable in kind, quantity, and quality.
4. Physical activities and athletic opportunities must be equally available to members of both sexes. It is the duty of physical educators and coaches to determine the interests and abilities of students and, insofar as the school can afford it, meet the needs of all students. Separate athletic teams are required if both men and women express sufficient interest. Opening teams to both sexes is insufficient as men would dominate many teams and the result would not effectively accommodate the interests and abilities of women. Contrary to common thought, schools are not required to offer identical programs for both

sexes; neither do money expenditures have to be identical. But publicity, travel expenses, number and salary of coaches, athletic scholarships, athletic training services — the items necessary to develop a total athletic program for men and women — must be comparable.

As you may suspect, Title IX will mean drastic changes in many existing programs. For years some physical educators and coaches have said that if vigorous physical activity and athletic competion is good for males, it is equally good for females. In many schools and colleges the male program will be reduced to provide equal opportunities, causing a drastic change in money, activities, and number of coaches. Some schools are still fighting; the NCAA spent money lobbying and filing lawsuits to prevent enforcement of the regulations. But the law is clear, and the majority of U.S. society is united in the belief that the nation is best served if all persons have equal opportunity to participate and/or compete. Title IX is a perfect example of how society influences physical education, and vice versa.

ECONOMIC INFLUENCES

The economic force of sports is enormous, whether one considers money spent or received. Millions of dollars are spent annually on athletic equipment, fishing supplies, etc. A recent survey revealed that the two fastest growing leisure time pursuits in the U.S. were bicycling and camping (Forbes 1972). Table 10-1 shows results of a Harris Poll on the sports watched or read about by American sports fans. Note that interest in all but boxing and skiing increased from year to year in the first question asked, whereas there are several yearly changes when fans were asked to select one favorite sport.

Table 10-2 presents the results of an older survey of 2000 boys and girls (grades 10-12). Students were asked to check those sports in which they regularly participated, either in or out of school. As will be noted, swimming was the most popular with both boys and girls, with sex differences being apparent in the other choices.

It is reasonable to conclude that interest in sporting activity will eventually translate into economic gain for manufacturers of equipment and for sport administrators who hope to raise money through gate receipts. There is evidence that this conclusion is true, as a Gallup Poll of 1973 shows.

The impact of mass media has always been a social and political influence on American sport. Recently, however, it has been the most dominant economic factor for some particular sports. Publicity from radio, television, newspapers, and magazines are the primary sources of sports information for most of us — and television is the main financial supporter for almost all professional teams. The live coverage of the Super Bowl, or made-for-television athletic events such as "Super Stars" are programs seen by millions only because advertisers pay up to $250,000 per minute for the privilege of having a huge audience. The advertisers are more concerned with economic facts than either social or political matters. Collegiate budgets are enhanced by televised games. Public interest in sporting events has, for dozens of years, caused newspapers to devote more space to this topic than any others. There are many who believe media coverage is responsible for recent dramatic increases in sports interest among the American public. Bowling and tennis are prime examples. It is said that the Billie Jean King vs. Bobby Riggs match was the most important single factor behind the tennis boom (a three-fold increase in the last five years), but if it were not for the television, radio, and press, it would have been of no more significance than many similar matches played between men and women over the past years.

Assuming that sports interests of persons are eventually translated into paid admissions to sporting events, into buying products of sporting goods companies, and

TABLE 10–1. INTEREST OF 1324 SPORTS FANS.

	1972 %	1971 %	1970 %	1969 %
Question: Which of these sports do you follow?				
Football	63	60	60	52
Baseball	60	57	56	47
Basketball	51	46	39	38
Bowling	29	27	21	26
Golf	28	23	21	24
Boxing	24	31	17	X
Hockey	24	17	14	17
Auto racing	24	22	21	19
Horse racing	21	17	17	17
Skiing	18	19	X	X
Track and field	19	18	18	16
Tennis	17	11	10	8
Boating	14	14	13	X
Question: Which one of these is your favorite sport?				
Football	28	28	30	31
Baseball	23	25	27	29
Basketball	14	14	11	10
Bowling	7	7	6	7
Auto racing	4	8	10	9
Golf	3	3	3	5
Boating	3	X	X	X
Boxing	2	3	2	1
Hockey	2	2	2	2
Tennis	2	2	2	2
Skiing	2	X	X	X
Track and field	1	X	X	X
None	5	6	5	2

x = not asked.

TABLE 10–2. PERCENTAGES OF HIGH SCHOOL STUDENTS REPORTING REGULAR PARTICIPATION IN VARIOUS SPORTS.

SPORT	RANK	TOTAL (%) (N=2,000)	BOYS (%) (N=964)	GIRLS (%) (N=1,036)
Baseball	3	41	49	34
Basketball	2	44	47	41
Billiards	11	14	26	2
Boxing	17	2	5	0
Bowling	4	33	34	32
Football	6	27	47	8
Golf	15	7	11	4
Horseback riding	8	23	18	28
Hockey	16	5	6	5
Ice skating	5	29	26	32
Roller skating	7	25	19	30
Skiing	13	9	10	9
Tennis	10	15	12	18
Track	12	12	21	3
Swimming	1	55	52	58
Wrestling	14	8	15	1
Other, or none	9	17	16	18

From Warren S. Blumenfeld and H. H. Remmers, Sports preferences of high school students as defined by reported participation, *Research Quarterly* 36 (May 1965) : 205-6. Used by permission.

TABLE 10–3. PERCENTAGE OF ADULT ATTENDANCE AT SELECTED SPORTING EVENTS, 1959-1972.

	1959 (%)	1972 (%)
Question: Which of these sports have you attended in person in the last year? (Includes high school, college, professional sports)		
Baseball	28	30
Football	23	33
Basketball	18	23
Stock car racing	9	2
Horse racing	9	10
Wrestling	6	7
Boxing	4	14
Hockey	4	7
Dog racing	2	4
Tennis	2	2
Track & field	2	6
Soccer	1	13

Gallup Poll, Princeton, N.J.

into reading sports magazines, the amount of money spent is staggering. There are even economic benefits which are unplanned. For example, the weekend motel business was once booming in those cities 80 to 100 miles from a home game of a National Football League team. Because of the home-city blackout that was in effect and the scarcity of tickets, people drove to a motel and rented a room with a color television set to see a game.

Exercise has also been used as an economic force. The famous Canadian 5BX (five basic exercises) program was devised by a physical educator in response to the Canadian Air Force request for a quick, daily exercise regime designed to reduce the coronary problems of pilots. The Canadian Air Force approached this from an economic point of view. Too many of the pilots were suffering from heart problems in their early forties after the Air Force had spent thousands of dollars training them. Adult physical fitness programs became very popular in the U.S. when the 5BX program was published.

Many large and small companies now promote physical fitness and recreation programs for their employees. For example, Firestone Rubber Company owns a country club used solely by employees. Increased productivity and less employee turnover are thought to result from these measures. The President's Council on Physical Fitness and Sports promotes the fitness programs conducted for business employees. National conferences designed to show top business executives that fitness programs are important are held. In 1974 six firms with outstanding programs (Exxon, Brunswick, Flick-Reedy, Owens-Corning Fiberglass, Xerox, and Life Insurance Co. of Georgia) were asked to explain why they support such efforts. Better physical and mental health, which leads to higher morale and productivity, were cited. There are literally dozens and dozens of companies that are convinced that the promotion of fitness programs makes sense from an economic as well as social standpoint.

A humorous incident about the economic impact of physical fitness is that at one time there was a suggestion in the British House of Lords that all persons who were grossly overweight be taxed at a higher rate. This was proposed because mortality tables showed that obese people do not live as long as other people, and do not pay the average amount of taxes. (The measure did not pass!)

Our ever-changing society forces change upon us. It is no longer adequate for physical educators to know how to play golf; they must also know why golf is important to many people and unimportant to others. The political environment affects performance, as does both the social and economic environment. In other words, a physical educator must be aware of the nonschool environment before he can function effectively in the gym, pool, or athletic field. Ten years ago no long-haired football player was ever seen. Now? Court decisions have been rendered on whether or not this is an area where the coach's rules must be followed. Some decisions have been in favor of the coach's rules, while others have indicated that the player's rights must be respected. Two years ago, sharing the gym with the girl's teams would presumably have ruined the boys' teams chances for victory. Time marches on — the physical educator who does not have an awareness of political, social and economic forces is soon out of step.

LEARNING ABOUT POLITICAL, SOCIAL AND ECONOMIC INFLUENCES

Customarily, all physical educators must take general education courses in the social science area. Quite often you can select the courses that you please. Logical choices are these:

1. *Political science.* This is the study of government and politics, its structure and its policies. In most every school there is an introductory political science course. Material covered in this course represents the very minimum that a physical educator should know.
2. *Sociology.* This is defined as the scientific study of human social behavior and the organization and functions of groups. An introductory course, such as Principles of Sociology or Social Problems, represents the minimum preparation a physical education major should possess.
3. *Economics.* This discipline enables a physical educator to become familiar with such economic problems as growth, income, employment, governmental budgets, and allocation of resources. Courses entitled Principles of Economics or Economic Problems certainly should be taken.
4. *Sport sociology.* Ordinarily, physical education departments would like their majors to take the above-listed courses. These are all taught by other departments in the college or university. They are necessary for a basic understanding of political, social, and economic problems, but they may not relate directly to sport. In 1953 Cozens and Stumpf published *Sports in American Life* and tried to awaken a deeper understanding in this area. It took a long time, but now many departments are convinced that physical educators must better understand how their discipline fits into American society. On the undergraduate level, courses such as Sport and Society or Socio-Cultural Aspects of Sport are being offered. Typical units in such a course cause one to consider how sport relates to such topics as social organization, social status, economics, communication, school athletics, women's and children's sports, drugs, and personality. If you do not find this course to be of importance, then perhaps your interest in physical education is not as great as it should be.

ASSESSING YOUR CURRENT STATUS

There are no published tests which can be used by physical educators to assess their current status regarding knowledge of political, social and economic forces. But perhaps a subjective judgment might be reached by asking yourself these questions.

1. How much of the sports page in the daily paper do you regularly read? What other parts of the paper do you regularly read?
2. What other general sports periodicals (e.g., *Sports Illustrated, womenSports, Sport,* sport sections of *Newsweek*) do you regularly read?
3. What specific sport periodicals (e.g., *Mentor, Coach and Athlete, Scholastic Coach, Athletic Journal, Swimming World, Modern Gymnast*) do you regularly read?
4. What have you read about the political, social, and economic aspects of sport?

In summary, to become aware of the political, social, and economics forces as a segment of our body of knowledge means that you must be aware of the total environment in which you live. A current issue on many campuses is whether athletic programs should be financed by all students through a required fee or financed out of general funds by those who wish to pay. At one major school, the student body president (a graduate student in physical education) believed that it should be voluntary. The athletics department disagreed. What is your stand? On what educational, political, social, and economic principles do you make your decision?

Bibliography

Bennett, B. L. Critical incidents and courageous people in the integration of sports. *JOHPER* 42 (Apr. 1971):83.

Blumenfeld, W. S., and Remmers, H. H. Sports preferences of high school students as defined by reported participation. *Research Quarterly* 36 (May 1965):205-6.

Bressett, S. M. Is amateurism dying? *JOHPER* 44 (June 1973):21.

Briner, B. Making sport of us all. *Sports Illustrated* 39 (Dec. 10, 1973):36. (Commercialism in professional sports.)

Brown, G. Jeepers! Peepers is in charge now. *Sports Illustrated* 37 (Oct. 23, 1972):40-49 (Jack Scott, controversial athletic personality.)

Brown, R. The black gladiator — The major force in modern American sport. *NCPEAM Proceedings* (1973):43-50.

Carol, J. TV talk. *Sports Illustrated* 39 (Apr. 9, 1973):9. (Discussion of baseball television exposure.)

Carry, P. Going to bat for Taiwan. *Sports Illustrated* 41 (Aug. 19, 1974):64-74.

Cozens, F., and Stumpf, F. 1953. *Sports in American life.* Chicago: University of Chicago Press.

DeBacy, D., et al. What do men really think about athletic competition for women? *JOHPER* 41 (Nov.-Dec. 1970):28.

Deford, F. Mrs. Billie Jean King! *Sports Illustrated* 42 (May 19, 1975):70-82.

_____. Religion in sport. *Sports Illustrated* 44 (Apr. 19, 1976):88-102.

_____. The word according to Tom. Part 2 of Religion in sport. *Sports Illustrated* 44 (Apr. 26, 1976):64-69.

_____. Reaching for the stars. Part 3 of Religion in sport. *Sports Illustrated* 44 (May 3, 1976):42-60.

Gilbert, B., and Williamson, N. Sport is unfair to women. *Sports Illustrated* 38 (May 28, 1973):88-98.

_____. Are you being two-faced? Part 2 of Sport is unfair to women. *Sports Illustrated* 38 (June 6, 1973):44-54.

_____. Programmed to be losers. Part 3 of Sport is unfair to women. *Sports Illustrated* 38 (June 13, 1973):59-65.

_____. Women in sport: A progress report. *Sports Illustrated* 41 (July 29, 1974): 27-31.

Eitzen, S., and Yetman, N., Immune from racism? *Civil Rights Digest* 9 (Winter 1977):3-13.

Henry, G. T. A bibliography concerning Negroes in physical education, athletics, and related fields. *JOHPER* 44 (May 1973):65-70. (Good source to locate an article.)

Johnson, W. Defender of the faith. *Sports Illustrated* 37 (July 24, 1972):32-43. (Avery Brundage, recent president of the International Olympic Committee.)

_____. Faces on a new China scroll. *Sports Illustrated* 39 (Sept. 24, 1973):82. (Sport and physical education in Red China.)

_____. An eager people in the swim. Part 2 of Faces on a new China scroll. *Sports Illustrated* 39 (Oct. 1, 1973):43.

_____, and Williamson, N. Whatta Babe! Part 1 of Babe. *Sports Illustrated* 43 (Oct. 6, 1975):112-29.

_____. Babe: An unreal pro. Part 2 of Babe. *Sports Illustrated* 43 (Oct. 13, 1975):48-57.

_____. Babe: Tee to green. Part 3 of Babe. *Sports Illustrated* 43 (Oct. 20, 1975):48-62.

Kennedy, R. 427: A case in point. *Sports Illustrated* 40 (June 10, 1974):87-100. (Athletic illegalities in college.)

_____. The payoff. Part 2 of 427: A case in point. *Sports Illustrated* 40 (June 17, 1974):24-30.

_____. The man who stood sports on its head. *Sports Illustrated* 42 (Apr. 28, 1975):22-24. (Jack Scott, controversial figure in sports.)

Kenyon, G., and Loy, J. Toward a sociology of sport. *JOHPER* 36 (May 1965):24.

Kirshenbaum, J. Voting to snuff the torch. *Sports Illustrated* 33 (Nov. 20, 1972):44-55. (Denver's rejection of the 1976 Winter Olympic Games.)

Kusserow, J. Games as a medium for world understanding. *JOHPER* 42 (Jan. 1971):46.

Loy, J. W. Case for the sociology of sport. *JOHPER* 43 (June 1972):50.

Lowe, B. The sociology of sports — A basic course outline. *The Physical Educator* 28 (May 1971):79.

Lucas, J. Open letter to Lord Killanin. *JOHPER* 44 (Feb. 1973):8-10. (Proposal for restructuring the Olympic Games.)

Moore, K. Not on the up and up. *Sports Illustrated* 43 (Oct. 27, 1975):16-19. (Anti-American biases in Pan American Games.)

Olsen, J. The black athlete — A shameful story. *Sports Illustrated* 29 (July 1, 1968):15-27.

_____. Pride and prejudice. Part 2 of The black athlete. *Sports Illustrated* 29 (July 8, 1968):19-31.

_____. In an alien world. Part 3 of The black athlete. *Sports Illustrated* 29 (July 15, 1968):28-43.

_____.In the back of the bus. Part 4 of The black athlete. *Sports Illustrated* 29 (July 22, 1968):28-41.

_____. The anguish of a team divided. Part 5 of The black athlete. *Sports Illustrated* 29 (July 29, 1968):20-35.

Rahrig, D. Race and races: American participation in the Olympic Games of 1936 and 1968. *The Physical Educator* 27 (Mar. 1970):58.

Reed, J. D. The Louisiana Purchase. *Sports Illustrated* 40 (July 22, 1974):66-80. (Superdome construction and financial woes.)

Stein, B. E. Cultural crisis in American sports. *JOHPER* 43 (Apr. 1972):42.

Telander, R. A voice for those long silent. *Sports Illustrated* 32 (June 30, 1975):60-63. (U.S. Olympic athletes complain about our Olympic Committee.)

Wilson, B. The battle between the sexes on physical education. *The Physical Educator* 29 (Oct. 1972:139.

Student Activities

1. Read more in this area by finding books or periodical articles on topics such as these:
    a. Recent progress in Title IX
    b. Financing school sport programs
    c. Sports during the Renaissance
    d. Sports during the Industrial Revolution
    e. Sports in early American life
    f. Avery Brundage — Olympic dictator or savior?
    g. Sports in emerging nations
    h. Franchise moves in professional sports
    i. Arguments before, during, and after the 1976 Olympics
    j. Pay TV and its impact on sports viewing
2. Look in the medical journals available in your school library for articles which show the relationship (if any) between exercise and longevity.
3. Look in the business journals available in your school library for articles which show the relationship of the economy to sport.
4. Visit an adult physical fitness class. Do you think this type of program has social or economic benefits for the participants? For the nation?

Statements for Class Discussion

1. Sports are the best way a person can rise from the ghetto to a better life.
2. The changes that are being made because of Title IX are long overdue.
3. Title IX is a great idea, but should be implemented more slowly.
4. If more people took "exercise breaks" rather than "coffee breaks," they and the nation would benefit socially, not just economically.

CHAPTER 11

TEACHING PHYSICAL EDUCATION AND DANCE IN SCHOOLS AND COLLEGES

INTRODUCTION

Teaching physical education or dance seems to be the professional goal of virtually all students who enter our discipline. Helping students improve their biological development, their application of mechanics for everyday living and moving, their learning of movement skills, their understanding of political, social, and economic forces, and their attitudes toward self and others is the same regardless of where the teaching takes place. This chapter will begin with a listing of concepts to be gained, followed by an awareness of how the body of knowledge relates to the basic purposes of physical education in schools. Definitions of common terms used in teaching are given. Detailed discussions of what physical educators do as they work with various age levels constitute an important part of the chapter. Courses which will help your own professional education in the teaching of physical education are described. Finally, various means of evaluating your status with regard to teaching are given.

CONCEPTS TO BE GAINED FROM THIS CHAPTER

When you have mastered the material in this chapter, you will be able to demonstrate comprehension of these concepts:

1. The purposes of physical education in the schools, as stated by AAHPER, are directly related to the body of knowledge given in Chapters 5-10 of the text.
2. Numerous terms (required and elective programs, low-organized games, tenure, etc.) must be understood before you can discuss your future involvement in physical education or dance.

3. At this point, teaching physical education or dance is or is not an appropriate career goal for you. This concept is based on a tentative understanding of:
   a. the age level (e.g., preschool, K-6) you would or would not prefer to teach
   b. the qualities of successful physical education teachers that you possess or lack
   c. the activity skills you will need to develop to conduct a varied physical education or dance program

PURPOSES OF PHYSICAL EDUCATION IN THE SCHOOLS

In Chapter 5, the ideas of Fraleigh concerning the disciplines of physical education are presented. Subsequent chapters (6-10) amplify the knowledge and understandings that are our body of knowledge. Most people think that physical education is only a subject taught in school. We would prefer that you think of physical education as a discipline, and that you realize professional educators apply the body of knowledge in such a way that students will profit now and in later years. Consider how the purposes of school physical educators relate to our body of knowledge. Educators try to:

1. Condition heart, lungs, muscles, and other organic systems to respond to increased demands by imposing progressively greater demands upon them.
2. Help children learn to move skillfully and effectively not only in exercise, games, sports, and dances but also in all active life situations.
3. Enrich understanding of space, time, mass-energy relationships, and related concepts.
4. Develop understandings of voluntary movement and the ways in which individuals may organize their own movements to accomplish the significant purposes of their lives.
5. Extend understanding of socially approved patterns of personal behavior, with particular reference to the interpersonal interactions of games and sports. (AAHPER, 1962, pp. 2-4).

Comparing these purposes with the material in Chapters 5-10 (as shown in Figure 11-1) depicts a remarkable similarity! It is seen that for physical education to affect people's lives, we must be concerned with the three domains that relate to all learning. Concepts and facts must be discovered and organized into a body of knowledge. Then professional teachers, who understand both the body of knowledge and effective teaching techniques, determine what and how students should be taught to be better prepared for the many years ahead. The purposes of physical education in the school must agree with the basic philosophy of society regarding education. Society determines the ultimate goals of education, but professional physical educators determine the best way to achieve them.

DEFINITIONS RELATED TO THE TEACHING OF PHYSICAL EDUCATION

There are many terms you should understand before beginning your study of the teaching of physical education. These are given below.

1. *Required program* refers to physical education classes taken because either the state law or local school district requires it.
2. An *elective program* means students may elect to take physical education if they wish. The option usually is granted only to those in grades 11-12.
3. A *required elective* program is one in which students must take physical education but may choose what activity they wish to learn.

FIGURE 11-1. Relationship of physical education body of knowledge to the purposes of school physical education.

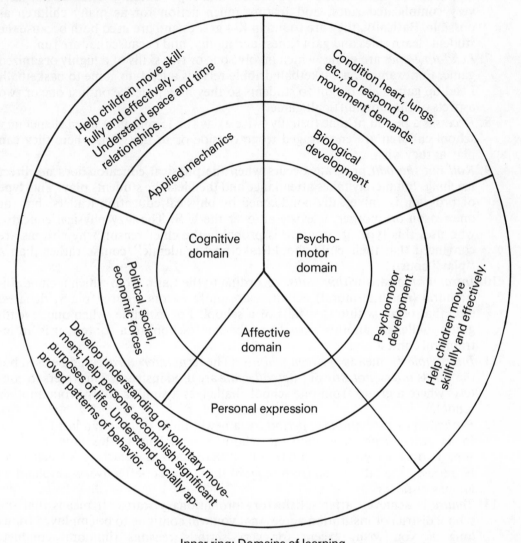

Inner ring: Domains of learning
Middle ring: Body of knowledge in physical education
Outer ring: Purposes of school physical education

4. *Teacher certification* refers to the requirements you must meet to receive a license (or certificate) to teach from the State Department of Education. All teachers from kindergarten through high school must be certified by the state in which they teach. Upon successful completion of certain required courses, your college verifies to the state that you have met all requirements and should receive a certificate. Interestingly enough, there are no certification requirements to teach in four-year colleges; a college could (and sometimes does) hire persons without a college degree.

5. *Education courses* are those courses which deal with teaching. They are offered by the Department of Education, and generally involve principles of learning, growth and development, measurement and evaluation, and student teaching.

6. *Low-organized games* are sometimes called elementary games. Examples are tag, drop the handkerchief, hop scotch, and rope jumping. They do not have very complicated rules, and feature much action for as many children as possible. Basically, they are found in K-4 grades and are used both because the students learn rules and gain fitness and agility, and because they are fun.

7. *Lead-up games* are games which involve one or two skills of a highly organized game. For example, a basketball dribble relay is a lead-up game to basketball. Lead-up games are taught to students so they may practice on just one or two aspects of the more difficult game.

8. *Recess* is a period of time (usually twice a day for 15 minutes) when elementary school children are encouraged to go outside or to the gym, where they can play as they wish.

9. *Roll out the ball* program occurs when the physical educator does no direct teaching, but merely takes attendance and then lets the students play. This type of program is universally condemned by physical education leaders, but for one reason or another, it exists all over the U.S. The lazy physical educator who uses this type of program is probably the chief reason why citizens are convinced that their child should take an "academic" course rather than a "play" course.

10. *Intramural* means *within walls,* according to the Latin from which it came. Intramural (not inter*mural*) activities are those events (sports, plays, debates, etc.) that occur within the walls of a school. For example, when one seventh grade challenges another class from the same school to a contest, it is an intramural contest.

11. *Interscholastic* means *between schools.* (The term *intermural* could be used but the words *interscholastic* or *intercollegiate* are used instead.) This refers to contests where a group from one school challenges a similar group from another school.

12. *Probation* or *probationary period* for a newly hired teacher can last from one to six years, depending upon the school system. During this time, teaching supervisors are trying to evaluate your effectiveness as a teacher. A teacher can be released (i.e., dismissed from the job) if the teacher-effectiveness evaluations are unsatisfactory.

13. *Tenure* is achieved after satisfactory probationary status. It means that the school district or institution agrees that you will continue to be employed for as long as you wish, except for very serious reasons (immoral conduct, alcoholism, etc.).

14. *Salary schedule* refers to agreed-upon salary figures between the district and the teachers' association. The salary is dependent upon your degrees and years of experience. Usually each year of experience means an increase in salary. In years past, salaries were set by negotiation between the superintendent and each teacher, but now salary schedules are found in most school districts. A common misconception is that teachers in elementary schools are paid less than high school teachers — not so, if there is a salary schedule. All teachers in that district, regardless of where they teach, are paid according to the agreed-upon figure and their position on the salary schedule.

TEACHING PHYSICAL EDUCATION IN PRESCHOOL PROGRAMS

Currently, the great majority of physical education programs begin with kindergarten-age children, but there is a strong trend toward providing such programs for preschool children (ages three to five). At this point, these programs are not usually part of the public or parochial school system, and thus could be discussed in Chapter 13 of the text. However, since they ultimately will be part of the school system, they will be considered here.

A child first learns through the senses, and then at about age three becomes interested in other people and things. The child is beginning to experience socialization in various aspects of play — talking, singing, writing, etc. Motor movements (running, hopping, etc.) should be emphasized, both for their psychomotor value and for socialization purposes. "Ceaseless activity" (Werner 1975, p. 181) describes children at this age. Gradually psychomotor movements are directed toward organized group activities (tag, cops and robbers, hide and seek). At age five, the child begins kindergarten, hopefully ready to cope with an increasingly structured social setting.

We all know that psychomotor development of children from ages one to five will occur with or without the help of a physical educator. So why is there a strong trend to providing such a specialist in nursery or other preschool settings? First, there is reason to believe that psychomotor skills must be developed if school instruction is to be of optimal help to the child. Balance, locomotion, and manipulative skill all help in drawing, making letters, and playing in a group. Hand-eye and foot-eye coordination are useful in other situations than batting or kicking a soccer ball! Rhythmic experiences or swimming are not advocated specifically to develop outstanding young dancers or athletes. How are these best taught? Most of us learned through trial and error as we played around the home, but logic indicates that a specialist should teach skills better, quicker, and more correctly than would occur with aimless experimentation on the part of a three-year-old. We believe that learning difficulties that plague some children due to vision or auditory problems might be alleviated with proper psychomotor training.

Teaching preschool physical education is more than watching children scamper around a playground, hanging upside down on monkey bars. It is a directed series of psychomotor activities designed to improve coordination of gross and fine muscle movements, to ensure that the socialization process is begun, and to remedy (if possible) those conditions which hamper a child as he or she starts kindergarten. Should you undertake this task, you will need much patience, along with a vast knowledge of various psychomotor activities suitable for different developmental stages.

TEACHING PHYSICAL EDUCATION IN ELEMENTARY SCHOOL (K-6)

Elementary schools (usually kindergarten through sixth grade) often employ specialists to teach physical education. These specialists are either physical education majors with a certificate to teach K-6 or elementary education majors with an emphasis in physical education. If you major in elementary education with an emphasis in physical education, you could either teach a regular class (say, fifth grade) or teach physical education. It is quite common to teach in the classroom part of the day and teach physical education the rest of the day.

The usual day of the elementary school physical educator can be described in one word — busy! Classes are about 30 minutes long, with students coming to the gym from their classroom. Seldom are regular gym clothes worn. The classes are coeducational, and vary from 20-35 students. In some schools you will see this group only two or three times a week, although they will have daily recess. The lessons tend to be active; hopefully, all students will practice many times, under direct supervision, an effective way to perform gymnastic skills, dances, basic movements, and low-organized games. As children reach the higher grades, the emphasis on lead-up games increases, since their physical and social maturity has reached the point where they are almost ready for the more highly organized team games. Girls are every bit as accomplished in performing activities as are boys, so expectations should be the same for both sexes. Students are eager to learn skills and even more eager to participate. The more you talk, the less they accomplish! Facilities may not be as spacious as those found in junior and senior high schools.

Few elementary schools have a well-organized intramural sports program; those that do find enthusiastic student response. Administrative problems (lack of money, shortage of facilities, and bussing of students) make it difficult. However, an enthusiastic, dynamic physical educator sees the tremendous value of these activities, and usually gets such a program organized during the noon hour or after school. A recent trend is for elementary physical educators to coach in junior or senior high schools; the tremendous need for coaches necessitates this in some districts.

There are special joys and problems connected with elementary school physical education. By far the greatest joy is the enthusiasm of the students. The problems usually revolve around the lack of facilities and the great number of students you see each week. Often beginning physical education majors fail to seriously consider teaching at this level. Our experience is that about 40% of the majors prefer the K-6 age once they have experience in working with these students.

Perhaps you remember that when you were in grades K-6 your regular classroom teacher "taught" you physical education. This is still the pattern in many schools, but there is some evidence to show that students taught by a physical education specialist achieve greater results. (If this weren't true, it wouldn't speak very highly of our specialists, would it? However, there are some studies which show no specialist superiority.) Most classroom teachers would prefer not to teach physical education, but until the financial situation is eased, there is apt to be only a modest increase in the number of specialists in the near future.

The training of the teacher of elementary physical education is fairly standard throughout the U.S. Education courses (featuring characteristics and problems of children ages 5-12) and physical education courses (featuring rhythmic activities, movement education, gymnastics, games of low organization, and lead-up games) are commonly taken. In the better programs, you will be required to work with K-6 children outside of school, such as in local recreation agencies, the YMCA-YWCA, or Little League. Experiences like this are essential, because they help you determine if you wish to teach, and whether you wish to work with this age group. You may have forgotten what K-6 physical education is like; for many, trying it is liking it!

TEACHING PHYSICAL EDUCATION IN MIDDLE SCHOOL (6-10) OR JUNIOR HIGH SCHOOL (7-9)

Physical educators at these levels have approximately the same years of training as do those who teach in the earlier grades: a four-year bachelor's degree. In those states where many out-of-state teachers apply for jobs, often the M.A. or M.S. is necessary. Usually a physical education specialist is employed, one for each sex. Currently there is a change from the coeducational program offered in elementary school; except for rhythms, the classes are seldom of mixed sex. Title IX will alter this. There is virtually no emphasis on movement education skills, although the rapid physical growth and development often cause students to be less coordinated than they were earlier. The main activities taught by the physical eudcator in the six or seven classes per day are team sports and fitness activities. This is the age where team membership is important for social reasons, so these activities are stressed. Rhythms, aquatics, gymnastics, and individual activities are important. Extracurricular activities are primarily team-oriented, with at least a few athletic teams for both boys and girls sponsored by most schools. Intramural programs have been extremely popular where they are offered, but the increased number of school teams has reduced this program. It is quite common for physical educators to have coaching as one of their duties. (Not too many years ago, coaching was a part of the job. However, the majority of schools now pay extra for any extracurricular assignments.)

The special joys and problems of the 7-9 or 6-10 program are several. In general, the attitude of the students is decidedly in favor of any type of activity. This decreases discipline problems greatly. Most schools have better facilities and equipment than in elementary schools, although the size of the classes may be drastically increased. The problems revolve around the tremendous physical growth spurt found in this age group; the students are so varied in coordination, strength, and social and emotional maturity that it is sometimes difficult to determine just what will most benefit the students. Those students who are poor in physical education class begin to dislike it, because they are gradually becoming more concerned with peer status than with personal skill attainment. This makes it important for all students to have some degree of success.

This age group, despite its peer-influence problems, lends itself to some individualized programs. Varied activities should be offered. Students need to be exposed to a wide number of activities with the intent that specialization will occur in the next few years as each student develops greater interest in a few. If the program contains only the standard four or five sports, many students will lose interest as they achieve a skill level that satisfies them.

TEACHING PHYSICAL EDUCATION IN SENIOR HIGH SCHOOL (10-12 or 9-12)

Possession of a bachelor's degree is universally required to teach in high school. Highly desirable schools (because of location, size, salary schedule, or facilities) can be more selective of the great many applications they receive each year; quite often a master's degree plus teaching experience is required for employment. (Ironically, in these days of financial problems, some districts are not hiring teachers with master's degrees. The salary schedule indicates that those with a master's will earn more money so the school district saves money by hiring those with only bachelor's degrees.) The teaching load is six or seven periods a day, which is similar to that of the other teachers. There is still an emphasis on team sports and fitness, but the better programs will feature the individual, dual, and rhythmic areas even more. The carryover sports should receive the main emphasis, because this is the last time many of the students will take physical education. Many schools combine physical education with health, driver education, and/or first aid. Physical educators or health educators tolerate this arrangement, but many are convinced these should be separate courses, each taught by a specialist. Intramurals and interscholastic activities are very much a part of the high school teaching position; again, teachers usually receive extra pay for these extra duties.

In most high schools, the joys outnumber the problems in teaching physical education. On the negative side the most common deterrents to learning are too many students in class, and poor and insufficient facilities. Student attitude toward class may be poor, especially if the activities are the same ones that have been taught since grade school. High school students usually do not like required uniforms, and the class details (calisthenics, tests, drills, etc.) often cause discipline problems. Individualized programs, mini-courses (units only three to six sessions long), and contract grading are all techniques employed by successful teachers.

The joys and satisfactions come with being able to work with and see progress in students — those who are skilled, strong, and coordinated and who can learn many skills, and those initially uninterested students who later find success. When the K-12 program shows progression and variety, when it is based on student interests and needs, and when students are expected to meet logical and individualized standards, then many of the problems become minute.

TEACHING IN INNER CITY SCHOOLS

Up to this point, the material in this chapter has been about the teaching of physical education in the majority of schools in the U.S. We believe it is a realistic and accurate portrayal, although it obviously is a composite picture. However, the majority of Americans live in the 25-30 larger cities — and schools in these cities are sometimes strikingly different from those portrayed here. The students are somewhat different; the schools are different. It stands to reason that the programs are different, too.

In financially burdened inner city elementary schools, there are often no physical education specialists. The classroom teacher is forced to conduct physical education either on a small asphalt playground or in a multi-purpose room that also serves as a lunchroom and assembly hall. The outdoor facilities (smaller), the class size (larger), the bilingual students who do not understand one another, the student non-participation in class, the poor nutrition and inadequate rest, and the lessened parental guidance or concern all combine to cause active but unmotivated children. Teaching physical education in inner city elementary schools is harder, more discouraging, and more frustrating than in other situations — but probably more essential.

In junior and senior high schools, the student problems are compounded by even greater overcrowding in old buildings. White flight from the cities has caused minority children to become the majority, usually increasing school population dramatically. Racial clashes are common, often with tragic results. The problems of the elementary schools are all present, plus greatly increased pregnancies, drugs (including alcohol), tobacco and a high dropout rate. As essential as psychomotor skill development is for all students, human development is even more important to these children. The successful secondary teacher, according to Ridini and Madden (1975), must provide meaningful motivation, a diversified and relevant curriculum, awareness of how physical education activities can carry over into leisure pursuits, and help to those students who can't perform basic skills at minimal levels. Possessing the attitudes and skills of a counselor is perhaps more important for a successful inner city physical educator than being a skilled activity teacher. Special techniques are needed, because students just won't line up in clean uniforms, dutifully go through five minutes of calisthenics, and move quickly and silently to their squad positions. This is not to say that you wouldn't teach skills or emphasize the cognitive domain. The point is that the affective domain is more crucial; inner city (especially ghetto) children have so many environmental handicaps that physical education class must be more than merely learning the skills and rules of a sport. An excellent source of information on this topic is Ridini and Madden's book (1975), *Physical Education for Inner City Secondary Schools,* which describes the problems and also suggests realistic solutions.

TEACHING PHYSICAL EDUCATION IN COLLEGE

Junior (or community) colleges are springing up all over the U.S. These schools almost always offer activity courses for nonmajors and a few courses for majors. Teachers in junior college invariably have the master's degree, and often have had experience in the K-12 program. Coaching and/or supervising intramurals is virtually a universal assignment for both men and women. The junior colleges usually offer such courses as introductory physical education, first aid, anatomy, and physiology for the prospective major, as well as activity courses for all. Junior college teachers should be motivated toward teacher preparation, as well as toward general teaching. The junior college is often a part of the local district and its teachers are on the same salary schedule as other teachers in the district.

The primary difference you would note when teaching in college is the absence of discipline problems. Most teachers find this a refreshing change! It is common for the junior college to require all students to take one (sometimes two) years of physical education activity courses. Since these are apt to be single courses (e.g., beginning tennis), the junior college teacher begins to specialize. A shortage of expert teachers in gymnastics, karate, SCUBA, fencing, and rhythms exists, while those with expertise in team sports are plentiful.

The physical education department at a four-year institution has two main missions — to offer service courses to the general student body, and to offer courses for physical education majors. College teachers in these institutions will spend part of their time teaching activities and part teaching the body-of-knowledge courses which are required for majors. Very rarely are teachers without master's degrees hired for the four-year colleges; the doctorate is highly desirable if a person is to be promoted and receive an adequate salary. The small college hires generalists (persons who can teach or coach a variety of different activities), whereas the larger college or university can hire biomechanic experts along with gymnastics, aquatics, individual sport, and dance teachers. Demand for these specialists will probably continue for several years.

Coaching as an extracurricular duty is most often combined with teaching at the smaller schools. Men's athletics has grown into such a large business at the major universities, however, that often there is no connection between physical education and athletics. Coaching at all levels will be discussed in detail in the next chapter.

As at other levels, teaching in college has both joys and problems. Discipline problems are minimal, and the facilities and equipment are superior to most high schools. The teaching load is somewhat less than in the K-12 grades, ranging from 12 classroom hours per week to about 20. This figure varies greatly depending upon coaching duties, teaching of graduate courses, administrative responsibilities, and the institution.

TEACHING DANCE

The teaching of dance in schools is a growing career opportunity for many prospective physical educators. Many four-year colleges and universities have dance minors and there are several schools which offer a dance major. The purpose of these programs is to educate persons for qualification in one of these three areas: dance education, dance performance, and/or dance therapy. Dance performance and dance therapy will be discussed in greater detail in Chapter 13, since these two careers occur primarily outside the school.

For those persons who wish to specialize in dance education, there are growing career opportunities. One of the most obvious careers would be teaching in private dance studios, which will also be discussed in Chapter 13. Teaching dance in the schools, however, is a distinct possibility. For those who prefer to work in preschool through grade six, the students (boys and girls) are customarily taught basic rhythms, simple folk dances and beginning square dancing. The purpose is to make students aware that dancing is rhythmic movement to music. Some students may look upon dancing as something inappropriate for themselves, but in fact a large number of successful athletes have improved their coordination, skill, and agility through dance courses. The teacher of dance in these grades tends to travel from class to class throughout the week, inasmuch as dance specialists hired to work with students of this age serve as consultants to classroom teachers. Most dance and rhythmic activities for this age group are taught by the classroom teacher or by the physical education specialist.

In grades 7-12, it is more common to employ a dance specialist who does little else but teach this particular activity. It is almost universal that girls have dance units in their physical education program, while all of the better physical education programs have at least social dance for both boys and girls. A dance specialist works primarily with girls, teaching modern dance, ballet, tap, and jazz dancing. Title IX will affect the composition of these classes, as it will no longer be possible to restrict them to girls. It is probable that an increasing number of boys will take advantage of class offerings in dance. The dance specialist is invariably called upon to help when school plays and musicals are staged; the choreography for such theater productions is almost always his or her responsibility.

The facilities for teaching dance in any of the K-12 grades usually are adequate at best. Dance teachers customarily have to use large gyms or smaller rooms adjacent to the gym. In neither case are the acoustics very good, the floor really suited for dancing, or the size of the room appropriate to the size of the group.

It is quite common for the dance units taught in physical education classes to be extremely popular — particularly social dancing. Many students in grades 7-12 do not dance well, but they would like to learn if it can be done without embarrassment. A superior dance teacher can, within the space of a few weeks, turn antagonistic groups into enthusiastic groups that look forward to dancing. The secrets seem to be in teaching dances that will be used in social settings as well as dances which are taught for rhythmic or cultural values, and in being able to relate to students. If these two essentials are considered, the dance teacher's job is especially rewarding.

In some four-year institutions, dance majors or minors are part of the physical education department, while in other schools they are part of the fine arts or theater departments. In either case, dance specialists must be certified to teach before they can be employed by a school district. It is wise for them to be able to teach in another area or to be reasonably skilled in a variety of physical education activities. While there are full-time jobs for dance specialists, it is more common that a person spends part of the time teaching dance and part of the time teaching other subjects or activities.

OTHER CONSIDERATIONS — SALARY AND MINORS

Salaries have always been of interest to prospective employees! The salaries of beginning teachers have risen more than 50% (to an average of $8,000) since 1965. Beginning salaries of those with the M.A. and Ph.D. degree have risen about 54% (to about $8,600 and $9,300, respectively) in the same time. The Southeast region of the U.S. (Alabama, Arkansas, Florida, etc.) seems to be below the national average. The highest beginning salaries are paid in the Mideast (Delaware, Maryland, and New

York) and the Great Lakes area (Illinois, Indiana, Michigan, Ohio). However, remember that these are averages, and that each local district sets its own schedule. The average salary for all teachers was about $12,500 in 1976.

A minor area of study is highly desirable for physical education majors. Why? Consider these 1974 statistics (NEA, 1975):

Elementary PE-Health graduates equaled about 95% of the demand.

Secondary PE-Health graduates (male) equaled 428% of the demand.

Secondary PE-Health graduates (female) equaled 310% of the demand.

True, the continuing rise in women's sports will create a demand for coaches, but there just is not an adequate number of full-time physical education jobs for all graduates. In the past it was common for our majors to graduate with a combined major in physical and health education and thus be qualified to teach either or both disciplines. Health educators have long been dissatisfied with this arrangement, preferring to have enthusiastic, informed health teachers instead of apathetic, "lukewarm" physical educators teaching the class. As certification laws become stricter, more and more states now recognize these as two separate disciplines, and require certification in each. Think about it — what would you teach besides physical education?

WHAT WAS — AND WHAT MIGHT BE

Statistics are dated by the time any text is printed, but they are useful in predicting what might happen in the future. As a way of summarizing the job opportunities available to you, consider Table 11-1 as a general guide.

LEARNING ABOUT SCHOOL PHYSICAL EDUCATION

The theme of this text is that physical education is a discipline and that professional teachers should understand all of its aspects. Thus, teachers of physical education should first be conversant with the foundations of our area, and in addition, learn about the special techniques which pertain to teaching. Courses in both categories are listed and/or described below.

1. *Human anatomy, physiology, physiology of exercise.* These courses have been mentioned in Chapter 6.
2. *Activity courses* in various sports, *psychomotor learning,* and *teaching methods.* These courses were described in Chapter 7, although it is obvious that a discussion of methods courses might just as well have been done in the present chapter.
3. *Psychology of coaching* (Chapter 8) related very much to the teaching of school physical education.
4. *Physics, mathematics, kinesiology.* These courses have been described in Chapter 9.
5. *Economics, political science, sociology,* and *sport and society.* These were presented in Chapter 10.
6. *Organization and administration of physical education.* There are numerous policies and details which must be considered when conducting a school physical education program. These include the activity program, the staff, the facilities, intramural and interscholastic athletics, class routines, public relations, and safety precautions.
7. *Measurement and evaluation in physical education.* For many, the most difficult problem in teaching is assigning grades. Because we can use so many ob-

TABLE 11–1. PROFILE OF K-12 PHYSICAL EDUCATION TEACHERS.

WHAT WAS IN 1970–76	*WHAT MIGHT BE BY 1984*
Where do physical educators teach? About 35% teach in K-6 classes, about 50% in 7-10, about 15% in 10-12.* About 75% of all physical education teachers have taught at each level (elementary, middle school, high school) at some time in their career.* Secondary physical education teachers compose about 8.3% of all secondary teachers.† Elementary physical education specialists who regularly teach physical education are found in 69% of school districts. About 55% of the districts employ specialists who only teach. Elementary specialists who act as consultants and also teach are found in about 5% of school districts. The larger the district, the more likely the consultant or consultant-teacher role is found.‡ About 74% of all districts have elementary physical education teachers.‡ *What do physical educators teach?* About 33% teach health and/or first aid.* Only about 10% provide an adaptive or corrective program.* About 50% of the men have, at some time in their careers, taught girls.* About 25% of the women, have at some time in their careers, taught boys.* Team sports are emphasized in grades 7-11.* Lifetime sports in grades 10-12.*	By 1984, school age population will decrease (ages 5-13, 11%; ages 14-17, 15%). Enrollment will decrease (K-8, 8%; 9-12, 13%). Teacher need will increase in K-8 by 6%; will decrease by 9% in 9-12 grades. § The percentage of physical education teachers at each level will probably remain about the same. Many large districts require that teachers (whether new or experienced) begin in the elementary program, and move to the upper grades as positions open. If economic pressures lessen, more elementary specialists will be hired in school districts of every size. It will be advantageous for physical education majors who expect to teach in high school to have a second teaching area (minor). Schools need persons to help coach, but will have relatively few full-time physical education openings. Elementary physical education consultants will invariably be those who have had 2-10 years of successful experience. Versatility will continue to be a desirable quality. Great rise in coed, lifetime sports will mean that male and female students in each class will be the norm rather than the exception. There still will be combination physical education-health teachers, but health special-ists will be required in many states. Recreation responsibilities will be given to recreation specialists, except for summer-only physical activity programs. Rise in outdoor recreation (hiking, skiing, mountain climbing) calls for persons to teach these activities. Increased need for dance, aquatic (especially SCUBA), gymnastic experts. Increased need for those trained to work with the mentally, emotionally and physically handicapped.

Material for the "What Was" column was gathered from various sources of 1970-76 data. Material in the "What Might Be by 1984" column is an interpretation by a national group and by the authors of this text.

TABLE 11–1 CONT.

WHAT WAS IN 1970–76	WHAT MIGHT BE BY 1984
What about coaching athletics, intramurals, cheerleaders?	Great increase in the number of coaching jobs for both men and women. Women especially will probably be required to coach if they want to teach physical education in grades 7-12.
About 60% of the men coach one or more varsity sports.*	
About 45% of the men are an assistant coach in at least one sport.*	Pattern will be to have two athletic directors (one male, one female).
About 25% of the men are also athletic directors.*	Intramural participation will probably decrease as many more school teams for formed.
About 41% (women) and 33% (men) are also directors of intramural sports.*	Directing the cheerleaders may still be a required duty for some.
About 42% (women) and 5% (men) coach cheerleaders.*	Rise of sport and recreation clubs means the need for sponsors, teachers.
What do physical educators perceive as their teaching weaknesses?	The rise of opportunity to specialize while an undergraduate will help prepare persons in a chosen activity area.
Lack of proficiency to teach adaptive-correctives, dance, rhythms, and elementary physical education.*	More schools will offer an opportunity to specialize in elementary, secondary, or adaptive physical education.
Lack of early (sophomore or junior year in college) professional experiences in school.	Early field experiences (internships, practicums, pre–student teaching) will be common.
Lack of experience in successfully coping with other situations than white middle-class suburban students.	Student experiences (student teaching, internships, practica) in inner city, and small rural schools will be "strongly recommended" by the department.

*Elba Stafford, et al., *Educational characteristics of physical education teachers in Wisconsin public schools* (Madison, Wis.: Wisconsin Dept. of Public Instruction, 1970), pp. 8, 9, 13, 18, 21, 31.
† *NEA Research Bulletin* (March 1972):4.
‡ *NEA Research Bulletin* (May 1972):45, 46.
§ National Center for Education Statistics, 1976.

jective devices (stop watches, tape measures, and the like) it is comparatively easy to measure physical performance. Evaluating and grading is another matter. In the measurement course you will learn elementary statistics, the administration and interpretation of all types of skill and written tests, and the principles of testing (by administering those tests listed in Chapter 6 and 7 to new majors).

8. *Field experience.* As mentioned earlier, it is essential that you have early experience in schools. We have known students who, after student teaching in their senior year, decided that they didn't want to teach. This is a tragic waste of time and money for both the student and the department. Summer recreation experience or coaching Little League is not the same as teaching children in a school setting. There is no substitute for actually helping a teacher, or teaching under competent supervision.

In addition to the physical education major courses, about one-eighth of the credits required for graduation will be in education. Many students feel that the courses are too general and irrelevant to physical education. Not so — a teacher must know about children in general as well as physical education.

IS TEACHING PHYSICAL EDUCATION FOR YOU?

The problem which all teacher-training institutions have is attempting to identify students who are potentially successful teachers as early in their college careers as possible. Usually, colleges require a certain GPA before students are permitted to take upper division education courses or student teaching, yet the GPA is not a very reliable measure of predicting how well a student will teach. Three broad categories of information, described below, might help you and the department make a logical decision in your career choice.

Comparison with Peers or Successful Teachers

The first category of information you might consider consists of comparing yourself with peers, or with successful teachers. Quite often comparisons are made in conjunction with personality tests.

Personality is a large factor in teaching success, but no one has devised a completely valid and reliable way to measure this crucial quality. One method of obtaining a rough estimate of personality is to take a published test, and then compare your score with those of similar groups. The two tests mentioned below have been selected because they have been found useful when counseling prospective teachers. Your score will *not* predict how successful you would be as a teacher; it will only indicate your comparison with others. If your instructor can make arrangements with your counseling center, you might take one or both of the tests. The counselor will help you interpret your score.

Minnesota Multiphasic Personality Inventory (MMPI). This test has been used by thousands of persons. Two investigators (Gowen and Gowen 1955) have selected 98 questions from it, and through various try-outs and statistical procedures, have determined that these items are useful in counseling prospective teachers. Should your instructor arrange for you to take this test, compare your score with your appropriate group on Table 11-2. Remember, the norms presented will compare you with other prospective majors. Past experience tells us those who score somewhere above the 35th standard score are usually successful at least through student teaching.

Cattell 16 PF. This test, which purportedly measures 16 personality factors, has likewise been extensively used for many years. Mattsson (1970) has studied student teachers in various disciplines, using the Cattell 16 PF as one device to gather data on what might be called a "successful" group of prospective teachers (successful in that they have completed at least three years of college, have achieved at least a 2.5 GPA in their major, and are motivated enough to student teach). Because of the 16 different factors mentioned in this test, it would be usual for you to find some of your scores above the mean, and others below. This test needs interpretation by a trained counselor. Table 11-3 shows the means and standard deviations for various groups on this test. As mentioned in Chapter 8, the whole is more than the sum of its parts — which is another way of saying that traits must be considered in clusters rather than individually. Ogilvie and Tutko warn, "We have been particularly wary of the exaggerated use of any single trait deviation because of the tendency to respond in an exaggerated way and over-generalize with regard to the personality make-up of a given individual. There has been a tendency for a significant number of physical educators . . . to overreact to specific high or low traits without due consideration for the total psychological picture." (Ogilvie and Tutko 1972, p. 218.)

The means and standard deviations in Table 11-3. indicate where successful (as defined above) physical education students have scored on each of the traits. Note the variance between all the student teachers and the physical education majors in B, C, F, G, I, O, and III.

TABLE 11–2. NORMS FOR GOWEN AND GOWEN ADAPTATION OF MMPI TEST (MALE AND FEMALE).

STANDARD SCALE	FRESHMEN	SOPHOMORES	JUNIORS	SENIORS
100				
95				
90				
85				
80	97.		96.	
75	91.	94.	92.	95.
70	86.	89.	87.	90.
65	81.	84.	82.	84.
60	75.	79.	77.	79.
55	70.	74.	73.	73.
50	65.	69.	68.	68.
45	59.	64.	63.	62.
40	54.	59.	58.	57.
35	49.	54.	54.	51.
30	43.	49.	49.	45.
25	39.	44.	44.	40.
20	33.	39.	40.	34.
15	27.	34.	35.	29.
10	22.	29.	30.	23.
5				
0				
MEAN	64.575	68.727	67.878	67.583
SD	13.357	12.458	11.843	13.916
N	214.0	55.0	82.0	72.0
H. S.	96.0	93.0	92.0	93.0
L. S.	22.0	32.0	34.0	26.0
RANGE	74.0	61.0	58.0	67.0
8SC	1.069	.997	.947	1.113
MAX. SCORE	98.0	98.0	98.0	98.0
NO. TRLS	1.0	1.0	1.0	1.0

TABLE 11–3. MEANS AND STANDARD DEVIATIONS OF VARIOUS GROUPS ON THE CATTELL 16 PF TEST.

16 PF FACTOR DESCRIPTIONS (−) (+) LOW SCORE – HIGH SCORE	ALL STUDENT TEACHERS (K–12) IN STUDY* (N=769)	STUDENT TEACHERS IN JUNIOR OR SENIOR HIGH SCHOOL PE		
		FEMALE (N=19)	MALE (N=23)	TOTAL (N=42)
A: Reserved–Outgoing	11.77	11.90	11.35	11.60
	3.09	2.94	.2.81	2.85
B: Dull–Intelligent	8.58	8.05	7.00	7.48
	2.09	1.47	1.76	1.70
C: Emotionally immature–Mature	15.59	16.16	16.74	16.48
	3.55	3.72	3.14	3.38
E: Submissive–Dominant	11.97	11.00	12.96	12.07
	4.18	2.75	3.46	3.27
F: Sober–Enthusiastic	16.61	18.26	16.91	17.52
	4.33	3.00	3.49	3.31
G: Expedient–Conscientious	13.15	13.84	14.26	14.07
	4.55	3.72	3.35	3.48
H: Shy–Venturesome	13.89	13.37	13.65	13.52
	4.96	4.40	4.72	4.52
I: Tough minded–Sensitive	11.18	10.84	9.39	10.05
	3.69	3.04	2.79	2.96
L: Trusting–Suspicious	7.19	6.90	7.78	7.38
	3.14	2.31	2.92	2.67
M: Conventional–Imaginative	12.36	12.37	11.30	11.79
	4.12	3.32	2.06	2.72
N: Forthright–Shrewd	9.94	9.21	9.74	9.50
	2.59	2.32	2.03	2.16
O: Confident–Apprehensive	10.00	10.11	9.04	9.52
	3.54	3.43	3.10	3.26
Q_1: Conservative–Experimenting	9.86	9.69	9.74	9.71
	2.66	2.63	2.49	2.52
Q_2: Group dependent– Self-sufficient	9.76	8.95	9.30	9.41
	3.28	3.05	2.87	2.92
Q_3: Casual–Controlled	11.04	10.37	10.74	10.57
	2.91	2.75	2.72	2.71
Q_4: Relaxed–Tense	12.13	12.47	11.48	11.93
	4.57	4.55	3.99	4.23
I: Low anxiety–High anxiety	1.60	1.83	1.07	1.41
	3.82	3.55	3.24	3.36
II: Introverted–Extroverted	17.87	18.13	18.20	18.17
	4.78	3.65	4.34	3.99
III: Responsive–Tough poise	−2.64	−2.33	−.86	−1.52
	3.38	3.02	2.33	2.73
IV: Dependent–Independent	11.30	10.37	11.12	10.78
	3.61	3.01	2.52	2.74

Data (1970) through the courtesy of Dr. Kenneth Mattsson, professor of education, Mankato (Minnesota) State University. The study was made possible by a grant to Dr. Mattsson from the ESSO Education Foundation.

TABLE 11–4. PERSONALITY TRAITS OF FEMALE AND
MALE AAHPER PHYSICAL EDUCATORS.

	TRAIT	*FEMALE AAHPER*	*MALE AAHPER*
		Members were Different from the Control Group of Females in that they were more:	*Members were Different from the Control Group of Males in that they were more:*
A:	Reserved and aloof	X	
B:	Intelligent	X	X
C:	Emotionally stable		X
E:	Assertive and dominant	X	
G:	Conscientious and persistent	X	X
I:	Tender minded and sensitive		X
I:	Tough minded and realistic	X	
L:	Trusting and adaptable		X
N:	Naive and unpretentious		X
O:	Confident and placid	X	X
Q_1:	Experimenting and analytical	X	
Q_3:	Controlled and exacting	X	X
Q_4:	Composed and relaxed	X	

From Polly Cabe Roberts, Personality characteristics of groups in physical education and related professional areas, in *Abstracts of Research Papers* (Washington, D.C.: AAHPER, 1972), p. 104. Used by permission.

Should you have the opportunity to take the Cattell 16 PF test, you could compare yourself to the general population, and to physical education members of AAHPER. Roberts compared female and male AAHPER members to a group of adult non-physical educators, and found differences as shown in Table 11-4. Your results might show similar differences.

Self-concept is a very important component of personality. The stereotype of the physical education major (not too intelligent, overmuscled, unaware of anything except sports) has caused some prospective majors to change to other careers. But what do we think of ourselves?

Vincent (1976) compared female college athletes, nonathletes, physical education majors, and general students, and also female high school athletes and nonathletes in self-concept. Women physical education majors, and high school athletes, had significantly higher self-concept scores than the others. This coincides with findings by Brown, Roberts, and Mulumphy, but is in some disagreement with Snyder and Kivlin. Data for males is lacking, but there is reason to believe that they too are satisfied with themselves. A teacher with a poor concept would be very undesirable, as students are influenced as much by how we act as by what we teach.

Self-examination of Past Experience

A second way to assess your status with regard to teaching is to examine your past experience. Figure 11-2 is a very concise survey of one year of high school physical education. If possible, your instructor will have you complete it and then discuss in class some of the "best" answers. Remember that these "best" answers depend upon your instructor's philosophy.

One thing should be emphasized. Chances are that your high school physical education program may not rate too highly when compared to an ideal program. Overcrowded classes, administrative obstruction, inability to improve poor facilities, inadequate budget, and/or a poor instructor may all contribute. Answer the survey truthfully, but be hesitant to assume that your instructor is totally responsible for the rating.

Comparison with Outstanding Teachers

Finally, a way to assess your status with regard to teaching physical education is to compare yourself to outstanding physical education teachers. Two such persons were described in *Update*. The comments are selected to show the qualities desired in an elementary and a secondary teacher, plus a description of their duties.

"Just the Kind of Man You'd Like to Teach Your Own Children"

H. Edwin Lanehart, a 38-year-old physical education teacher at Woodmoor Elementary School in Baltimore County, Maryland, has been named the Maryland Teacher of the Year.

His principal said, "He is the kind of person that any time you ask him to do something, or even mention it to him, it is done. He doesn't think of himself, but of the children and the program. He is just the kind of person I would want to teach my children if I had them."

Lanehart teaches kindergarten through sixth grade. Lanehart involves himself in the activities, especially in rhythms and dance. He and the children have a lot of fun. He says he tries to draw the parallel, especially for boys and older children, between rhythm and athletic ability. Sometimes he has them dribble basketballs to music.

In addition, Lanehart is the physical education helping teacher for the Southwest District elementary schools of the county school system, which means he is responsible for keeping in touch with all elementary physical educators in his area and giving them the benefit of his experience. He says he tends to spend his time with the first year teachers in his area. Fridays are the prescribed day for these duties. There are 23 schools with 17 physical educators including himself. He visits them on a rotating basis and is on call whenever a teacher wishes to request help or advice on program, curriculum or special problems. This year, 9 of his 16 colleagues are first year teachers.

He also spends 1½ days each week at Special Education Centers for children with learning disabilities. He gives physical education classes at two such centers: Lansdowne and Hebbville. He also conducts a perceptual motor workshop and clinic weekly on Wednesday nights. Because he now has only 2½ days to spend at Woodmoor it has been necessary for the authorities to appoint a second physical education teacher to Woodmoor part-time. Dr. Merson says that there have been requests and suggestions from the county that Lanehart be transferred wholly to special duties. She has resisted this successfully until now. She believes he is a stabilizing influence in the school; not only that, "Ed does a tremendous job in changing the way children feel about themselves. He improves their own self-concepts. That is something it is hard to put a finger on, but it is what makes a truly great teacher."

Lanehart has resisted being moved entirely into special education, also. He believes that a teacher must teach, and he values his daily contacts with the youngsters, who certainly respond to him in a most satisfying way.

Every year since he became a teacher, Ed Lanehart has put on a program for the Parent Teachers Association because he believes in keeping in touch with parents.

Through these programs he can indoctrinate the parents in the values of movement education.

He has always been active in the state association, and has been editor of the Maryland AHPER Newsletter for several years, a responsibility he had to relinquish this year because of all his other duties. He was a member of the editorial committee that worked on *Promising Practices in Elementary Physical Education,* a book published by AAHPER.

"She Makes Sports Fun" (A letter from students)

We would like to bring to your attention the outstanding qualities of Miss Dorothy Hill. Miss Hill is head of the physical education department at Shaker Heights High School. It is an exceptionally well-organized and respected part of the school.

Besides being head of this department, Miss Hill is also supervisor of the Girls' Leaders Club of Shaker Heights High, a nationally rated official, and organizer of all intramural, interclass, and varsity games.

Miss Hill's patience in class, combined with her demonstrations of skills, inspire confidence in her students and promote class participation. We feel that these qualities are most important in any physical education teacher. (Signed by 53 students.)

Accompanying the letter were the following three statements:

Miss Hill's ability to teach extends beyond most. She makes a sport fun and exciting to be included in because of the fact that she makes it be like a sport and not like a class requirement. Also, she cares about how her students do in her classes. When necessary she will participate in the game to illustrate how a certain technique is executed instead of just trying to explain. I feel it's important if a teacher can participate like this.

Miss Hill's successful teaching is partly due to the fact that she cares for her students. Her concern for them reaches far beyond that which is called for. In her classes, she teachers so that the sport being played becomes fun, and not only something that is just required from the students. The students enjoy her methods and seldom take advantage of her kindness. On the whole, Miss Hill is a warm and friendly person, traits seldom found in gym teachers today. She really makes my gym classes fun, and I look forward to having them every day.

Shaker Heights High School has a very good, competent staff of girls' physical education teachers. But one of the teachers, Dorothy Hill, stands out in my mind. She not only does an excellent job of teaching the classes, but is somehow able to inspire confidence and friendship between herself and the students. She is able to motivate the teams to play hard and to play together as a team, not as individuals.

SUMMARY

To end the chapter, we summarize qualities which two physical educators say should be possessed by professionals. In Table 11-5 they have said succinctly what those of us in teacher preparation know — that only taking the courses required for graduation does not make a person ready to teach, nor a professional. In Table 11-5 Crase is talking to those who would teach physical education majors, while Crawford is talking to those who will be teaching K-12 physical education. Both sources serve to remind you that teaching physical education requires more than playing ability in a few sports.

FIGURE 11-2. Survey of high school physical education experience.

Please comment upon your high school physical education class by writing "yes" or "no" in the space ahead of each statement. Select any one year you took the course. You are welcome to add comments in the space between each statement.

_____ 1. Did you actually take the physical education class (as opposed to being excused because of athletics)? (If no, you need not answer any more questions.)

_____ 2. Did your physical education class meet at least three days per week?

3. Did you have instruction (at least 4-5 periods each) in the following:
_____ a. Team sports (basketball, soccer, volleyball, etc.)?

_____ b. Individual sports (tennis, golf, gymnastics, wrestling, etc.)?

_____ c. Rhythms (social, dance, modern dance, etc.)?

_____ d. Aquatics (swimming, lifesaving, etc.)?

_____ e. Conditioning (calisthenics, exercises, physical fitness, etc.)?

_____ 4. Did you spend at least 80% of class time in instruction, and 20% in play?

_____ 5. Were most of the activities each year new ones, i.e., not taught last year?

_____ 6. Did you have to have a physical exam before taking physical education class?

_____ 7. Did you have a separate health class?

_____ 8. Did your school have an extensive intramural program for _all_ students (boys and girls, many activities, great percentage of participation)?

_____ 9. Did you ever have to make up missed work in physical education after you were absent?

_____ 10. Were there some students who failed or got low grades in physical education?

_____ 11. Did you ever have skills tests (other than physical fitness tests) in physical education class?

_____ 12. Did you have written tests in physical education class?

_____ 13. Did your class put on a demonstration every one or two years for the parents?

In general, how do you think your high school physical education class would rate when compared to the program recommended by your state?

_____ Excellent _____ Good _____ Fair _____ Poor _____ Terrible

IF TIME PERMITS, YOUR INSTRUCTOR WILL INDICATE THE "DESIRABLE" ANSWERS.

TABLE 11–5. DESIRABLE CHARACTERISTICS OF PHYSICAL EDUCATION TEACHERS.

Whoever would be a professional college teacher possesses these qualities: *

1. Sees dignity in teaching physical education and is not apologetic. That person knows that the discipline is important, and that lives will be enriched if persons understand our body of knowledge. He or she *wants* to teach.

2. Has a personal philosophy which "practices what is preached." If it is important enough to teach, it is important enough to do.

3. Exudes a personal aura of sureness, optimism, self-confidence. This, coupled with a captivating teaching style, will cause students to look forward to class.

4. Has a thorough knowledge of whatever is being taught. This knowledge is broad and deep enough to motivate and captivate learners of all levels, yet permits creativity to be displayed.

5. Has a humanistic philosophy which, when combined with a sense of humor, makes students feel they are an important part of the group. The professional cares about and for people.

6. Is fair and consistent in dealing with students. We demand these qualities in officials of athletic contests; the teaching process demands this likewise.

7. Has constant pursuit of psychomotor, cognitive, and affective excellence. This relates to no. 5 below.

Whoever is ready to teach physical education possesses these qualities: **

1. Expertise in one or more activities. Currently, experts in aquatics, gymnastics, dance and coaching individual sports are most in demand.

2. Versatility. Many schools want persons who can teach in the classroom *and* in the gym. Being an expert (see no. 4 above) is fine, but you should be able to teach a variety of activities.

3. A pleasing personality and appearance. You are judged first by your outward appearance and then by your personality. These qualities have a great deal to do with teaching effectiveness and, more often than not, are the determining factors in obtaining a job.

4. Above-average command of the English language. You are also judged on both oral and written communication. A successful interview depends upon written skill and verbalization of your beliefs.

5. Desire to grow professionally. Becoming an active participant in local, state, district and national professional groups is easy—we never have enough workers! Attendance at clinics and summer sessions is necessary. Some teachers go back to school because they are forced to by state law; professionals want to because they realize that it will make them better educators.

6. Realization of similarities and differences between teaching physical education and athletic coaching. You should be as concerned about the below-average and average students as with the gifted. Teaching is hard physical and mental work; "rolling out the ball" is easy.

7. Loyalty to the administration and cooperation with your colleagues. Human, not professional problems cause most teaching failures. No two persons will act, think, or teach alike, yet must cooperate even if not in the gym at the same time. Decision by superiors will not always meet with your approval, but as long as you teach there, you are expected to support them.

*Adapted from Darrell Crase, In search of greatness, *The Physical Educator* 28 (Oct. 1971):130-32. Used by permission.
**Adapted from Wayne Crawford, Are you ready to teach? *JOHPER* 36 (Jan. 1965):87.

Bibliography

General.

AAHPER. *Physical education careers for women.* (Pamphlet); *Careers in physical education and coaching for boys.* (Pamphlet); *Dance careers for men and women.* (Pamphlet). Washington, D.C.:AAHPER.

_____. 1962. *This is physical education.* Washington, D.C.:AAHPER.

Alexander, R. How to prevent the student teaching blues. *JOHPER* 41 (Mar. 1970):93-95.

Carter, J. A. Is education preparing teachers for the future, or simply perpetuating the past? *The Physical Educator* 28 (May 1971):81.

Check, J. F. Is creative teaching for the physical educator in vogue? *The Physical Educator* 28 (Dec. 1971):192.

Coplan, A. The ugly gym teacher. *The Physical Educator* 21 (Oct. 1964):106.

Crase, D. In search of greatness. *The Physical Educator* 28 (Oct. 1971):130-32.

Crawford, W. Are you ready to teach? *JOHPER* 36 (Jan. 1965):87.

Douglas, J. Skills necessary for an effective teacher. *The Physical Educator* 26 (Mar. 1969):37.

Henry, C. D. The black physical educator: Is he different? what does he want? *The Physical Educator* 26 (Oct. 1969):110.

Jewett, A. E. 'Would you believe' public schools 1975: Physical education for the real world. *JOHPER* 42 (Mar. 1971):41.

Jordon, T. C. Micro teaching: A reappraisal of its value in teacher education. *Quest* 15 (Jan. 1971):17.

Klesius, S. E. Physical education in the seventies: Where do you stand? *JOHPER* 42 (Feb. 1971):46.

NEA. Teacher supply and demand in public schools, 1974. *NEA Research Memo* (May 1975):8.

Pelton, B. Competency based teacher education: Implications for physical education *The Physical Educator* 29 (Oct. 1972):147.

Schochet, M. We can't remain just a high priced repetitive recreation program. *JOHPER* 41 (Apr. 1970):24.

Stark, B., et al. Young teachers write. *JOHPER* 42 (Jan. 1971):40.

Stafford, E.; Seefeldt, V.; and Jensen, G. 1970. *Educational characteristics of physical education teachers in Wisconsin public schools.* Mimeographed. Madison, Wis.: Wisconsin Department of Public Instruction. (See also *JOHPER* 42 (May 1971):51.)

Updyke, W. A backward glance at priorities. *JOHPER* 42 (Mar. 1971):79.

Preschool.

Becker, J., et al. Childhood education program. *JOHPER* 45 (June 1974):20-21.

Herkowitz, J. A perceptual motor training program to improve the gross motor abilities of preschoolers.*JOHPER* 41 (Apr. 1970):120.

Ward, B. Implications of physical education for preschool children. *The Physical Educator* 32 (May 1975):80-83.

Werner, P. H. Movement experience for preschool children. *The Physical Educator* 32 (Dec. 1975):182-85.

Elementary school.

AAHPER. Essentials of a quality elementary school physical education program. *JOHPER* 42 (Apr. 1971):42.

Masche, K. A. Effects of two different programs of instruction on motor performance of second grade students. *Research Quarterly* 41 (Oct. 1970): 406-11.

Trimble, R. T. Selected research findings with implications for elementary school physical education. *The Physical Educator* 29 (Oct. 1972):123.

Weber, J. D. Motivational wizard. *JOHPER* 44 (Apr. 1973): 51-55. (Elementary physical education specialist.)

Whitehill, P. Major in elementary physical education at Eastern Washington State College. *JOHPER* 41 (Feb. 1970):81-83.

Workman, D. Comparison of performance of children taught by the physical education specialist and by the classroom teacher. *Research Quarterly* 39 (May 1968):389-94.

Middle school.

Bird, J. Physical education and the middle school child. *JOHPER* 44 (Mar. 1973):25.

Stafford, E. Middle schools: Status of physical education programs. *JOHPER* 45 (Feb. 1974):25-28.

Secondary schools.

AAHPER position paper. Guidelines for secondary school physical education. *JOHPER* 42 (Apr. 1971):47.

AAHPER. New physical education. *JOHPER* 42 (Sept. 1971):24. (Eleven short articles, each describing an innovative program.)

Regna, J. Teaching gymnastics: A most satisfying experience. *The Physical Educator* 32 (Dec. 1975):188.

Inner city schools.

Bell, J. A. Plato, the ghetto, and physical education. *The Physical Educator* 29 (May 1972):87.

Ezersky, E., and Thiebert, P. R. City schools without gyms. *JOHPER* 41 (Apr. 1970):26.

Ridini, L. Physical education for the inner city. *The Physical Educator* 28 (Dec. 1971):176-79.

_____, and Madden, J. E. 1975. *Physical education for inner city secondary schools.* New York: Harper and Row.

Wagman, E. Physical education and the disadvantaged. *JOHPER* 44 (Mar. 1973):29.

College.

Hodges, P. B. Status and structure of physical education in public two-year colleges of the Midwest. *JOHPER* 45 (June 1974):13-16.

Dance.

Burton, D., and Armstrong, D. People should love to dance. *JOHPER* 45 (Oct. 1974):65-66.

Faulkner, T. R. An approach to the study of ethnic dance for American students. *JOHPER* 44 (May 1973):55-56.

Poll, T. L. Jazz dance in secondary school physical education. *JOHPER* 44 (Jan. 1973):33-34.

Sebantine, J. Jazz dance in the secondary school. *JOHPER* 43 (Feb. 1972):69.

Schroeder, C. B. Expanding the dance program for boys. *The Physical Educator* 28 (Mar. 1971):52-53.

Varga, G. J. Definition of social dance and an argument for its inclusion in the elementary school program. *JOHPER* 43 (Feb. 1972):38.

Young, J. Using streamers to introduce creative dance. *The Physical Educator* 32 (Dec. 1975):207.

Personality.

Gowen, J. C., and Gowen, M. S. Teacher prognosis scale for the MMPI. *Journal of Educational Research* 49 (Sept. 1955):1-12.

Just the kind of man you'd like to teach your own children. *Update* (Mar. 1972):3.

Ogilvie, B., and Tutko, T. 1972. Motivation and psychometric approach in coaching. In *Psychological aspects of physical education and sport,* ed. J. E. Kane, pp. 209-231. Boston: Routledge and Kegan Paul.

Roberts, P. C. 1972. Personality characteristics of groups in physical education and related professional areas. In *Abstracts of Research Papers,* p. 104. Washington, D.C.: AAHPER.

She makes sports fun. *Update* (Mar. 1972):14.

Vincent, M. F. Comparison of self-concepts of college women: Athletes and physical education majors. *Research Quarterly* 47 (May 1976):218-25.

Widdop, J. H., and Widdop, V. A comparison of the personality traits of female teacher education and physical education students. *Research Quarterly* 46 (Oct. 1975):274.

Student Activities

1. This chapter has outlined different levels on which to teach. Select the one that interests you the most, and submit a written report containing as much of the following as possible:
   a. observation of the actual situation
   b. interview with someone who is now working (or has worked) in that area

c.   written information obtained from the employer or library
d.   interview with older students who are preparing to enter the area

Statements for Class Discussion

1. Anybody who knows sports can teach elementary school physical education.
2. Teaching physical education would be OK if it weren't for the kids — the elementary students are too wild, and the older ones too lazy.
3. Physical education should be fun. Instead, all we do is practice skills and never get to play.
4. Physical education is no fun because the athletes get all the attention from the coach.
5. Why should the school hire physical education teachers? All they do is watch kids play games they already know.
6. Those that can, do. Those that can't, teach. Those that can't teach become physical educators and coaches.
7. Teaching physical education is a racket.

CHAPTER **12**

OTHER OPPORTUNITIES IN SCHOOL-RELATED PHYSICAL EDUCATION

INTRODUCTION

Chapter 11 has indicated some of the opportunities available in teaching physical education at various school levels. However, most physical educators continue working when the last class ends, because activities which occur outside regular class hours are an important facet of the job. This chapter will discuss such possible activities as intramurals, coaching, sports administration, and athletic training. Two other areas which could need full-time persons, depending upon the school, are adapted physical education and aquatics; these are also discussed.

CONCEPTS TO BE GAINED FROM THIS CHAPTER

When you have mastered the material in this chapter, you will be able to demonstrate comprehension of these concepts:

1. Physical education, intramurals, athletics, and recreation are related, even though all have distinct goals and methods.
2. For both theoretical reasons (program enrichment) and practical reasons (getting a teaching job), physical educators should consider becoming qualified for such possible out-of-class activities as intramural (IM) or sports programs, coaching, or athletic training.
3. Other full-time careers related to school physical education include those of being a specialist in adapted physical education or being an aquatic director.

4. Even though goals may change, you should know a great deal about at least one of the opportunities mentioned in this chapter. Your knowledge should include the goals of the program, the usual duties, parts of the job that appeal to you (and parts that do not), the training and experience required to be a success, and the probable need for qualified people at the time of your graduation.

THE RELATIONSHIP OF PHYSICAL EDUCATION, INTRAMURALS, ATHLETICS, AND RECREATION

For years we have considered physical education classes in schools as the foundation of our program. Since all students take physical education at some time in their K-12 years, it is here they are exposed to learning the skills, strategies, knowledges, and fitness techniques which are deemed necessary. The intramural program is organized to permit voluntary participation by those who wish competition in a variety of·activities, and is a chance to apply skills learned in physical education class. For those who are gifted in physical skills we have athletics; up until recently, the number of participants here has been smaller than in intramurals. The triangle shown below has been used to depict this relationship of three programs, and most physical educators would heartily subscribe to it.

Athletics

Intramurals

Physical Education Program

However, the triangle depicts an idealistic rather than realistic picture in most schools. Almost all schools have physical education classes and athletics. A much smaller percentage have an adequate intramural program, and an organized recreation program is seldom found in schools. Jones (1971) has proposed that we be honest with ourselves, and that if we really believed in the "triangle," we would enhance the basic instruction and intramural programs before emphasizing athletics. He uses a four-sided diagram, which shows that each part is related, yet separate, and that no part is more important than the other.

Regardless of the model one prefers, it is apparent that the components (physical education, intramurals, athletics, and recreation) are interrelated in that they each do different things for students. On the model, instruction and recreation are interchangeable, as are athletics and intramurals. Most physical educators feel that a balanced life, student or adult, will include a portion of these four related factors.

In the past, the terms *curricular* (any subject taught during regular school hours) and *extracurricular* (any voluntary school-sponsored activity which is not a regular school subject) were used. In this classification, the physical education program is curricular, while IM, athletics, recreation are extracurricular. However, the school organizes its programs to benefit the students in every way, and thus *all* school-sponsored activities (e.g., classes, newspapers, athletics, clubs, and intramurals) really are part of the curriculum. Even though this concept is sound, the various programs are still called extracurricular in most schools.

INTRAMURALS

Intramurals are theoretically a part of every good school program. It is interesting to remember that in the 1800s students in American boarding schools were given permission to organize their own athletic teams as a means of relieving tension built up after spending all day in school. Thus, dormitory teams played intramural contests. Then came the idea to select an all-star team to play the best team from another school. This was the birth of interscholastic athletics.

Usually, intramurals refer to a variety of physical activities (i.e., basketball, volleyball, softball), but actually, they can be any activity organized and conducted for the students enrolled in that school. Since the goal of a good intramural program is to have a student-run group which involves 100% of the students, it is obvious that the more activities there are, the greater should be the participation. From angling to wrestling, badminton to tumbling, vigorous activities (sports) to quiet activities (checkers) — all are part of the program. There is a very fine line between a good recreation program and a good intramural program.

Intramural activities are handicapped because of space, money, and athletics. Athletics relates to all the problems. IM programs usually get second choice of time and space in the school, and do not raise money. These facts, coupled with the increase in athletic teams for both boys and girls, will usually prevent much student participation.

Depending upon the director and the school administration, intramural programs may be held before school, at noon hour, immediately after school, in the evening, on Saturday, or during an activity period as a part of the regular school day. The director can either receive extra pay for the duties (ranging from $50 to $500), or can receive time off from regular classes as payment.

Who is selected for the job as intramural director? Often it is the physical educator who has no coaching or other extra duties during that time of year. However, the primary qualifications are training through courses and experience, organizational ability, ability to work with students, and an intense desire to promote activities that will interest the majority of students. Almost all colleges offer at least one course in intramurals, sometimes requiring it for physical education majors. To adequately prepare for an IM position requires on-the-job experience. Since virtually all colleges offer some type of IM-recreation program, this experience can be obtained. Related courses which might be offered at your school include Intramural Management, Officiating, Intramural Internship, Administration of Parks and Recreation, Sports Administration, and Athletic Management and Control. For further information contact the National Intramural Sports Council, c/o AAHPER, 1201 Sixteenth Street N.W., Washington, D.C. 20036.

COACHING

Coaching is the teaching of sports skills and strategies to those students who are participating in an organized team. It usually is done in a school situation, but numerous coaches of Little League baseball, age-group swimming, softball, and gymnastics are found.

You might be surprised to realize that most nations of the world do not include athletics as part of their school programs. These countries do not feel that sponsorship of school teams meets their educational goals. We believe differently, and organize all kinds of college, high school, junior high school, and elementary school teams. Most nations have out-of-school-experiences similar to our Little League baseball, age-group swimming, Biddy Basketball, and gymnastic clubs. We view athletics as educational in nature, designed to improve students in physical, social, and emotional areas. We think the schools can do this better than local sports clubs or government-sponsored gymnasiums.

Despite our idealistic view that athletics is educational, there are growing signs that public support of school programs is decreasing. Steinmetz and Bowen (1971) surveyed two main groups: voter and taxpayer officials, and school administrators and athletic officials. Some of their finds are disturbing to those who are interscholastic athletic advocates.

1. Only 51% of voter-taxpayer officials and 67% of school-athletic officials felt that competitive teams sports will *always* be an important component of all public school systems.
2. Only 47% of voter-taxpayers and 35% of school-athletic officials felt that money spent on competitive athletics in the school would remain the same or increase in the next few years. Despite inflation and Title IX, 22% of the voter-taxpayer group and 32% of the school-athletic group were certain it would go down. (This relates to our discussion of Title IX in Chapter 10; programs for girls and women *must* be relatively equal to those for boys and men.)
3. Some cuts in school athletic programs were forecast by 43% of the voter-taxpayer group and 66% of the school-athletic group.
4. Perhaps most importantly, only 57% of voter-taxpayer group and 61% of the school-athletic group were certain that the "American way of life" would suffer if we did not have sports.

It seems that a sizable minority of Americans, including school-athletic officials, are not convinced that the time, effort, and money spent on athletics are justified. Yet we see a great increase in student participation in virtually all high school sports. The 1976 Interscholastic Sports Participation Survey (Table 12-1) clearly shows this, especially for females. All girls' sports show participation increases (one of 2779%) since 1971, while 15 of the 28 boys' sports show increases. Despite what some citizens say, most school officials believe that involvement of more students is desirable — and if the economic picture brightens, there will be even more increases. There is still a great difference in the number of boys on teams compared to the number of girls, but Title IX may cause that gap to eventually disappear.

What do these facts and trends mean for you? First, there now is, and will be for some time, a need for more coaches at all levels. When you consider that each team has at least one coach and some have several, do you wonder at the need? Secondly, there are traditionally a surplus of male basketball, football, baseball, and track coaches, but a drastic shortage of coaches for female teams in all sports. Professional educators prefer female coaches for female teams, and we must concentrate on meeting this need. Thirdly, for both sexes, there is a shortage of qualified gymnastic, soccer, and tennis coaches.

As mentioned earlier, the majority of males who major in physical education do so with the intent of coaching. More and more female majors see this as one of their goals. Since virtually all majors have participated in at least one high school athletic team, you undoubtedly are familiar with the duties and responsibilities of coaching.

TABLE 12–1. 1975 INTERSCHOLASTIC SPORTS PARTICIPATION SURVEY.

	BOYS			GIRLS		
	NUMBER OF SCHOOLS	NUMBER OF PARTICIPANTS	% CHANGE IN PARTICIPANTS SINCE 1971	NUMBER OF SCHOOLS	NUMBER OF PARTICIPANTS	% CHANGE IN PARTICIPANTS SINCE 1971
Archery	48	550	NR*	171	1,735	NR*
Badminton	595	7,104	− 27	1,205	18,110	NR
Baseball	13,394	399,900	− 1	33	1,038	NR
Basketball	18,874	688,410	+ 6	14,931	387,507	+ 194
Bowling	811	9,478	− 20	676	8,136	+2000
Cross country	10,018	204,087	+ 25	2,631	30,798	+1690
Curling	374	4,095	− 1	336	3,363	NR
Decathlon	128	916	+ 29	-----	------	-----
Drill teams	41	1,417	NR	352	9,371	NR
Fencing	64	1,018	+214	36	333	NR
Field hockey	160	936	− 59	1,675	59,944	+1307
Football						
11 man	14,740	1,058,533	+ 21	-----	------	-----
8 man	552	12,295	− 22	-----	------	-----
6 man	3	40	−994	-----	------	-----
9 man	143	4,178	+ 33	-----	------	-----
12 man	73	2,553	−910	-----	------	-----
Golf	9,954	154,457	+ 29	2,596	32,190	+2779
Gymnastics	1,464	34,516	− 15	3,379	79,461	+ 361
Ice hockey	646	17,544	− 22	38	269	NR
Lacrosse	251	6,487	+ 84	155	5,318	+1081
Pentathon	52	75	NR	-----	------	-----
Riflery	297	4,477	+114	101	1,279	NR
Rugby	10	250	− 82	-----	------	-----
Skiing	348	8,662	− 11	271	5,367	+ 102
Soccer	4,195	112,743	+ 44	599	11,534	+1548
Softball	1,154	14,816	+270	6,496	133,458	+1260
Swimming	4,198	125,234	+ 37	3,285	85,013	+ 394
Table tennis	264	2,033	NR	164	1,180	NR
Tennis	8,421	143,970	+ 48	6,991	112,166	+ 331
Track & field						
(Indoor)	1,344	46,319	− 7	565	17,142	NR
Track & field						
(Outdoor)	16,279	644,813	− 1	12,636	395,271	+ 535
Volleyball	2,215	49,677	− 22	10,607	245,032	+1265
Water polo	367	12,187	+ 89	2	24	NR
Weightlifting	56	1,144	NR	-----	------	-----
Wrestling	9,288	334,107	+ 26	-----	------	-----

Compiled by the National Federation of State High School Associations, Elgin, Ill. Used by permission.

*NR = not reported in 1971

In bygone days, physical education teachers often coached three sports as a part of their job, and in addition often conducted the intramural program — all without extra pay. It is now common for coaches and intramural directors to be paid in one of two ways: a salary ranging from as little as $100 to as much as $2000 for one sport, or a reduced teaching load (a person would teach one or two fewer classes than other teachers).

There is a unique problem in obtaining a coaching job. Despite the obvious need for more coaches, some superintendents will not hire physical educators as head coaches in the "pressure" sports. The reason is simple: too many of these coaches spend their time and energy in coaching, and give second priority to teaching. They may simply let students play games, and/or they may work only with the athletes who are in the class. Superintendents acknowledge that physical education majors are probably the best trained coaches they can find, but feel that their attitude toward coaching harms the physical education program.

In many high schools of moderate size or smaller, there is but one male and one female physical educator. At the same time, there is a need for head and assistant coaches in many sports, and in many states these people must be certified as teachers first and as coaches second. Thus, superintendents need coaches, but may not need physical educators. There is a strong trend to hire persons certified to coach (by having a minor in physical education, or a coaching certificate) rather than hiring physical education majors. The coaching certificate is a relatively new program; it was created specifically to offer training to those men and women who wish to coach but do not want to teach physical education. In states which have this certification, the law reads that to be a coach in most sports, the person must either be a physical education major, a physical education minor, or possess the coaching certificate. Because of the overcrowded field in physical education and the great need for coaches, there is an ever-expanding number of coaching-certified people. Regulations vary from state to state, but usually the coaching certificate requires courses in principles of physical education, human anatomy and/or physiology, organization of athletics, athletic training or first aid, and coaching theory courses. If your school offers the coaching certificate, the exact regulations will be given in the college catalog.

Many persons do not remain in coaching a long time. As in any other job, there are many reasons. First, there is the personal and public pressure of continually striving to win. Granted, this is an important objective, but often it is hazardous to educational goals. Another reason for ceasing to coach is the changing values which students put on athletics. More and more students are deciding that the sacrifice, the training, the hard work is not worth the effort. A third reason is the time required to coach successfully. Your desire to spend 20-40 hours a week on athletic matters may decrease as other responsibilities grow. There may be other reasons, such as inadequate budget, poor facilities, or uneven competition which results in continual losses. For most coaches, however, these reasons are forgotten because of the satisfactions of associating with students, and watching and helping them grow in many ways. For further information, contact NAGWS or NASPE, c/o AAHPER, 1201 Sixteenth Street N.W., Washington, D.C. 20036.

SPORTS ADMINISTRATION

As we have discussed, many physical educators enter our field because they want to coach, but eventually lose their enthusiasm. One possible job which allows a person to remain close to athletics is sports administration. The tremendous expansion of athletic teams means that an administrator must take the responsibility for the overall direction of a sound program. The goal, of course, is the efficient administration of a total sports program. The athletic director is one who arranges schedules, supervises and administers the finances, arranges transportation, makes certain medical exams are taken, etc. In short, the director is responsible for the myriad of details which occur with several coaches and dozens of athletes.

A recent development will have significance for women physical educators. The rise in women's sports has created some sports administration jobs for women. Title IX and its implications will further expand the opportunities for females. Minnesota, for example, has a woman who is an assistant director of the state group that controls athletics. Her job is to promote and supervise the interscholastic sports program for women. While jobs at this level are few, there is already a demand for women athletic directors at colleges and high schools. There are a growing number of these jobs, because the women's athletic groups clearly state that women administrators should be in charge of the program.

How do athletic directors learn about administering a total program? In the past, an ex-coach with seniority was often appointed to the position and learned most of the details through trial and error. These qualifications are still valid, but a number of schools are offering specialized training (usually for a master's degree) in this area. This training encompasses study in physical education and athletics, business law, journalism, public relations, and human relations.

ATHLETIC TRAINING

The athletic trainer is a person, qualified by training and experience, who supervises the preventive and rehabilitative aspects of athletes. He or she acts as a liaison between the coach, physician, and player, seeing that the coach's routine procedures (taping, etc.) are carried out, and that the physician's orders are followed. In years past, the coach was his own athletic trainer, but it was obvious that most coaches lack the knowledge and the time to properly perform the needed tasks. The goal of an athletic trainer is simple — to prevent injuries, or to treat and supervise the rehabilitation of injured persons so they can participate in athletics without doing further damage to themselves.

The future demand for athletic trainers appears to be great for both men and women. There are so many teams sponsored by the school that it makes sense to have at least one qualified trainer there. Within 5 to 10 years all schools will be required by law to have an athletic trainer if they have any athletic teams. This will prove a great benefit both to coaches and to players. The extra money received for serving as a school athletic trainer is comparable to that of a coach.

What courses are taken by athletic trainers? Aside from the sciences, anatomy, physiology, chemistry and/or physics, courses are required in first aid, athletic training, medical aspects of athletic training, nutrition, and kinesiology. In addition, all recognized programs require several hundred hours of practical experience in the training room.

What education is required of athletic trainers? Some (especially those who work in colleges or with professional teams) are registered physical therapists. Physical therapists have a graduate degree in physical therapy, and are qualified to administer all types of rehabilitative procedures. **Their** training is thorough, primarily because of the rigorous standards required to **earn** the certificate. For further information about physical therapy, see Chapter 13.

Most athletic trainers, though not physical therapists, have taken physical therapy courses as a supplement to their regular undergraduate degree. Excellent training may be secured at one of the colleges and universities in the United States where the basic requirements of the Certified Athletic Trainer award may be met. These schools conform to the standards of the National Athletic Trainers Association. After graduation, students have to pass the national certification examination. This certificate is a distinct advantage when seeking a job. For further information, contact Athletic Trainer, Indiana State University, Terre Haute, IN 47809.

ADAPTED PHYSICAL EDUCATION

In Chapter 13, several different nonteaching careers in the activity and therapy fields are mentioned, and most are discussed in some detail. But because two of them relate primarily to the school, they are discussed in this chapter. One part-time position, athletic training, has already been examined. The other, teaching adapted physical education, may be either a part-time or full-time position.

Adapted physical education consists of a diversified program of developmental activities, games, sports, and rhythms suited to interests, capacities, and limitations of students with impairments, disabilities, or handicaps who may not safely, successfully, or with personal satisfaction engage in unrestricted activities included in general physical education programs (AAHPER 1975, p. 5).

Obviously the scope of this program is very broad because it serves such a variety of students. Its necessity is readily apparent when you realize that adapted physical education is needed by 20%-25% of all students. It deals with persons with vision, hearing, and social problems in an attempt to show them education skills (Winnick 1969, p. 46).

Most of us think about teaching physical education to average or gifted persons (as on athletic teams). However, adapted physical education is becoming more prominent each year, as we discover the great value of physical movement in the lives of the handicapped. The goal of such a program is to adapt a physical education program to the needs and abilities of the students. These adaptations are of many types: emphasis on basic coordination, revising rules of regular games, physical fitness activities, and rehabilitation exercises. Because of the interest initiated by the Kennedy Foundation — President Kennedy, you might remember, had a sister who is mentally retarded — there has been an upsurge of interest in this specific area.

For those of you that plan to work in adapted physical education programs, the job opportunities are great. Schools must meet stricter governmental regulations which require *all* students to be educated, sometimes within the regular class ("mainstreaming" is the currently used term). In large enough schools, special classes are taught by specialists. These people have the regular physical education major background, supplemented by such courses as psychology of exceptional children, learning disabilities, perceptual-motor development, remedial exercises, etc. Practical work while an undergraduate is a necessity. Many physical education departments sponsor programs specifically for the handicapped, and local school districts are supposed to do the same. The opportunities for such practical experience are numerous; after participating in them you would have a good idea if teaching adapted physical education is the right career for you.

Specialists working in schools receive the same pay and benefits as the regular staff with similar education and service, and are expected to meet the same standard of education. It is likely that only very large districts will hire full-time adapted physical education specialists. For further information, contact Consultant, Programs for the

Handicapped, c/o AAHPER, 1201 Sixteenth Street N.W., Washington, D.C. 20036; or Physical Education and Recreation Officer, Division of Personnel Preparation, Bureau of Education for the Handicapped, 7th and D Streets, S.W., Washington, D.C. 20202.

AQUATIC SPECIALIST

At present, the only activity which could become a full-time job is aquatics. Because of the great rise in public interest in aquatics, many schools have built pools and are finding it necessary to employ aquatic specialists. Even if there are no pools in the schools, a majority of cities over 5,000 in population have some sort of swimming facility (YMCA or outdoor pool, or nearby lake). It is usual for schools to make certain that all students can swim by the fifth grade, and for many types of aquatic programs (e.g., lifesaving, competitive teams, synchronized groups, survival swimming) to be offered for both students and adults.

Swimming is likewise the only activity in a physical education class which requires specific certification. The Red Cross Water Safety Instructor (WSI) or the YMCA Aquatic Director rating is the minimum requirement for a swim instructor; since relatively few physical education majors possess either certificate, those who do have a great advantage over the physical education generalist. When a pool is controlled by the school a qualified person (WSI, plus experience in aquatic facility management) is hired to be the director. This person is responsible for the complete operation of the facility: instructional programs, teams, water sanitation, hiring of personnel, recreational use by the community, etc. The pay is generally higher than teachers with the same experience, but it is a 12-month assignment with all-week responsibility.

How do you become an aquatic specialist? Obviously, the ability to swim and teach others to swim is the universal requirement. Beyond that, skill in such aquatic activities as springboard diving, SCUBA, synchronized swimming, and lifesaving are highly desirable. Experience as a competitive swimmer certainly would be advantageous. All aquatic experts attend workshops and clinics where teaching methods, pool management, public relations, water sanitation and similar topics are studied. For further information, contact the Aquatic Council, c/o AAHPER, 1201 Sixteenth Street, N.W., Washington, D.C. 20036.

Bibliography

Intramural director.
Anderson, D. Intramural sports in a changing society. *JOHPER* 42 (Nov.-Dec. 1971):67.
Barnes, S. Sports clubs. *JOHPER* 42 (Mar. 1971):23-24.
Gerou, N. The intramural director. *JOHPER* 42 (May 1971):61.
Gilbert, B. Imagine going to school to play. *Sports Illustrated* 43 (Oct. 13, 1975):84-89. (New intramural program.)
Hillman, W. H. Intramurals via the physical education class. *JOHPER* 43 (Apr. 1972):63.
Hyatt, R., ed. The intramural story. *JOHPER* 45 (Mar. 1974):39-53.
Jones, T. R. Needed: A new philosophical model for intramurals. *JOHPER* 42 (Nov.-Dec. 1971):34-35.
Lannon, M. J. Community involvement in elementary school intramurals. *JOHPER* 43 (Nov.-Dec. 1972):67-69.
Leider, F. Intramurals in the junior high school. *JOHPER* 44 (Mar. 1973):71-72.
Pollack, B. Student involvement in the college intramural program. *JOHPER* 46 (Mar. 1969):36-37.
Stewart, R. E. Brief history of the intramural movement. *The Physical Educator* 30 (Mar. 1973):26-28.

Stumph, P. The expanded intramural concept. *JOHPER* 30 (Mar. 1973):55.

Underwood, J. Beating their brains out. *Sports Illustrated* 42 (May 26, 1975):84-96 (IM program at MIT.)

Coach — Age group.

Bula, M. Competition for children: The real issue. *JOHPER* 42 (Sept. 1971):40.

Frank, J. Elementary school — Not too early for interscholastic sports. *The Physical Educator* 22 (Mar. 1965):9-11.

Kaplan, J. A wintry heritage. *Sports Illustrated* 44 (Feb. 9, 1976):30-36. (Age-group ice hockey.)

McCarthy, J. Little League lunacy. *National Elementary Principals* 44 (Nov. 1963):80-83.

Pileggi, S. Everybody gets to play. *Sports Illustrated* 43 (Nov. 3, 1975):47.

Underwood, J. Taking the fun out of a game. *Sports Illustrated* 43 (Nov. 11, 1975):86-98. (Age-group football.)

Coach — School.

AAHPER. The coaches and the courts. *JOHPER* 41 (June 1970):10.

Ashton, S. The athlete's changing perspective: A student view. *JOHPER* 43 (Apr. 1972):46.

Barry, J. M. It's all a part of the game. *Sports Illustrated* 43 (Oct. 6, 1975):40-52.

Bonnette, A. R. Should there be separate curricula for coaches and physical educators? *The Physical Educator* 40 (Oct. 1969):127.

Briggs, P. W. Opportunity to be relevant. *JOHPER* 41 (May 1970):41.

Bucher, C. A. After the game is over??? *The Physical Educator* 30 (Dec. 1973):171-75.

Crase, D. Athletics in trouble. *JOHPER* 43 (Apr. 1972):39.

Cratty, B. Coaching decisions and research in sport psychology. *Quest* 13 (Jan. 1970):46-53.

Heck, A., et al. Ethics of competition: Three viewpoints. *JOHPER* 42 (Mar. 1971):87.

Hoehn, R. The coach as a psychologist. *Scholastic Coach* 40 (Apr. 1971):78.

Johnson, W. Not such an ordinary Joe. *Sports Illustrated* 39 (Nov. 19, 1973):47-55. (Joe Paterno, football coach.)

Jordan, P. Fight, ladies, fight! *Sports Illustrated* 42 (Mar. 10, 1975):62-72. (Penn State women's teams.)

McNight, D., and Hult, J. Competitive athletics for girls! We must act. *JOHPER* 45 (June 1947):45-46.

Neal, P. Psychological aspects of coaching women in sports. *JOHPER* 41 (Oct. 1970):75-81.

Ogilvie, B., and Tutko, T. 1972. Motivation and psychometric approach in coaching. In *Psychological aspects of physical education and sport,* ed. J. E. Kane, pp. 209-31. Boston: Routledge and Kegan Paul.

Pelton, B. Athletic coaching, a challenging profession. *The Physical Educator* 26 (May 1969):69.

Porter, C. M. The coach as character builder. *The Physical Educator* 29 (Mar. 1972):36.

Rosato, F. The group process — Some suggestions for athletics. *The Physical Educator* 31 (Mar. 1974):87-89.

Sheehan, T. J., and Alsop, W. L. Educational sport. *JOHPER* 43 (May 1972):41.

Sisley, B. Laboratory experiences for developing coaching competencies, the preparation of women for coaching responsibilities. *The Physical Educator* 30 (Dec. 1973):182-84.

Snyder, E. A study of selected aspects of the coach's influence on high school athletes. *The Physical Educator* 29 (May 1972):96.

Stein, B. E. The cultural crisis in American sports. *JOHPER* 43 (Apr. 1972): 42-44.

Steinmetz, L. L., and Bowen, D. H. Sports in schools: Jeopardy and uncertainty. *Selling Sporting Goods.* Pamphlet (Nov. 1971).

Stier, W. F. The coaching intern. *JOHPER* 41 (Jan. 1970):27-29.

Sport administrator.

AAHPER. Professional preparation of the administrator of athletics. *JOHPER* 41 (Sept. 1970):20

Deford, F. No death for a salesman. *Sports Illustrated* 43 (July 28, 1975):56-65. (Successful big-time athletic director.)

Kelly, T. B. Athletics: Leadership or management. *JOPER* 46 (Apr. 1975):21.

Richardson, D. E. Preparation for a career in public school athletic administration. *JOHPER* 42 (Feb. 1971):17.

Sisley, B. Challenges facing the woman athletic director. *The Physical Educator* 32 (Oct. 1975):121-23.

Athletic trainer.

Arthur Croft Publications. Suggested medical services for school sports programs. *Physical Education Newsletter*, Mar. 15, 1971.

Delforge, G., and Klein, R. High school athletic trainer's internship. *JOHPER* 44 (Mar. 1973):42.

Koenigsberg, R., and Arrighi, M. Women athletic trainers. *JOPER* 46 (Jan. 1975):51-52.

Kram, M. The face of pain. *Sports Illustrated* 44 (Mar. 8, 1976):58-66.

Kumph, R. The training room staff. *JOHPER* 45 (Oct. 1974):30-31.

LeCava, G. The role of sport in therapy. *Journal of Sports Medicine and Physical Fitness* 7 (June 1967):57-60.

Prokop, L. The struggle against doping and its history. *Journal of Sports Medicine and Physical Fitness* 10 (Mar. 1970):45-48.

Schwank, W., and Sayers, J. M. New dimensions for the athletic training profession. *JOHPER* 42 (Sept. 1971):41-432.

Wilson, H., and Albohm, M. Women athletic trainers. *JOHPER* 44 (May 1973):57-59.

Adapted physical education instruction.

AAHPER. Adapted physical education. *JOHPER* 40 (May 1969):45-49.

———. Swimming for the handicapped. *JOHPER* 41 (Oct. 1970):65.

———. 1975. *Careers in activity and therapy fields.* Washington, D.C.:AAHPER.

Auxter, D. Teacher of individually prescribed instruction in perceptual motor development. *JOHPER* 42 (June 1971):41.

Berges, S. A. Teaching physical education in the schools for the deaf. *JOHPER* 43 (Apr. 1972):81.

Buell, C. Physical education for visually handicapped children. *JOHPER* 42 (Apr. 1971):63.

Carlson, R. B. Status of research on children with perceptual-motor dysfunction. *JOHPER* 43 (Apr. 1972):57.

Cousen, C. Adapted sports and recreation for the handicapped child. *JOHPER* 43 (Nov.-Dec. 1972):53.

DeBonis, E. The master's program in physical education with a specialization in physical education for the handicapped. *JOHPER* 42 (June 1971):42-43.

Ersing, W. Current directions of professional preparation in adapted physical education. *JOHPER* 43 (Oct. 1972):78.

———. An approach in teaching swimming to the developmentally disabled and mentally retarded. *The Physical Educator* 31 (May 1974):72-74.

Freischlag, J. Competition and physical education for the handicapped: How compatible are they? *The Physical Educator* 31 (Mar. 1974):42-43.

Funk, D. C. Effects of physical education on fitness and motor development of trainable mentally retarded children. *Research Quarterly* 44 (Mar. 1973):30.

Geddes, D. Physical activity: A necessity for severely and profoundly mentally retarded individuals. *JOHPER* 45 (Mar. 1974):73-76.

Huber, J. H., and Vercollone, J. Using aquatic mats with exceptional children. *JOPER* 47 (Jan. 1976):44-46.

Johansen, G. Integrating visually handicapped children into a public elementary school physical education program. *JOHPER* 42 (Apr. 1971):61.

Pettit, M. H. Physical education for orthopedically handicapped children. *JOHPER* 42 (Feb. 1971):75.

Seaman, J. Attitudes of physically handicapped children toward physical education. *Research Quarterly* 41 (Oct. 1970):439-45.

Stein, J. Sense and nonsense about mainstreaming. *JOPER* 47 (Jan. 1976):43.

Vodola, T. M. New Jersey Special Olympics: Boon or bane? *JOHPER* 44 (Jan. 1973):93.

Waggoner, B. E. Motivation in physical education and recreation for emotionally handicapped children. *JOHPER* 44 (Mar. 1973):73-76.
Winnick, J. Issues and trends in training adapted physical education personnel. *JOHPER* 43 (Oct. 1972):75.

Aquatic instructor.
Alexander, R. M., and Shields, D. A. University of Florida aquatic specialist program. *JOHPER* 45 (Nov.-Dec. 1974):69.
Cahill, P. J. Cortland's professional preparation in aquatics. *JOPER* 47 (May 1976):58-59.
Lindeman, J. Aquatic specialists program at the University of Michigan. *JOHPER* 43 (Sept. 1972):88.

Student Activities

1. This chapter has discussed several possible job positions. Select the one which interests you the most, and try to find out more information by doing one or more of these things:
    a. Interview someone who is currently performing that job.
    b. Talk with a senior who is preparing to enter the field.
    c. Look at printed and visual material. (See instructor, counselor, guidance center.)

Statements for Class Discussion

1. How do you react to this conversation?
    Person 1: I am a physical educator.
    Person 2: How nice! What do you coach?
2. Should a physical educator (who does not coach) be addressed by students as "coach?"

CAREERS

CHAPTER 13
NONTEACHING CAREERS
IN PHYSICAL EDUCATION

INTRODUCTION

Chapters 11 and 12 have dealt at great length with the opportunities available for a physical educator who aspires to teach or be affiliated with educational institutions. However, one of the central themes of this text is that there are many opportunities for a physical educator outside of the schools. This chapter will discuss the positions available in six major categories: professional sports; sales; media; therapeutics; health; and governmental agencies. Probably at this time the great majority of you are planning for a career in teaching and coaching, but there are other factors to consider: the teaching profession presently has a surplus of qualified persons at most levels, and changing careers after graduation is becoming as common as changing majors while in school. It may well be that both school and nonschool physical education careers will be in your future.

We strongly emphasize again that practical experience gained during undergraduate years should be required by your school. Participation in local situations where you can learn about careers in sports, therapy, and media work, is essential. Students who are too busy with studies or athletics or student government to participate in meaningful pregraduation experiences are running a real risk of preparing for a career that sounds good but in fact does not hold their interest. Consider these experiences as valuable (if not more so) than courses taken; consider them a part of your college requirements.

CONCEPTS TO BE GAINED FROM THIS CHAPTER

When you have mastered the material in this chapter, you will be able to demonstrate comprehension of these concepts:

1. There are more than two dozen physical education careers outside of the teaching field, found in six broad categories.
2. It would be wise to know much about at least two nonteaching careers in physical education. Knowledge should include need for professionals in this career, usual duties, basic requirements and future advancement.

PROFESSIONAL SPORTS POSITIONS

There are two main categories of careers related to professional sports: 1) an active participant, or 2) a coach, official, trainer, or administrator. The professional athlete is well publicized; his or her skills are constantly on display, with the salary or winnings a subject of public interest. Undoubtedly there will be some of you who become professional athletes. You should realize that the majority of such persons have a relatively short career and although virtually any sum of money looks large to the college student, competent legal advice prior to signing a professional contract is essential. Also important to consider is the uncertainty of a professional career; this means that forethought concerning your career after retirement is extremely wise.

There are obviously positions with professional teams which would appeal to you. Top sports administrators (general managers, ticket and promotion managers, etc.) are seldom ex-professional players. Business ability is far more important than years of competition on the court or field. On the other hand, ex-performers are most apt to be coaches or field managers or officials. Off season employment is usually the stepping-stone to a career in a front office. As mentioned in Chapter 12, there are a few schools in the U.S. which offer master's degrees in sports administration. The courses in these programs are both physical education and business, and generally include an internship experience. A person with both professional and academic training would be more apt to obtain a position of his or her choice.

The coaching of professional teams is seldom entrusted (excepting perhaps baseball) to persons without high school or college coaching experience. Usually, service as an assistant coach and then as a head coach in college is necessary before one reaches the professional ranks. While salary and fringe benefits are considerably above teacher salaries, the lack of job security is a major drawback. Teacher-coaches must be prepared to teach, which means finishing at least the bachelor's degree (for high school) or the master's (for college coaching).

As we said in Chapter 13, athletic trainers are an integral part of professional teams. Service as a high school or college trainer is customary before being hired by professional teams. Salaries and fringe benefits are greater than those of teachers, but again job security is lacking.

Officials, despite what you may believe, are intelligent, well-trained, conscientious persons. There are a few officials (basketball, baseball) who devote full time to officiating. Attendance at a baseball officiating school, owned by former major league officials, is the best way to be a baseball official. Other officials invariably start working high school games, then progress up through college games to the professional leagues. The pay is excellent, once these latter jobs are reached.

Quite a few persons combine sports with business by owning sports schools. Former professional athletes have the initial advantage in attracting clients because of their names, but good teaching at reasonable prices is the characteristic of successful enterprises. All major cities have at least seasonal sport schools but there are many year-round operations. Parents are willing to pay for top-flight (not necessarily big name) instruction and many physical educators make this instruction available. For positions in these schools, technical competence in a sport, plus the ability to teach, are the primary requirements. It is common for majors to work in summer or part time during the year in such schools, in order to gain valuable experience as well as income. Ownership of such sport schools is usually by persons who started as employees and combined this experience with financial and management skills. To prepare for eventual ownership, courses in business law, public and human relations, accounting, and journalism are suggested.

Careers are available as instructors in the specialized sport schools or similar enterprises. Pros in bowling, golf, SCUBA, tennis, swimming, gymnastics, skiing, skating, and dancing are able to earn a good living if they are skilled teachers with a special ability to relate to whomever they are teaching. The obvious preparation for these positions is extreme competence in the sport with as much on-the-job experience as possible. These careers seldom last a lifetime, but are usually steps toward something else.

SALES POSITIONS

The positions discussed below are those for which a major or minor in physical education would be considered adequate preparation. None are occupations in which great numbers of physical educators are needed, yet each is a possible career choice which warrants consideration.

Successful salespersons are quite like successful coaches — they have a thorough knowledge of their product, they are tireless and aggressive, and they enjoy meeting the public. The most obvious job for a physical educator is with a sporting goods company, or with a gymnasium clothing manufacturer. Every state has from one to a dozen athletic supply companies that employ salespersons. They travel a certain territory throughout the year, calling on physical education instructors, athletic directors, and owners of sporting goods stores. All manner of goods are sold, ranging from team and class uniforms to equipment. Most companies start beginning salespersons on salary and fringe benefits equal to those of a beginning teacher. Usually, the salesperson is paid on a commission basis after two or three years, with earnings substantially more than a teacher's.

At least one pharmaceutical company (Upjohn) actively seeks physical education majors as salespersons. These employees are called *detail persons;* they visit doctors and pharmacists, trying to convince these persons to use their particular brand of drugs and medicine. Why are such companies attracted to physical education majors? Because of their scientific background coupled with their ability to meet the public. Salary and fringe benefits are equal to those described above for athletic company salespersons.

Sales of physical education texts (such as this one) and sports-related books usually account for a great share of a book company's profits. Salespersons are employed to travel a certain geographic area, calling on college instructors and bookstore managers. There are several book companies that have numerous books in the physical education, health, recreation, and athletic fields; notice the advertisements for specific companies in *JOPER.* Salespersons invariably have college degrees plus the ability to establish rapport with potential users of the text. Salary and fringe benefits are equal to that of teachers.

Preparation for a sales career includes, besides the courses required for a major, courses in salesmanship, accounting, business law, human relations, and psychology. At this point, there are very few saleswomen employed in these positions; however, the recent upsurge in women's sport programs will cause a greater demand for them.

MEDIA POSITIONS

It would be superfluous to dwell very much on the need for sports journalists. More space in the newspapers, more TV time is devoted to sports than to any other single topic. Magazines such as *Sports Illustrated, womenSports,* and *Sport* enjoy circulations of millions. Television sportcasters such as Howard Cosell, Chris Schenkel and Jim McKay are national celebrities, while every TV station has its own local sports person.

Sports journalism includes both written and visual communication. Basic educational requirements usually include majoring in journalism (now called *media* in some colleges), although talent and ability are more important than a degree *per se.* In addition, sports journalists need to know about physical education topics — athletic training and conditioning, sport skills, anatomy and physiology, and athletic administration and organization. There are numerous opportunities for practical experience, as junior and senior high school papers have sports reporters, and all colleges and universities have sports information offices. Almost all college sports departments could use your services, even though it might be on a volunteer basis. Contact the media or journalism department of your college or university for more details. In general, majoring in sports journalism would be preferred by many prospective employers, but if your media department does not provide sports journalism, you should at least get a nonteaching major in physical education.

Sports photography is a limited but viable career option. In additon to basic media education, the obvious job requirement is knowledge of photography. It is possible to free lance (be self-employed), but most photographers work for a television station or a newspaper.

Your salary and fringe benefits in a media position may not be equal to those of teachers until you have shown ability and gained experience. The working hours are long and irregular and when others are enjoying sport as spectators, you will be working. Regardless, most sports media persons believe that their topic is the most interesting and exciting of all the possible areas in journalism.

THERAPY POSITIONS

Therapy is the alleviation of illness or injury using one or more accepted means of treatment. In Chapter 12, mention was made of two school-related physical education programs that were part of the therapy group. Careers in athletic training and adaptive physical education are sought by those who combine their interest in sports or physical education with an interest in helping students overcome physical problems. There are at least four other therapeutic programs which might appeal to you. These — corrective therapy, physical therapy, recreational therapy, and dance therapy — are well-organized, certified careers which will be described below. A good source for information on all therapy fields is the AAHPER publication, *Careers in Activity and Therapy Fields;* information below is gathered primarily from that source. Addresses of specific groups are given at the end of each description.

Corrective Therapy

A corrective therapist assists individuals with either physical or mental disabilities to overcome or alleviate these handicaps. A corrective therapist uses medically oriented physical education techniques to accomplish this. Corrective therapists have become increasingly involved in adapted physical education and perceptual-motor programs for children. All treatment is given under the direction of physicians.

The basic education requirement is a bachelor's degree from an accredited school with a physical education major. Certification may be earned after completing 400 hours of approved clinical training under the supervision of qualified therapists. Although certification is highly desirable, it is not required for all jobs. As an undergraduate, you will take the usual requirements for the physical education degree plus additional courses in psychology, health, corrective and adapted physical education, and programming for the physically and mentally handicapped. Graduate and advanced degrees are offered by some colleges and universities.

Jobs may be found in hospitals and clinics, governmental agencies, rehabilitation centers, camps, colleges and universities, and public and private schools. Salaries and fringe benefits are comparable to those of teachers. At the present time there is a need for corrective therapists, especially in hospital and rehabilitation centers. For further information contact the American Corrective Therapy Association, 6622 Spring Hollow, San Antonio, TX 78249.

Physical Therapy

Physical therapists are likewise part of the health care profession. They work with patients who have been disabled by illness, accident, or at birth. Physical therapists evaluate patients with regard to respiratory, cardiovascular, neuromuscular, neuroskeletal, and sensorimotor functions. On the basis of this evaluation, they and a supervising physician or dentist select the appropriate treatments.

Treatment given by physical therapists includes exercises for strength, agility, coordination, motion, and endurance; activities for motor learning; instruction in daily living and use of assistive devices; and application of agents such as heat and cold, sound, and water for pain. An important part of a therapist's job is motivating patients, their families, and those who might help during the treatment period.

There are three levels of physical therapy practitioners: 1) professionally qualified physical therapists, 2) physical therapy assistants, and 3) aides. All programs leading to professional certification require the basic health sciences, clinical sciences, and supervised administration of evaluative and therapeutic procedures. There are three common patterns of education as follows: 1) completion of a regular bachelor's degree program (four years) in physical therapy, 2) completion of a bachelor's degree in physical education, corrective or occupational therapy followed by a 12-16 month physical therapy program, or 3) completion of a bachelor's degree in a related field followed by a two-year master's degree in physical therapy. Regardless of the route chosen, it is very difficult to enter professional physical therapy schools because of the great number of applicants. A high GPA is essential, and additional practical experience in a related field (e.g., athletic training) is highly desirable. Licensing is required in all 50 states; 49 states require an examination before the license is awarded.

Physical therapist assistant training programs are found in junior and community colleges. A graduate earns an associate degree in physical therapy via a special two-year college program. These persons are skilled technical health workers who assist a physical therapist in treatment and in providing other therapy services.

Physical therapist aides are not licensed, but have completed training in a hospital or clinic. Their primary job is to do routine tasks and activities which have been determined, assigned, and supervised by a professional physical therapist.

Opportunities for the employment of physical therapists are found in hospitals, clinics, nursing homes, rehabilitation centers, the armed forces, private and public schools, homes for the aged, and day care centers. Many of the best athletic trainers in college or professional athletics are physical therapists; their special background makes them invaluable partners on a sports-injury medical team.

The demand for physical therapists is greater than the supply, and will be so for years to come. Salaries and fringe benefits are equal to those of teaching. For further information, contact the American Physical Therapy Association, 1156 Fifteenth Street N.W., Washington, D.C. 20005.

Dance Therapy

Using dance as a therapy for the improvement of mental health is one of the emerging nonteaching professions which is proving attractive to dance persons. The purpose of such therapy is to use dance (movement) as a psychotherapeutic means of physical and emotional expression. Communicating through dance has been shown to be very helpful in alleviating some social, emotional, and physical problems.

A bachelor's degree is a prerequisite for advanced professional study in dance therapy. Undergraduate courses include psychology, anatomy, individual body mechanics, group dynamics, as well as extensive movement training. These latter courses will emphasize a variety of dance forms, techniques, and theories of dance, as well as choreography and improvisation. Modern, folk, and ethnic dancing are invaluable parts of the training of a dance therapist. Introductory dance courses and field trips will be a part of the educational experience. At the present time there are less than a dozen undergraduate degree programs in the United States. On the graduate level, you would take courses in theory, practice, and methods in dance, along with research emphasis on human behavior. The graduate experience includes an intern position, under supervision, in a clinical setting.

Persons with interest and education in dance therapy will find places of employment among rehabilitation centers, geriatric facilities, psychiatric centers and hospitals, correctional facilities, and mental retardation and developmental centers.

The demand for dance therapists will slowly grow in the United States as more medical and psychiatric professionals discover their effectiveness. Salaries and fringe benefits are comparable to those of teachers. For more information, contact the American Dance Therapy Association, Suite 230, 2000 Century Plaza, Columbia, MD 21044.

Therapeutic Recreation

The objective of therapeutic recreation is to bring about desirable behavior changes and promote individual growth and development. This career is discussed in Chapter 15, but since it is part of the therapeutic field, brief comments are made here. Recreation therapists organize and direct activities (sports, drama, nature, games, arts and crafts) adapted to specific needs. They also work with both the community agencies and governmental groups to expand services and facilities for the ill, impaired, handicapped, and disabled.

There is a well-defined six-step career procedure in therapeutic recreation. The first three levels do not require a bachelor's degree. A therapeutic recreation leader, or a therapeutic recreation specialist leader require the bachelor's degree, while the master therapeutic specialist has had graduate preparation and a minimum of three years of work experience.

There are job opportunities among the following: child and day-care, nursing homes and homes for the aged, city recreation departments, YMCA, YWCA, hospitals and clinics, camps, and private agencies. Salaries and fringe benefits are comparable to those of teachers. For further information contact the National Therapeutic Recreation Society (a branch of NRPA), 1601 North Kent Street, Arlington, VA 22209, or the Physical Education and Recreation Office, Division of Personnel Preparation, Bureau of Education for the Handicapped, 7th and D Streets, Washington, D.C. 20202.

HEALTH-RELATED POSITIONS

Chapters 6, 10, and 12 have described the increased interest in physical fitness and physical rehabilitation in the United States. It is obvious that this interest is created and sustained by professional workers in the health fields. Physical fitness is more than a school responsibility, and becomes even more important after students leave school. This section will describe various career possibilities primarily related to preventive health procedures.

According to many, the physical education teacher serves as a liaison between the medical profession and the general public. There are certain professions in the sports medicine field that are concerned with scientific discovery and application of medical matters. A fast growing specialty area is preventive medicine, wherein a physician is interested primarily in maintaining the good health of patients. The tremendous rise in adult physical fitness has encouraged this interest. The preventive medicine specialist may be typified by Kenneth H. Cooper, M.D., who is responsible for the aerobics programs, or Bill Bowerman (physical educator) and William Harris, M.D., (cardiologist) who have popularized jogging in the United States. This is a very logical step, since we recall that the earliest American physical educators were physicians. While very few current physical educators have chosen medicine as a profession, it is interesting to note that some schools (the universities of Wisconsin and Kentucky, for example) have physicians as members of their physical education departments.

Currently, physiologists in the discipline of physical education are very common. Most good departments of physical education have a physiology laboratory, where trained specialists work with treadmills, physiographs, oxygen analyzers, bicycle ergocycles, and all types of strength-testing equipment. The best trained of these persons have had training in medicine or physiology and are able to follow or lead the medical efforts to enhance the qualify of life enjoyed by modern society. All medical schools have physiologists; some of these persons are becoming much more interested in the types of problems facing physical educators and coaches. While there will always be a demand for well-qualified and capable physiologists in physical education departments, there is no current shortage of these specialists.

For years most of the physical fitness work in the U.S. was done by physical education workers. McCloy, Steinhaus, Cureton, and Clarke have made this their main academic interest. William Orban (a Canadian physical educator) devised the Canadian 5BX program, which was the first adult exercise regime to achieve nationwide popularity in both the United States and Canada. Cureton has, for several years, spent weekends conducting adult fitness clinics in YMCAs all over the United States.

Physicians are beginning to recognize the help that a well-trained exercise specialist can give them. For instance, Cooper has opened a preventive medicine clinic in Dallas and has hired a physical educator as supervisor of gymnasium facilities. The clinic offers short courses to train persons to help the physician in administering certain laboratory tests, interpreting the results, and supervising physical rehabilitation.

For many people over 35, a thorough physical examination now means an exercise stress test (a carefully supervised exercise bout, tiring enough to put stress on the heart and lungs). Stress-testing technicians are becoming vital components of the physician's staff. Some preventive medicine clinics (e.g., Cooper's) and some hospitals train persons for this position. As more and more physicians use stress tests as a routine part of adult physical exams, the number of technicians needed will continue its steady rise.

In Chapter 10, mention is made of several companies which provide fitness and recreation programs for their employees. The President's Council on Physical Fitness and Sports has published a pamphlet, *Physical Fitness in Business and Industry* (1972), which provides management with reasons why fitness is important and with specific activities through which fitness might be achieved.

Corporations have adapted goals such as Xerox's, which is to "improve the physical fitness of our employees so that they may live longer lives, have better performance records and participate more fully in life."[1] One estimate (Malena 1976, p. 2) is that 50,000 U.S. companies spend $2 billion annually on recreation and fitness programs. Some companies purchase membership for their employees in local YMCA-YWCAs or health spas, while others spend money within the organization. Malena also says that over 300 companies have full-time fitness and/or recreation directors. These positions are for both men and women, since the company gyms are available to all employees. Some companies have both inside and outside facilities; one insurance company has a running track on the roof of its downtown building! Duties of industrial fitness directors include organizing and supervising of exercise programs, teaching sport skills, motivating employees to begin or continue activity participation. Some companies have their fitness programs under the supervision of their medical department. This is desirable because physicians give stress tests and prescribe desirable fitness programs, while the fitness directors ensure that the advice is followed. Salaries and fringe benefits are, in most cases, superior to those of teachers. Basic requirements for employment are undergraduate majors in physical education or recreation, depending upon which is the main thrust of the program. Fitness directors need extra preparation in fitness techniques and exercise physiology laboratory experiences. For further information, contact the National Industrial Recreation Association, 20 North Wacker Drive, Chicago, IL 60606.

One fast growing segment of health-related careers is a part of the business world, but is discussed here because health benefits result. It is said that there are over 800 health spas and women's slimnastic studios in the U.S. (Henschen 1975). These are well-equipped, clean, and efficiently run gymnasiums and pools, with features (saunas, carpeted floors, chromed equipment, and soft music) designed to attract and keep paying customers. They offer the same type of program (exercise and participation in activities) which could be available to adults after school hours at many school gyms. Some physical educators consider such commercial establishments as undesirable, claiming that the operators are untrained in physical education and are only interested in making money. This charge contains some truth, but if the public is willing to spend money for such purposes and the school or community government fails to provide the facilities and program, where must the public turn? Trained leadership, both male and female, is needed; physical educators can provide it.

---

[1] Quotation from Xerox Recreation Association Inc., mimeographed communication, no date.

Currently the best trained leadership provided in the health spa field is by the YMCA, which often has an adult health club as part of its program. Most YMCA physical directors are specifically trained in fitness programs, some being qualified to assist physicians in stress testing. The YMCA sponsors regional clinics for physical directors; in some cities, cardiac rehabilitation programs are a part of its services. An effort has been started in at least one U.S. institution (the University of Utah) to prepare qualified commercial health spa operators through a certification program. The courses taken are combinations of physical education, business, psychology, health, physical therapy, and recreation.

Salaries and fringe benefits depend solely on the financial condition of the enterprise, but are generally below those of teachers. Further information and a good discussion of this whole topic is found in Henschen's article, "Health Spa Certification." (See Bibliography.)

Along this same line, a small number of fraternal organizations (Elks, Eagles, etc.) are establishing exercise rooms for the benefit of their members. As yet, there is no established trend for trained physical educators to be employed, but as physical educators become more capable of intelligently supervising and organizing adult physical fitness programs, the opportunity will present itself.

Leslie and McClure (1972) point out that activity needs of citizens extend from preschool through retirement, and that physical educators have not recognized the potential careers awaiting them, especially in the older age setting. The need exists for exercise programs for older citizens who are neither ill nor handicapped; physical educators with training in adult fitness programs, recreation activities, and psychology and motivation will be able to fill this need.

GOVERNMENTAL AND AGENCY POSITIONS

There are at least four different types of positions available to physical educators within the federal government. (Foreign readers of this text might be reminded that their governments have programs similar to those discussed below.) The two which have received the most publicity are the Peace Corps and VISTA. As you might know, the Peace Corps enlists persons 18 years of age or older to serve overseas in a variety of positions. Peace Corps volunteers (male and female) are given 12-14 weeks of training in the language and customs of a particular country before being sent overseas. All expenses are paid by the government, and $75 for each month of service is later given as final pay.

There is actually a segment of the Peace Corps dubbed the "Sports Corps." According to its director, the Sports Corps was:

created to enlist sportsmen and physical educators to fill host country requests for coaches, physical education organizers and instructors. In 1971, there were over 200 coaches or physical educators working with young people in more than 20 developing countries.

There are four categories of work possible for a Sports Corps Volunteer. They are: staffing and directing physical education and recreation programs in universities and municipalities, serving on the staff in elementary and secondary schools, setting up sports clubs and testing programs where school programs do not exist, and coaching national teams.[2]

VISTA (Volunteers In Service To America) is similar to the Peace Corps, except that the assignment is in the United States. It has no Sports Corps. VISTA volunteers

[2] From a letter by Glenn Randall, director of Sports Corps, October 21, 1971.

are given training, then sent to areas of need. A small living allowance is given. There is a great need for health-oriented persons (e.g., health educators) in VISTA. In both the Peace Corps and VISTA, the need is great for persons who have training and expertise in certain areas, and thus a physical educator with a degree and/or experience in teaching is highly desirable. As you may expect, neither the Peace Corps nor VISTA is a long-term career prospect, but they are excellent ways to serve others and at the same time receive valuable professional training. The address for further information about either program is Peace Corps/ACTION, Washington, D.C. 20525.

The armed forces have both regular and civilian positions available to physical educators. Regular personnel may be assigned to the physical training program, or to Special Services. Physical training specialists are primarily leaders of calisthenics and other vigorous sport activities. All military services have a Special Services branch, and it is to these men and women that the sports program is usually assigned. Becoming a part of this group is much easier if you have a degree in physical education, but in part it depends upon being in the right place at the right time.

A position somewhat similar to the Sports Corps is the Sports Specialist program, which is a civilian position attached to a military base. (Contrary to public opinion, the armed services make a conscious effort to place persons in positions for which they are trained. If there is an opening, then the best available person is usually assigned.)

These positions are not great in number, but they do exist, especially if you are interested in starting out in one of the less desirable geographic areas. For a single person, these are positions which will enhance your professional training while you earn a good salary and travel throughout the world. This is most definitely a long-term career possibility for some persons.

One formal teaching career must be mentioned in this chapter. The Department of Defense hires a number of civilian teachers for positions in American K-12 schools overseas. In every country where we have a sizable complement of troops (e.g., Germany) there are such schools located on the military base. Usually the term of service is two years. Salary and other fringe benefits are at least equal to (if not better than) those in the United States. There are very few openings for full-time physical educators; a person with a physical education major or minor, combined with an academic area, would be much better qualified for employment.

Finally, the U.S. Government has temporary positions (from three months to two years) for athletic coaches. Many countries, especially the emerging nations, desire American sports knowledge and expertise. The State Department and AAHPER cooperate in fulfilling these requests. Usually these positions are filled with persons who have had successful teaching and coaching experience. Technical competence is the most important qualification. It is common to assign such a person as the national coach of a certain sport, who trains and then accompanies the teams to national and international sporting events, such as the Asian Games or the Olympic Games. Should a position such as this hold interest for you, a knowledge of foreign languages would greatly help in your selection. An overseas coach must be resourceful (facilities are poor by American standards), respectful of persons in other lands, and extremely conscientious. In other words, there is no place for an "ugly American" overseas. Salary and other fringe benefits vary tremendously. The number of such positions available is quite limited, but they are there for those who qualify.

Local government, as discussed here, includes all local and county governmental agencies, excepting schools. In most areas, these positions for physical educators are in the Parks and Recreation departments. At this point you probably think that recreation positions are a natural for a physical educator, but actually, physical educators are hired only when the services of a trained recreator are unavailable. Chapter 15 will discuss the relationship of recreation to physical education; the gist of the difference is that physical educators are usually skilled only in physical activities. For those recreation departments large enough to hire a sport specialist, however, the physical educator is the number one choice. For practical purposes, there are only so many openings in recreation in which physical educators can serve very effectively. Beginning salaries and fringe benefits available to employees of recreation departments are roughly comparable to those of teachers.

Another governmental position for physical educators is in correctional institutions. It is felt that a properly conducted and supervised physical activity program is of therapeutic value to inmates. A proper program is one that develops psychomotor skills and is more than mere free play. A background of physical education and social work, with emphasis on counseling skills, is desirable. Most of the present jobs are in maximum security institutions, but city and county jails need combination physical education-counselors, too. The number of careers in correctional institutions is not plentiful at this time, but will enjoy a steady growth. Salaries and fringe benefits are comparable to teaching. Persons in the social work department of your college should be able to help you and your adviser plan a suitable program. Hopefully, this will include an intern experience while you are an undergraduate.

An *agency* is a group of persons organized to provide service to others. Careers in 10 different agencies are outlined in Table 13-1, but some general comments might be useful to familiarize you with agency roles.

The Red Cross is constantly seeking field representatives who have special competence in aquatics and first aid. The agency is committed to sponsoring nationwide programs in these two areas, and thus needs persons to work in the many communities where the programs exist. Field representatives are employed by the Red Cross to train local leaders, to organize and supervise instructor classes in aquatics and first aid, and to represent the agency in many local affairs. The basic qualifications are a college degree (preferably in social work, education, physical education, or any social-related field) and a desire to work with volunteers. There are Red Cross positions overseas wherever the armed forces have a camp or base. These overseas positions, however, rarely call for the services of a trained physical educator.

The YMCA, YWCA, Boys' Clubs, etc., employ physical educators who organize and direct all sorts of physical activities — from archery to camping to wrestling. The work is varied and the hours are long, but the dedicated worker finds reward in personal satisfaction. It demands a very conscientious, resourceful person to be outstanding in this type of position, because success depends upon offering the public a program so good that people will gladly pay for it. In comparison with a school situation, the facilities and equipment are roughly comparable, but salaries and fringe benefits are apt to be slightly lower. One rewarding feature, however, is that because you are dealing with persons who attend because they want to, the discipline problems tend to be less than in many school situations.

It is common for physical education majors to secure field representative or physical education jobs in agencies and, after some years, move upward to executive positions. For example, the National Director of Safety Services of the American National Red Cross is a former high school and college physical educator. Because of his voluntary work in the aquatic and first aid field while teaching, he was asked to join the national organization. While it may be unusual to achieve such a prominent position of national leadership, it is quite common for physical educators to achieve local and state executive positions with agencies.

TABLE 13–1.
AGENCIES WHICH OFFER CAREERS
FOR PHYSICAL EDUCATION OR RECREATION MAJORS.

YMCA

A worldwide fellowship seeking to improve spiritual, social, recreational, and physical life of young people. Maintains residence facilities; conducts adult education classes; sponsors dramatic events, musical events and sports programs; provides swimming instruction; and offers personal counseling. For more information, write: YMCA, 291 Broadway, New York, NY   10007

YWCA

The Young Women's Christian Association is a voluntary membership organization with a local, national and international program of services for individual development and a goal of helping all women and girls make their full contribution to a society where justice and peace for all people shall prevail. Organized for women and girls over 12. Offers a program of health education, recreation, clubs and classes of all kinds, adjusted to community needs. Local units include community YWCAs, student associations, and YWCA residences. For more information, write: YMCA–National Board, HPER Consultant, 600 Lexington Avenue, New York, NY 10022.

BOYS' CLUBS OF AMERICA

Federation of 800 clubs serving more than 800,000 boys (ages 7-20). It promotes the health, social, educational, vocational and character development of boys. Clubs conduct a variety of activities every afternoon and evening. Committees: Citizenship and Leadership Development; Cultural Program; Individual Services; Outdoor Program; Physical Education; Program Planning and Development; Social Education. For more information, write: BCA, 771 First Avenue, New York, NY   10017.

BOY SCOUTS OF AMERICA

An "educational program for the character development, citizenship training, and mental and physical fitness of boys." Has packs, troops and explorer units organized in local councils. Maintains Boy Scout Museum; conducts studies on problems and needs of youth and operation of Scouting councils and districts; maintains library of over 6,000 volumes related to social studies, youth work, and history; compiles statistics. For more information, write: BSA, New Brunswick, NJ   08903.

AMERICAN NATIONAL RED CROSS

The American Red Cross serves members of the armed forces, veterans and their families; aids disaster victims, and assists other Red Cross societies in times of emergency. Activities include a blood donor program; training of volunteers for chapters and hospitals; community agencies; nursing, first aid, and water safety programs; international activities; service opportunities for youth. For more information, write: ARC, 17th and D Streets, N.W., Washington, DC 20006.

CAMP FIRE GIRLS

Organized for girls from age 7 through high school. Blue Birds (ages 7-8) have creative play, simple service, and social activities within the group and immediate community; Camp Fire Girls (ages 9-11) have a program of seven crafts (home, outdoors, creative arts, frontiers, business, sports and games, and citizenship); Junior Hi Camp Fire Girls (ages 12-13) have advanced activities ranging from art to zoology; Horizon Club Camp Fire Girls (14 and older), stress civic and community service projects, coed activities, and career opportunities. For more information, write: CFG, 65 Worth Street, New York, NY   10013.

GIRL SCOUTS OF THE U. S. A.

Organized for girls 7-17. Brownie Girl Scouts (ages 7-8); Junior Girl Scouts (9-11); Cadette Girl Scouts (12-14); Senior Girl Scouts (15-17); adult volunteers and professional workers (both men and women interested in service to girls). Purpose is "inspiring girls with the highest ideals of character, conduct, patriotism, and service that they may become happy and resourceful citizens." Program activities in the arts, home, out-of-doors and community projects. citizenship, international friendship, and health. Educational activities include leader training design, international friendship exchange program. For more information, write: GS, 830 Third Avenue, New York, NY   10022.

NATIONAL RECREATION AND PARK ASSOCIATION

Government and private recreation agencies and park departments, professional park executives and recreation leaders, zoological agencies, and citizens interested in recreation, parks, and conservation. "To develop nationwide recreation and park systems, standards for recreation space, activities, leadership and administration." Conducts numerous educational institutes, seminars and conferences. For more information, write: NRPA, 1601 North Kent Street, Arlington, VA   22209.

AMERICAN CAMPING ASSOCIATION

Camp owners, directors, counselors, camps, businesses and students interested in organized camping. Maintains library (5,000 volumes). Conducts Campcraft Certification program. Committees: Leadership, Program Services, Standards, Studies and Research. Divisions: Private Independent Camping, Agency Camping, Church, School Camping; Resident, Day and Travel Camping. For more information, write: ACA, Bradford Woods, Martinsville, IN   46151.

SPECIAL SERVICES SECTION, DEPARTMENT OF U. S. ARMY

Opportunities for Civil Service employment as professional workers in service clubs, crafts programs, youth activities programs, sports programs. Many jobs are overseas. Basic requirements include U.S. citizenship; excellent physical and mental health; desirable appearance, personality, and initiative; age 21 or over; college degree (bachelor's) in suitable area. Examination required for some positions. Excellent fringe benefits and travel. For more information, write: Recreational Directorate, HQ, Dept. of Army, ATTN: DAAG—KE, Washington, DC   20314.

Adapted from *Care Power*, a brochure published by AAHPER.

Bibliography

General.
Bryant, J. E. Some possibilities for employment in physical education's allied fields. *The Physical Educator* 31 (Dec. 1974):193-95.
Scott, P. M. A crystal ball. *The Foil* 54 (Spring 1974):2-9.
Professional sport positions.
Garry, P. The highest accolade is silence. *Sports Illustrated* 39 (Oct. 15, 1973):135. (Professional basketball officials.)
Gilbert, B. Net result: A capital game. *Sports Illustrated* 43 (June 2, 1975):36-44. (Tennis pro in Washington, D.C.)
Kennedy, R. On his mark and go-go-going. *Sports Illustrated* 42 (May 12, 1975):80-98. (Pro athletic agent.)
McDermott, B. If your game feels sick, visit Dr. Swing. *Sports Illustrated* 43 (June 2, 1975):61-64. (Golf pro.)
Wendel, R. E. Occupational programs are the future. *JOHPER* 37 (Oct. 1972):17.

Yates, B. Shall we gather at the squash courts? *Sports Illustrated* 38 (May 7, 1973):90. (Private athletic club created by local businessmen.)

Sales positions.

Marshall, J. Heroes with feet of clay. *Sports Illustrated* 39 (Nov. 5, 1973):42. (A former boxer who has become the pre-eminent sport sculptor.)

Reed, J. D. How about a game? *Sports Illustrated* 41 (Dec. 12, 1974):78-85. (AMF, manufacturers of sporting goods.)

Media positions.

Deford, F. It's not the game. *Sports Illustrated* 38 (Apr. 9, 1973):117. (Joe Gargiola, television personality.)

Fimrite, R. Lucky devil, he found heaven. *Sports Illustrated* 42 (May 12, 1975): 32-41. (Radio sportscaster.)

Olsen, J. Virtue is its own reward. *Sports Illustrated* 38 (Jan. 22, 1973): 64-74. (Television sportscaster Chris Schenkel.)

Therapy positions.

AAHPER. 1975. *Careers in activity and therapy fields.* Washington, D.C.: AAHPER.

Hoffman, F. Physical Therapy. *The Physical Educator* 23 (Mar. 1966):2.

Schmais, C. Dance training for the dance therapist. *JOHPER* 44 (Oct. 1973):67-68.

_____. What is dance therapy? *JOPER* 47 (Jan. 1976):39.

Health-related positions.

Fortune magazine. Keeping fit in the company gym. *Fortune* (Oct. 1975):136-43.

Franklin, B. Exercise stress testing as a means of detecting potential coronary heart disease. *JOHPER* 45 (June 1974):35-37.

Henschen, K. 1975. Health spa certification. In *Careers in physical education,* ed. N. J. Daugherty, pp. 47-55. Rutgers, N.J.: NCPEAM.

Johnston, R. W. Take heart in the long run. *Sports Illustrated* 40 (May 27, 1974):76-78. (Marathon running for postcardiac patients.)

Leslie, D. K., and McClure, J. W. The preparation of physical educators for expanded leadership and service roles. *JOHPER* 43 (Nov.-Dec. 1972):71-72.

Malena, D., ed. Just how fit are you? In *Datsun Action* 2 (1976):2-3.

Moore, K. A run for their money. *Sports Illustrated* 41 (Nov. 4, 1974):68-78. (Aerobics center in Dallas.)

Governmental and agency positions.

ACTION: Peace Corps. No date. *Physical education in Peace Corps.* Brochure. Washington, D.C.

Johnson, T. W. H. 1975. Preparing physical educators for employment in correctional institutions. In *Careers in physical education,* ed. N. J. Daugherty, pp. 11-16. Rutgers, N.J.:NCPEAM.

Student Activities

1. This chapter outlines several career possibilities outside the teaching profession. Select one that most interests you, and submit a written report containing as much of the following as possible:
    a. Observation of the actual situation
    b. Interview with someone who is now working (or has worked) in that area
    c. Written information obtained from the employer or library
    d. Interview with older students who are preparing to enter the area

Statements for Class Discussion

1. Physical "education" implies teaching people physical skills. Therefore, all careers in this discipline must be educational in nature.
2. It is more difficult to work in voluntary attendance situations (e.g., YMCA, Red Cross swim programs) than in required attendance situations (e.g., school).

CAREERS

CHAPTER 14

THE RELATIONSHIP OF PHYSICAL EDUCATION TO HEALTH EDUCATION

INTRODUCTION

The disciplines of health education and physical education are integrated in almost all facets of everyday living. This integration can be beneficial, but it may be that individuals can benefit more if the courses of study are separated. In the past, a physical education major could receive certification in both health and physical education by completing as few as nine credits in health education. Due to the growth of the health education field in the last 15 years, this is no longer possible at most colleges and universities. This expansion is probably due to the change in state requirements for teachers of health education. Since this field now includes both school and community (or public) health, health education has become a complete and separate course of study.

This chapter will define appropriate terms, list major concepts, briefly describe the historical background of health education and community health, review the courses necessary and the degrees obtainable in the field of health education (both school and community), and include an assessment of your current interest.

CONCEPTS TO BE GAINED FROM THIS CHAPTER

When you have mastered the material in this chapter, you will be able to demonstrate comprehension of these concepts:

This chapter was written by Dr. Laurna Rubinson, Health Education Department, University of Illinois, Champaign.

1. Health education involves the education of the individual and of the community in relation to physical, social, and emotional aspects of life.
2. The history of school and community health education has had direct influence upon the present status of health education.
3. Health areas, interests, and problems are the bases for health education.
4. Health education is essential for the individual to function effectively.
5. The health science courses of study encompass a wide variety of disciplines.
6. There are several health education career options.

DEFINITION OF TERMS

There are some terms that should be defined before the chapter continues.

1. *Health* — a quality of life that enables one to live effectively. Includes the physical, social, and emotional aspects of an individual.
2. *School health education* — the process whereby school health professionals provide experiences for individuals so that these individuals may favorably affect their own health behavior.
3. *Community health education* — the process whereby community health personnel provide leadership in the area of health education to members of a community.
4. *School health program* — those activities that are designed to promote health for both students and personnel. The program includes the areas of health instruction, health services, and the healthful school environment.
5. *School health services* — that part of the school health program that affects the health status of persons in that school. This includes health appraisals, counseling, prevention and control of disease, and emergency care.
6. *Health instruction* — the process of providing both planned and incidental health knowledge for students.
7. *Healthful school environment* — the promotion, utilization and maintenance of a safe, sanitary, and wholesome physical and emotional environment for students.
8. *Voluntary health agency* — any organization or agency that is nonprofit, supported by voluntary contributions, and is concerned about prevention, cure, or alleviation of a disease or group of diseases or disabilities. An example is the American Heart Association.
9. *Public (official) health agency* — a tax-supported organization that is mandated by law for the protection of the health of the public. An example is the New York State Department of Health (Nemir and Shaller 1975, p. 7).

HISTORICAL BACKGROUND

School Health Education

School health education in the United States had its early beginnings in Europe. The United States inherited from Europe the idea of the school's responsibility for supervising children's health, for promoting school sanitation, and the major objective of educating children about their health (Anderson and Creswell 1976, p. 6).

By 1850 schools in the United States became, for the most part, tax supported. In the mid-1860s Lemuel Shattuck's *Report of the Sanitary Commission of*

Massachusetts was issued, giving recognition to the school as being one agency for the promotion of health. A chronological outline of important events in the development of school health education from 1880 to the present is given below:

1880. The child study movement began.

1890. Instruction concerning the effects of alcohol and narcotics was required by all schools in every state.

1894. Health examinations in schools began in Boston, Massachusetts.

1910. Health education began to separate from physical education, both sectors believing that the students would be better served in this manner.

1910. The first White House Conference on Child Health was held.

1914. The school health demonstration project in Baltimore, Maryland, revealed that health instruction could alter health behavior.

1918. Health was named as the first of the seven cardinal objectives of education by the Commission on the Reorganization of Secondary Education.

1922. Behavior, growth, and development of school children were affected favorably by health instruction, as found in the school health demonstration project conducted by Dr. C. E. Turner in Malden, Massachusetts.

1920. The second White House Conference on Child Health and Protection convened.

1935. The school health education program became integrated into three phases: health services, health instruction, and healthful living.

1941. The text *Health Education* was written by the Joint Committee on Health Problems in Education (NEA) and the American Medical Association. This book presented current practices in school health education.

1942. The W. K. Kellogg Foundation sponsored a school-community project that established the importance of cooperation between school and community health professionals.

1949, -53, -55. National conferences were held to discuss professional training of personnel in health education.

1971. The formation of the National Health Education Organization occurred. This organization deals with health education programs and their effectiveness.

Community (Public) Health

Hanlon (1974, p. 39) categorizes public health modern history in three distinct periods: the 1860s when the Shattuck Report was written; the 1910s, when the groundwork was laid for further developments (U.S. Public Health Service and the Children's Bureau); and the 1960s, when public health began getting resources from Congress to make various programs available.

Shattuck's report stated the principal ideas and future modes of action that formed the basis of today's public health practices. Shattuck recommended, over 125 years ago, that there be (Hanlon 1974, p. 23):

1. establishment of state and local boards of health
2. a system of sanitary police or inspectors
3. the collection and analysis of vital statistics
4. a routine system for exchanging data and information, and sanitation programs for towns and buildings
5. studies on the health of school children and on tuberculosis, control of alcoholism, and supervision of mental disease
6. the sanitary supervision and study of problems of immigrants

7. the erection of model tenements, and public bathhouses and washhouses
8. the control of smoke nuisances and food adulteration
9. the exposure of nostrums ("quack" medicines)
10. the establishment of nurses' training schools
11. the teaching of sanitary science in medical schools
12. the use of preventive medicine in clinical practice, with routine physical examinations and family records of illness

In the second decade of the twentieth century there was a great increase in legislation and agencies in the field of public health. In 1912 the United States Public Health Service began, and the Act of 1912 established the Children's Bureau as an agency in the Department of Commerce and Labor. The Bureau was to be a center of research and information concerning the welfare of mothers and children (Hanlon 1974, p. 32), and its success led to the passing of the federal Child Labor Law in 1915.

The mid-1960s became the turning point in health legislation in the United States. The government widened the responsibility of the public sector (as exemplified by the Medicare legislation) and developed new patterns of medical service and continuing education exemplified by the Regional Medical Programs (Fogotson 1967, p. 394).

THE IMPORTANCE OF HEALTH EDUCATION

Health education is important for both social and personal effectiveness (Johns 1970, p. 11). There is a great deal of information regarding health practices that the general public receives, but is this information properly used by individuals? Health education helps to serve this purpose.

The interrelationship between health and education is an important one. If people are to learn, they must be healthy — physically and mentally. The quality of life can only be enhanced by practicing what is learned through health education.

Much has been written concerning the formation of attitudes and values. An integral part of health science education is enabling people to attain positive attitudes and values regarding their health. They must be able to solve problems and make correct decisions concerning their lives.

Acquisition of knowledge and formation of positive attitudes are only two of the three important factors involved in health education. The third factor is behavior change. Many people possess or acquire poor behavioral patterns concerning their health. For an effective life, these behavior patterns must be critically examined and, hopefully, changed to a positive mode of behavior. If behavior change is not apparent, acquired knowledge and attitude formation become of little importance. All three components — knowledge, attitudes, and behavior — serve as vital processes in the area of health education.

HEALTH ORGANIZATIONS

Some of the major organizations that have developed in school and community health are:

American Association for Health Education (AAHE)
American Alliance of Health, Physical Education, and Recreation (AAHPER)
American Public Health Association (APHA)
American School Health Association (ASHA)
Society for Public Health Education (SPHE)

The membership of these organizations comprises school health educators and community health educators. Each organization has specific roles, but the overall objective of the organizations is to improve the profession through an exchange of ideas. Ideas are exchanged through professional literature.

LEARNING ABOUT HEALTH EDUCATION

A student wishing to pursue a career in health education may elect either or both of two options. The person can major in school health education with the intention of becoming a professionally trained school health teacher, or emphasize community health in order to work in a health-related agency. It is also possible in some schools to become professionally trained in both areas; this is called school-community health education. A sample program from the University of Illinois Department of Health and Safety Education depicts the courses required and options available (Undergraduate Catalogue 1975-1977, pp. 368-69).

School Health Education Option

General Requirements	Speech communication or Rhetoric and a speech performance elective
	Natural sciences
	Physical sciences
	Social sciences
	History of the United States
	American government (state and federal constitutions)
	Physical education
	Humanities
Professional Educational Requirements	History and philosophy of education (education policy studies)
	Educational psychology
	Principles of education
	Techniques of teaching
	Educational practice
Health Education Specialty Requirements	Health and modern life
	Public health
	Nutrition
	Mental health
	Disease
	Organization of school health programs
	Principles of health education
	Emergency care procedures
	General safety education
	Education for human sexuality
	Drug abuse education
	Evaluation in health and safety
	Child development

Community Health Education Option

General Requirements	Speech communication or Rhetoric
	Natural sciences
	Physical sciences
	Social sciences

	Physical education
	Humanities
Health Education Specialty Requirements	Health and modern life
	Public health
	Nutrition
	Mental health
	Disease
	Organization of school health programs
	Principles of health education
	Emergency care procedures
	General safety education
	Education for human sexuality
	Drug abuse education
	Evaluation in health and safety
Allied Supporting Requirements	Educational psychology
	Processes and systems of communication
	Report writing
	Radio and television

If a student wishes to pursue a dual option, the community option is followed with additional course work to fulfill the education requirements.

As the need increases for public school health educators and as college-age people face critical health problems, the health educator at the college level becomes a necessity. Most colleges and universities require a Ph.D. or Ed.D. of a health educator.

The school health educator has the responsibility of planning and implementing the health education program in the schools, maintaining the healthful environment of the school, and supervising the health services. These health services include appraisal of student health, control and prevention of disease, health guidance and supervision, and emergency care.

The instructional portion of the program is usually the most time-consuming for the school health educator. The health educator may teach any or all of the following topics:

Consumer health education	Nutrition
Dental health education	Personal health
Drug use and abuse, alcohol	Prevention and control of disease
Human ecology and health	Public and environmental health
Sex education and family life	Safety education and disaster survival
Mental health and illness	Smoking and disease

Some of these topics may be controversial; the school health educator should be aware of the values of the community that he or she teaches in.

The community health option enables graduates to pursue careers in government. The graduate may work as a health educator, planner, or administrator in local, state, and federal government offices. The community health educator may also work for the World Health Organization, VISTA, Peace Corps, and the Public Health Service.

Organizations such as the American Heart Association, American Red Cross, American Dental Association, and American Medical Association afford varied opportunities for health educators. Hospitals and insurance companies are beginning to seek them out. Industry and business have also begun to employ those health educators who have specialized in safety and accident prevention.

Obviously, many career opportunities exist for the school and/or community health educator. Salaries for community health educators are usually higher than for school health educators. Fringe benefits may vary from organization to organization, but are usually similar to those of school health educators.

ASSESSING YOUR CURRENT INTEREST IN HEALTH EDUCATION

There are no standardized tests to assess one's interest in becoming a health educator. However, the future health educator has many points to consider. This person should have a genuine interest in people, in working with people, and in facilitating a change in people's attitudes, knowledge, and behavior to enable them to live more effective lives.

Scott and Carlo (1974, p. 1) issue a challenge to those students who protest the irrelevancy in today's education. These authors want prospective teachers to make a personal commitment to change the existing situation. To ensure that their protests are legitimate concerns and not just complaints, students should consider the following statements:

1. Do you actually want to get involved?
2. Are you vitally concerned about your prospective personnel and their problems?
3. Are you willing to devote the time that is necessary to challenge these persons?
4. Are you genuinely concerned that your personnel have the opportunity to be involved in meaningful learning experiences?
5. Can you relate to persons who have a life style different from yours?
6. Do you have the courage to try new approaches?
7. Are you willing to risk "failures" in order to venture toward new horizons?

Here are suggestions for obtaining more information concerning health education (school or community).

1. Write to a chairman of a health education department at the college and public school levels.
2. Interview a community health educator in your local health department.
3. Enroll in a freshman level, basic survey health course.
4. Read articles and books concerning the role of the field of health education.
5. Talk with students who are majoring in health education at the undergraduate level.

Bibliography

Anderson, C. L., and Creswell, W. H. 1976. *School health practice.* St. Louis: C. V. Mosby Co.

Fogotson, E., The turning point in public health law — 1966 reflections. *American Journal of Public Health* 57 (June 1967):394.

Hanlon, J. J. 1974. *Public health.* St. Louis: C. V. Mosby Co.

Johns, E. B., et al. 1970. *Health for effective living.* New York: McGraw-Hill.

Nemir, A., and Schaller, W. E. 1975. *The school health program.* Philadelphia: W. B. Saunders Co.

Scott, G. D., and Carlo, M. W. 1974. *On becoming a health educator.* Dubuque, Iowa: Wm. C. Brown Co.

University of Illinois at Urbana-Champaign. 1975-77. *Undergraduate Catalogue.*

Student Activities

1. Survey your community and determine the various health-related positions that might be available to you as a health educator.

2. Critically review and analyze at least one article from one of these journals in your school library:

Journal of School Health
Journal of American Public Health Association
Health Education Monographs
Journal of Human Sexuality
Journal of Drug Abuse
Journal of Health Education

3. Interview a recently graduated health education major and a community health educator. Attempt to determine if you might be interested in pursuing the career which they did.

4. Survey the schools in your local system to determine the extent of health education that is offered to the students.

Statements for Class Discussion

1. The community health educator is really a social worker.
2. School health educators are physical educators who are not well skilled in sports.
3. Controversial issues, such as sex education and abuse of drugs and alcohol, should probably not be taught by the school health educator.

CHAPTER **15**

THE RELATIONSHIP OF PHYSICAL EDUCATION TO RECREATION

INTRODUCTION

The relationship of physical education to recreation is an important one. Skills developed in physical education classes are incorporated into recreational athletics and other physical activities which are generally sponsored by recreation personnel — either as intramural programs in a school setting or as recreation department offerings in a municipal setting.

Within the last 10 years, a great number of specific curricula have been developed to train recreation personnel. This is a departure from an older philosophy which resulted in recreation personnel evolving out of a physical education curriculum. This new trend to train recreationists in specialized vocational areas is likely to continue but will be regulated to a great extent on the number of jobs developed within the various employment scenes.

CONCEPTS TO BE GAINED FROM THIS CHAPTER

When you have mastered the material in this chapter, you will be able to demonstrate comprehension of these concepts:

1. A difference in philosophy does exist between physical education and recreation personnel, yet the philosophies are compatible and complementary to each other.

This chapter was written by Dr. Donald Buchanan, dean of the School of Health, Physical Education, and Recreation, Mankato (Minnesota) State University.

2. Recreation participation is purely a voluntary act. You can simply engage in needs of all segments of the public.
3. Historical events of past years have contributed to a well-organized recreation movement and the development of a relatively new profession.
4. Careers in the recreation field are many and varied in training and application.

DEFINITION

A definition of recreation would be: "Recreation is the utilization of activities which are voluntarily selected and from which personal satisfaction is gained." After you have deliberated about acceptance or rejection of this definition of recreation, develop your own definition of recreation for a friend, another for your parents, one for your grandparents, or one for an ambitious youth of elementary age. And before we leave this thought-provoking exercise, how about writing a definition of recreation for a person who is serving time in a correctional institution?

A POSITION STATEMENT

Students desiring to gain insight into careers in physical education or recreation should acknowledge some fundamental facts:
1. Physical education is generally a required course of study in the elementary and secondary schools of the United States. The requirement varies from state to state; however, there is general agreement that physical education classes provide a setting in which physical skills are developed for use as personal gratification and/or to maintain a fitness level.
2. Recreation participation is purely a voluntary act. You can simply engage in vigorous or more passive activities at your discretion. You can have short periods of "recreation" or prolonged recreation experiences, such as a two-week backpacking and canoe trip.

Therefore, we could now engage in friendly debate as to the suggestion that "recreation" is an attitude. Explore the golf situation in which the skills are taught in a physical education class. Golf is also played on an afternoon for pure pleasure as "recreation" and, in addition, golf is played at the Augusta National Golf Course for work. Where is learning taking place?

The development of physical skills can occur in a recreational setting. In other words, learning new skills or perfecting others is not necessarily dependent on a formal atmosphere. The most important element for emphasis here is that the instruction needs to be conducted by trained personnel. The "teachable moment" could well be during the recreation period and, in the final analysis, *what happens to the participant* is the purpose for which recreationists and physical educators exist.

How does the recreation participant view this process? He or she is interested in participation for enjoyment. People tend to take active roles if they have physical activity success, and this is often accompanied by social involvement.

Who provides the setting for the participant is less important to him than to those who provide the learning setting. The most likely learning places are the home and the school. It is conceivable that the school laboratory cannot provide the needed time and supervisory personnel to enable the perfection of physical skills. At this point, municipal recreation departments can provide facilities for continuation of the perfection process. In other words, the physical education teacher and local recreation director need to work together.

The trained recreationist must be an analyst (to determine recreation needs of his or her constituency) and a programmer (to provide those services which will best satisfy those expressed needs). Categories of recreation activities have traditionally been the program areas of arts, crafts, dance, dramatics, education (skill development programs), hobbies, physical recreation (sports-games-athletics), music, outdoor education (nature-oriented activities), service activities, and social recreation and special events.

What then is the recreationist's ultimate responsibility? This professional needs two frames of reference: 1) what the participants seem to express as needs and interests, and 2) what he or she visualizes as activities which will extend their recreation interests beyond current expressed and developed levels.

Obviously, the tools of the recreation trade become the activities which can be administered as a program. Inherent in the program-offering decision, is the responsibility of analyzing the effects of program involvement on the participant.

The word *leisure* has deliberately been placed in the latter part of this segment of this chapter. Leisure may be defined as "a time period when freedom to choose what you wish to do is accomplished." We have read and heard about how much leisure we have. Actually, each of us perceives our own leisure time in contrast with our vocational choice. It can be argued that, after work commitments, we have only leisure remaining. However, if we subtract from 24 hours that time spent in maintenance functions (eating and sleeping) and employment, the remainder could be classified as leisure — that time which can be utilized to enhance our life experiences.

THE PAST AND PRESENT IN RECREATION

The concept of the importance of recreation had a modest beginning. In United States life, the Puritan work ethic frowned on "playing." It would appear that this opinion prevailed until urbanization and industrialization gained a substantial foothold. There were publicly accepted contributors to the recreation concept before 1900; however, such contributions began to be significant in the latter half of the 19th century.

It would be well at this time to acknowledge some notable "firsts" in the total recreation program structure in the United States. There is evidence to support such achievements as:

1. First city park, Boston, "Boston Common," 1634
2. First national park, Yellowstone, 1872
3. First church camp, Hinckley, Maine, 1880
4. First industrial recreation program, Allis Chalmers Company, 1882
5. First national body of professional recreation personnel, Playground Association of America, 1906

Prominent organizations which have assisted recreation in reaching its position today include: the United States Forest Service (1905), the Boys' Clubs of America (1906), the Boy Scouts of America (1910), the American Camping Association of College Unions-International (1914), the National Park Service (1916), the American Alliance of Health, Physical Education and Recreation (1937), Military Special Services (1941), and the National Industrial Recreation Association (1941).

A most significant and most recent step forward in the organized recreation movement occurred in 1966 when the National Recreation and Park Association was formed. This Association was the result of a merger of existing organizations and today the NRPA consists of the following branches.

1. American Park and Recreation Society. Composed of municipal and youth agency type personnel.
2. Commissioners and Board Members Branch. Those who serve on municipal and agency boards and whose boards affiliate with this branch.
3. National Student Recreation and Park Society. Designated for those students pursuing a bachelor's degree and/or graduate degrees in the field.
4. National Therapeutic Recreation Society. Professional recreation therapists who work within remedial-concerned institutions and programs.
5. National Society for Park Resources. County, state, regional, and Federal park employees.
6. Armed Forces Recreation Society. Personnel of each branch of the nation's military forces affiliate with the AFRS.
7. Society of Park and Recreation Educators. A branch for professional instructional personnel of departments within institutions of higher education.
8. Friends of Recreation and Parks. This newly created branch serves those persons who are not directly affiliated with a specific recreation and/or park unit but who are interested in promoting and playing supportive roles in the recreation movement.

Two significant new groups have been formed as affiliate "branches." The first of these groups is the Ethnic Minority Society. Its purpose is "to represent the recreational interest and rights of minorities while serving the same needs and desires of the public."

The second is known as COPARC: the Council of Parks and Recreation Consultants. This council acts in many ways with all efforts designed to upgrade or maintain high-level facilities and programs for the public.

The National Recreation and Park Association has its central office in Arlington, Virginia, and contributes the following publications to the field:

1. *Parks and Recreation* (magazine of general interest)
2. *Journal of Leisure Research* (research reports)
3. *Therapeutic Recreation Journal* (therapeutic recreation information)
4. *Washington Action Report* (legislative updates)
5. *Management Aids Series* (technical booklets)
6. *Park Practice Program* (designs of facilities, new concepts)
7. *Playground Summer Series* (program ideas)
8. *Guide to Books on Parks, Recreation and Leisure* (bibliography)
9. *SPRG-NRPA Curriculum Catalog* (complete listing of curriculum content of degree programs)

CAREERS IN RECREATION

The major in recreation is now offered by more than 300 colleges and universities. Many of these majors appear with different titles which offer insight into their major emphasis: recreation and park administration, recreation leadership, recreation resources management, recreation education, and leisure education. Although many of the current curriculums are interdisciplinary in nature, it would be appropriate for an interested student to review the summaries of the curriculum of any school; consult the *SPRG-NRPA Curriculum Catalog* for this information. This review would reveal the areas of specialization which most departments offer.

Several factors appear to justify a continued need for professional recreational and park personnel. Among the more prominent ones are: increased amounts of leisure time available to the public, more discretionary income, a vast number of recreational facilities created in recent years for public use, the realization of the importance of recreation activities as therapeutic tools, and the projection that our population numbers will continue to grow and that people will live longer. It seems logical that our natural resources will need better management. It would follow, then, that professional leaders, supervisors, and administrators will be needed to meet the management requirements of recreation and park programs in the public and private sectors, and that the availability of such positions will fluctuate with the economy.

Recreation and Government

The importance of governmental agency involvement in recreation cannot be minimized. The Federal government plays numerous roles; some of the more prominent agencies are:

1. The U.S. Department of Interior
    a. The National Park Service (national parks and other national recreational areas)
    b. Fish and Wildlife Service (fish and game management)
    c. Bureau of Outdoor Recreation (facility planning and funding)
    d. Bureau of Land Management (public land management)
2. The U.S. Department of Agriculture
    a. The U.S. Forest Service
        (1) National Forests
        (2) Wilderness Area
    b. Federal Extension Service (4-H Clubs)
    c. Soil Conservation Service (land management practices)
3. Department of Defense
    a. Corps of Engineers (river locks and dams, reservoirs)

The numerous job titles concerned with these agencies would connote the following types of preparation: recreation administration, forestry, biology, geography, and natural resource planning and engineering (both civil and special phases of engineering). Each agency has a formal application and testing program under civil service provisions. Students interested in the federal service programs should visit a civil service office and review job descriptions for positions which appeal to them.

State governments are also deeply involved in recreation with their principal role in providing facilities for public leisure time use. Two key governmental units involved with recreation facilities are the Department of Natural Resources (or similar state unit of similar name), and the state planning agency. Again, an interview with state employment office personnel regarding employment in a variety of positions is advisable.

County governments are following programs similar to those of their state government in providing outdoor recreation facilities — principally county parks.

Typical titles which may be found in this natural resource-based area are:

1. Park manager — city, county, regional, state, national
2. Land acquisition officer
3. Conservation organization positions
4. Interpretive specialist
5. Recreation specialist with Bureau of Reclamation and Bureau of Land Management and other federal agencies
6. Travel agent
7. Campground manager (private or public)

8. Public utility outdoor recreation specialist
9. Ice area manager
10. Theme park director

Municipal Recreation

The many municipal recreation departments across the nation present the best job opportunities for physical education students interested in a career in the recreation field. Examples of kinds of positions that would be available are: director of recreational athletics within a large municipal program, aquatics specialist, or specialist in working with the handicapped or in other phases of outdoor recreation. Here again, discussion with municipal recreation directors would give insight into the types of positions available in this extensive field.

An important consideration for persons interested in working with a governmental unit is recognizing that these agencies are in the public recreation business and their programs are supported by the tax dollar. The increasing demand on the tax dollar for a varied number of public purposes has somewhat deterred public recreation agencies from meeting the demands of public leisure. From this standpoint alone, the public agencies must assure broad programs for all segments of the public in order to justify their expenditures for personnel and for the development of additional facilities.

Job titles are extremely numerous in the municipal recreation sector.
A few are:
1. Director of municipal recreation
2. Director of department of recreation and parks
3. Recreation program supervisor
4. Recreation specialist
5. Community center director
6. Sports specialist

Recreation and the Schools

The old concept of recreation being a nonacademic discipline has recently been challenged by college and university faculty who have postulated that studies of leisure and programmatic attachments to leisure time use must become a reality in order to prepare citizens for a leisure-oriented world.

Two aspects of recreation need to be cited as positive contributions made by the schools. First, intramural programs at any and all levels of an academic institution meet many of the characteristics of recreation. One must note that these programs are normally highly physical in nature and do not meet the criterion of being broad in concept. It can be argued that there is really no reason why the broad recreational concept could not be incorporated into the school program except for the lack of available personnel to organize, supervise and administer the program.

The second of the school's contributions towards recreation lies within the community school concept. This type of program dictates that the school be made available to all persons within a neighborhood and/or community to allow further personal leisure-oriented development. Many facets of recreation are incorporated into community school programs, within adult education programs.

Students who desire this type of position should inquire about such requirements with the appropriate state Department of Education. Job titles which would be incorporated into this type of professional involvement are generally those of Community Education Director and Community School Director.

Industry and Recreation

As cited previously in the brief historical account of the evolution of the recreation movement, industry has made a significant contribution in meeting the leisure needs of its employees. Frequently, industrial firms have not only developed recreation facilities on their properties for employees and their families, but have additionally supported community recreation programs through sponsorship of teams. It is not unusual for a company to pay sports participation fees (or a portion thereof) of its employees, to sponsor an activity day in which an amusement park is opened to the employees' families at no charge, or to host parties for them during regular holiday periods.

The bachelor's degree in recreation leadership or administration is a common requirement for persons becoming industrial recreation directors. However, this is not a specific requirement in many instances, as directors of such programs come to these positions from personnel departments or other administrative areas. The director commonly becomes an *enabler* rather than a true recreation leader. This follows an accepted concept of having the employees organize interest groups for activity purposes, manage themselves in the activity program, and evaluate successes in the programs which they stimulate. The director is in a position to supply the necessary administrative detail to assure meaningful recreation experiences commensurate with the industry's commitment.

Voluntary Agencies and Recreation

Organizations such as the Boy Scouts, Girl Scouts, Campfire Girls, YMCAs, YWCAs, and Boys' Clubs are examples of youth agencies that employ persons with training in the field of recreation and physical education. While it is true that many of these positions are closely associated with physical recreation, it is also true that these personnel must have a broad background in personnel management, finance, community resources, and other training commensurate with youth problems and concerns of today. Requirements for leadership and administrative positions (of varying titles) with youth-serving agencies are frequently those requesting training for a recreation degree.

Therapeutic Recreation

Recreation can be considered therapeutic to all people as it offers renewal and change of pace. Emphasis is currently being placed on the leisure needs and rights of special groups of people such as the emotionally ill, physically handicapped, disadvantaged, and elderly. In the past, most career opportunities in therapeutic recreation were in the institutional setting. Similar positions and responsibilities in recreation administration and leadership were offered in activity therapy complexes to "captive audiences." The trend today is in the direction of municipal responsibility for special groups. Specialized programs for the handicapped are offered by many public and voluntary agencies as a part of the broad aim to meet the leisure requirements of the total community.

Students interested in careers in therapeutic recreation may choose the institutional environment where civil service positions and requirements are maintained. If the choice is to work at the municipal level, then application would be made through the superintendent of recreation.

Professional emphasis is placed in therapeutic recreation in many college and university recreation and park administration departments which lead to the bachelor's degree.

Typical jobs found in the therapeutic recreation field are:
1. Activities director — nursing homes
2. Recreation therapist — state hospital system, V.A. hospitals, private and children's hospitals
3. Recreation supervisor for special groups — municipal setting
4. Recreation specialist — day activity centers
5. Program director for senior citizens centers

IF YOU ARE INTERESTED IN RECREATION

Your initial reason for reading this text was a supposed interest in physical education. Now, however, you might be eager to investigate recreation more thoroughly. If so, the most obvious course of action is to do any or all of the following:
1. Contact the chairperson of the recreation department at a college or university. Ask him or her about the career prospects, program offered at a particular school, scholarship opportunities, etc.
2. Talk with several currently active recreation workers, especially those in a field in which you are especially interested.
3. Read articles and books concerning the role, programs, and future of recreation in the U.S. A selected bibliography is found at the conclusion of this chapter which may be of interest and help to you.
4. Observe a local recreation program. Better yet, become involved as a volunteer or paid worker.
5. Talk with students currently enrolled in a recreation curriculum at either the bachelor's or master's degree levels.

Bibliography

Artz, R. Community school movement: A progress report. *Parks and Recreation* 10 (Oct. 1975):37.

Bernheim, S. Don Quixote — Therapeutic recreation in the community. *Therapeutic Recreation Journal* 9 (3 Qtr. 1975):106.

Conrad, C. Help America get physically fit. *Parks and Recreation* 10 (Dec. 1975):38.

Curtis, J. E. Parks of the future. *JOHPER* 44 (June 1973):31.

Donaldson, G. W., and Donaldson, A. D. Outdoor education: Its promising future. *JOHPER* 43 (Apr. 1972):23-28.

Donnelly, K. Current trends in commercial recreation. *JOHPER* 44 (June 1973):33.

Evans, M. Recreation services for the inner city handicapped. *Parks and Recreation* 10 (Apr. 1975):33.

Ford, N. T. The recreation director syndrome. *JOHPER* 44 (May 1973):45-46.

Hodgson, J. D. Leisure and the American worker. *JOHPER* 43 (Mar. 1972):38.

Hutchinson, I. J. Federal programs in recreation and parks. *JOHPER* 44 (June 1973):27.

Johnson, J. Rangers get a touch of class. *Parks and Recreation* 10 (Jan. 1975):30.

Keller, B. Leisure education: Pathway to a better life. *Parks and Recreation* 11 (Jan. 1976):26.

Kerr, D. The status of women in parks and recreation. *Parks and Recreation* 10 (Apr. 1975):38.

Kraus, R. G. Today's crisis in urban recreation. *JOHPER* 44 (June 1973):29, 38.

Langman, R., and Rockwood, L. Be prepared . . . for a career in commercial recreation. *Parks and Recreation* 10 (July 1975):30.

Levy, J. Recreation at the crossroads. *JOHPER* 42 (Sept. 1971):51.

Littlefield, S. So, you're a recreation therapist. *Therapeutic Recreation Journal* 9 (3 Qtr. 1975): 106.

McKinney, W. C., and Ford, P. M. What is the profession doing about education for leisure? *JOHPER* 43 (May 1972):49.

Martin, A. Man's leisure and his life. *Quest* 5 (Dec. 1965):26-36.

_____. Leisure and our inner resources. *Parks and Recreation* 10 (Mar. 1975):1a.

Naus, B., and Adelman, H. Forecast for leisure. *JOHPER* 44 (Jan. 1973):61.

Nesbitt, J. A. Recreation for the ill and the handicapped. *JOHPER* 44 (June 1973):35-39.

Nierman, W. H. The community school and recreation. *JOHPER* 43 (Mar. 1972):53-55.

Prial, J. Rehabilitation through recreation. *Parks and Recreation* 11 (Feb. 1976):21.

Pollack, B. The university and the leisure needs of the inner city. *The Physical Educator* 27 (Oct. 1970):121.

Shivers, J. S. Recreational service in transition. *The Physical Educator* 27 (Oct. 1970):103.

_____. Recreational service: Overview and exceptions. *The Physical Educator* 30 (Dec. 1973):211.

Staffo, D. F. A community recreation program. *JOHPER* 44 (May 1973):47.

Strobbe, J. E. The year-round school and recreation. *JOHPER* 43 (Mar. 1972):51-52.

Young, S. K. Multicultural programming. *Parks and Recreation* 10 (Apr. 1975):40.

Wilkins, M. H., and Rayatz, R. L. Cultural changes and leisure time. *JOHPER* 43 (Mar. 1972):35.

Student Activities

1. Interview a recreation administrator or park manager and discuss the responsibilities of the position.
2. Analyze how the recreational needs of the handicapped are met in your local community.
3. Obtain a copy of your state's outdoor recreation plan and determine how your county's program fits within the plan.
4. Meet with your city administrator and gain insight about the recreation program benefits to the city's populace.
5. Interview several youth agencies' administrators and determine their job responsibilities.

COMMITMENT

CHAPTER **16**

A PHYSICAL EDUCATOR—
A CAREER CHOICE

INTRODUCTION

When you began to read this text, you were farily certain that you wished to pursue a career in physical education. You based your ideas mostly upon high school experiences, and what you thought physical educators' jobs involved. We have tried to expand your perception by discussing the concepts and the careers in physical education. In this final chapter, you are asked to make the decision as to whether you will continue in physical education. As mentioned earlier, this last chapter will help you assess your attitude toward physical education — with your actions being the criteria for judgment.

A MAJOR DECISION

You have almost finished your study of this text. By now, you should know which one of these statements best represents your view.
1. I have decided to remain in physical education, either as a major or minor, or to earn one of the various certificates.
2. I have decided, at least for the time being, that physical education does not provide a career interest for me.

The basic points made in the remainder of this chapter will apply to you, regardless of which statement you selected. The details (names of organizations, periodicals, etc.) are written for those who remain in physical education; but for those who choose otherwise, the seven major points and the listing of minors apply equally well.

ACTIONS LEADING TO A SUCCESSFUL CAREER

At this point you may have decided upon a career choice. Discussed below are a number of things that are done by professionally minded persons. The more you do, the greater is your zeal to become a professional.

1. *Complete courses and achieve above-average grades.* For years, both students and teachers have been saying that grades received might not necessarily be the best indicators of what a person has gained from a class. Yet, the GPA is the most important factor influencing a prospective employer — it simply cannot be overlooked. Requirements for a particular major or certificate must be met; while you will have to achieve a certain minimum GPA to graduate (usually 2.0 for all courses taken) it should be obvious that the higher, the better.

2. *Participate in intramurals and athletics.* In physical education we claim to favorably influence the physical, social, and emotional life of the individual; intramural and athletic experiences are designed to do this. Prospective employers are favorably impressed by physical educators who participate in such activities. If we claim they are beneficial to others, we certainly should participate ourselves. You might offer the excuse that you are too unskilled to play on the school team. Perhaps so, but lack of skill is no excuse for not participating in intramurals. A physical educator has two reasons for participating in intramurals — enjoyment (which usually comes from improved skill) and learning how these experiences are organized and administered. The professional physical educator understands both the intramural and athletic program.

3. *Obtain experience.* Some schools offer internship or practicum courses where a student can gain experience and college credit for working in a real situation. In our discipline, it may be helping in an elementary school physical education program (parochial schools especially need help), coaching athletics in elementary or junior high schools, working in the physical education program of the YMCA or Boys' Clubs, working in the summer as a playground director in a recreation program, working as an aide in the physical therapy department of a hospital, giving dance or swim lessons, helping children in day-care centers, or working with handicapped youngsters. The opportunities are endless! Sometimes these experiences can be more valuable than classroom credits. The most important thing is that they are an indication of great interest in your work.

4. *Join professional groups.* You remember that the term *professional* was defined as a person who obtains a broad education. The great majority of those persons who consider themselves professional realize that their education includes more than classroom experience. Thus, professional organizations have been organized for virtually every interest group imaginable. Indeed, one of the common complaints of professionals is that they find it difficult enough to keep up with the meetings and publications of the groups to which they belong, much less to broaden their knowledge by joining any new groups. Physical education is similar to other disciplines; there are at least a dozen special-interest groups. You can benefit greatly by at least reading their publications and knowing their

purposes, types of organizational structure, and membership requirements. A listing at the end of the chapter indicates addresses where you may obtain further information about a group.

a. *AAHPER.* The American Alliance for Health, Physical Education and Recreation is a national professional organization which brings together administrators, teachers, and leaders in these related fields, and is the largest of the various physical education groups. It was originally founded in 1885 by 60 people concerned with physical training. The main purpose of AAHPER is to strengthen and improve school and community programs in health education, recreation, outdoor education, physical education, and professional preparation.

   In organization, AAHPER has divided itself both by geography and by interest groups. The nation is divided into six districts, each district being composed of several states. Each state has its own separate association, with annual conventions being held at the state, district, and national levels. Associations of special interest areas are organized on the national level to focus attention on various aspects of our discipline. These seven associations are:

   1) AALR (American Assn. for Leisure and Recreation)
   2) ARAPCS (Assn. for Research, Administration, Professional Councils and Societies)
   3) AAHE (American Assn. for Health Education)
   4) ASCSA (American School and Community Safety Assn.)
   5) NDA (National Dance Assn.)
   6) NAGWS (National Assn. for Girls' and Women's Sports)
   7) NASPE (National Assn. for Sports and Physical Education)

   Like most organizations, AAHPER has a national headquarters (Washington, D.C.), several publications, many committees, and self-government by an Alliance Assembly and a Board of Governors.

   Membership (currently over 45,000, including more than 10,000 students) is open to all who are professionally engaged in any of the areas mentioned above. Student members are entitled to receive nine issues of *JOPER* each year, plus other fringe benefits. Recently, AAHPER has made special efforts to enlist student support as evidenced by:

   1) Employment of a consultant who can readily identify and be accepted by student groups. The person customarily spends half of the time meeting with student groups throughout the nation.
   2) Offering special bonus memberships (two years for the price of one) to graduating college seniors.
   3) Distributing teaching packets to graduating seniors.
   4) Holding special meetings in each of the districts to train student leaders.
   5) Distributing materials (pamphlets, etc.) to students.
   6) Securing an official place in the AAHPER structure for a council with student leaders, and an all-expense-paid meeting of these officers.
   7) Sponsoring meetings for students at state, district, and national conventions.

b. *Major's clubs.* For many years, AAHPER has encouraged colleges and universities to sponsor local clubs composed of major and minor students in the HPER areas. At present there are over 200 such chartered groups. Each club is free to set its own rules and decide its own activities. Most clubs are coeducational. As with many groups, the quality of student leadership varies from year to year, with a consequent variance of effectiveness. A major's club can add tremendously to a student's knowledge and professional competence. The purpose, therefore, is to favorably influence the student's knowledge and attitudes toward physical education as a discipline and profession. While some student clubs require members to join the AAHPER, encouragement, not coercion, is the normal procedure.

c. *Professional organizations.* These are composed of selected groups of persons who are involved as students or professionals in a particular area. Phi Epsilon Kappa (PEK) and Delta Psi Kappa (DPK) are the professional fraternity and sorority for physical educators. These are sometimes called honorary fraternities. Most members are students, although alumni chapters and membership are encouraged. The purposes of PEK and DPK are similar — to encourage greater professional competence through service with other persons who have the same interests.

PEK has over 60 chapters located in various colleges and universities, while Delta Psi Kappa has over 40 chapters. Chapters are organized according to the dictates of the national constitutions, which prescribe the officers and duties of each, the membership requirements, and the ritual. By definition, the professional fraternity exists for the professional benefits of its members. This means that various service projects (such as conducting sports' clinics, sponsoring touring sporting groups, attending conventions, and learning about new teaching methods) are its main activities. Social purposes are secondary to these activities. Each of these groups has a national publication: *The Physical Educator* (PEK), and *The Foil* (DPK). The chief difference between professional fraternities and major's clubs is that prospective fraternity members are selected by the active members. Merely majoring in physical education does not ensure membership.

d. *State physical education groups.* As indicated earlier, AAHPER has organized itself on a geographic basis and thus each state has its own Association of Health, Physical Education, and Recreation. The great majority of AAHPER members are much more active in state affairs than they are at district or national levels. Each state has an annual AAHPER Convention, sometimes in conjunction with the state teachers' convention. The convention is usually close enough for schools to encourage physical education students to attend as a group. Student memberships in the state association are available. Because it is a part of AAHPER, the purposes would be primarily the same — but with state-wide instead of national focus.

5. *Attend conventions and meetings.* Each state has meetings which involve physical educators. The most publicized of these are the annual meetings of teachers, but physical educators with interests other than teaching will find opportunities open to them. While AAHPER district meetings have a distinct emphasis, the national meeting truly represents all aspects of HPER. These meetings are rotated on a geographical basis from year to year. It is probable that at least one national convention will be held

reasonably close to you in the four or five years of your training. Here is your chance to gain knowledge and competence and to meet physical education leaders. The cost of attending meetings varies; almost all have a registration fee and most require membership in the Alliance. Quite often, an employer will pay part of the cost, but of course, this does not help the student. Remember that a characteristic of a professional is to seek further training at his own expense if there is no other way. There are numerous special interest meetings held each year in every state. High school athletic coaches, intramural directors, teachers in inner city schools, sport psychologists, athletic trainers, health scientists, swimming pool operators, parks and recreation workers — all of these groups try to meet occasionally. Contact your local HPER chairperson or the physical education consultant in your state Department of Education for information on interesting groups.

6. *Purchase books and subscribe to periodicals.* Why not begin your professional library the economical way with student subscriptions? If you become a member of AAHPER your membership includes subscriptions to *JOPER.* If you join Phi Epsilon Kappa, you would receive *The Physical Educator,* while Delta Psi Kappa members receive *The Foil.* Other periodicals which have great appeal and application (and sometimes student subscription rates) are *Sports Illustrated, Athletic Journal, Scholastic Coach, Coach and Athlete,* and *Psychology Today.* A list of their addresses is at the end of this chapter. A listing of books and pamphlets to be purchased would be lengthy and varied. Certain groups publish annual listings of their publications; send a letter for a catalog. A list of these sources is given at the end of this chapter.

7. *Observe and talk with professionals in the field.* Your professors and friends are two sources of information, but perhaps the person to offer the latest practical information is a *good* physical educator. Hopefully, the materials in Chapters 5-13 have given information on what physical education should be; if you find such a program, a professional will be nearby!

MINORS

Whether you major in physical education or not, selection of a minor to complement the major of your choice is important. If you desire to teach, you are undoubtedly concerned about the current facts relating to the supply and demand of teachers. The basic fact is that there is a surplus of teachers, including both male and female physical educators. However, you must realize that each year new physical educators are hired to fill new positions or as replacements. How can you make sure you are one of those hired? First, get good grades. Second, be able to show a prospective employer that you are attempting to be a professional. Join groups, attend meetings, build your library — in short, do those things discussed earlier.

Should you aspire to a nonteaching career in physical education, the future job prospects are difficult to predict. Some of the positions (e.g., Red Cross, YMCA, Peace Corps) mentioned in Chapter 13 are always available, while others (Armed Forces Sport Specialists, for example) are less frequently found. Nevertheless, obtaining good grades and seeking professional status will be essential in launching your career.

Regardless of whether or not you plan to teach, there is one other step you can take to improve your attractiveness to a potential employer. This is the selection of a minor. In most schools students have some elective hours required for graduation. Rather than take these in random fashion, why not take them in one or two disciplines? It is impossible to develop a list of desirable and undesirable minors, because the laws of supply and demand change yearly. For the latest information, consult your placement or counseling center. However, consider this listing of minors especially suitable for educators who do not plan to teach.

Psychology (motor learning specialists)
Social work (agency workers)
Sociology (sport sociology specialists)
Biology (exercise physiology specialists)
Computer science (laboratory research specialists)
Chemistry (exercise physiology specialists)
Physics (motor development specialists)

One last word. Selection of a minor should be done on the basis of your interests and capabilities. A surplus of persons does not mean that you should avoid something you really wish to do. A well-prepared professional will always succeed in a career.

Bibliography

AAHPER. Major day: A PEM club project. *JOHPER* 39 (Oct. 1968):101.

_____. Student involvement in AAHPER. *JOHPER* 40 (June 1969):65.

_____. Student involvement in the administration of sports program. *JOHPER* 41 (Feb. 1970):39.

_____. Challenges from the student action council. *JOHPER* 42 (Sept. 1971):56.

_____. SIN means Student Involvement Now. *JOHPER* 42 (Oct. 1971):6.

_____. What ever happened to the PEMM clubs? *JOHPER* 42 (Oct. 1971):6.

_____. Pilot project in student-directed interpretation to the campus community. *JOHPER* 42 (Nov.-Dec. 1971):61.

_____. North Carolina State student major conventions. *JOHPER* 44 (Mar. 1973):57.

Allison, E., and Weatherford, A. How to operate a successful PEM club. *JOHPER* 34 (Feb. 1963):67.

Bucher, C. A. Change and challenge. *JOHPER* 46 (Nov.-Dec. 1975):55-56.

Calhoun, L. Sophomores launch elementary school physical education program. *JOHPER* 42 (Feb. 1971):44.

Carmack, M. Open house for incoming freshmen. *JOHPER* 43 (Sept. 1972):81.

Clendennen, W. R. Career conference for future physical educators. *JOHPER* 43 (Jan. 1073):74-75.

Cody, C. Some thoughts about professional preparation. *The Physical Educator* 29 (Dec. 1972):193.

Colgate, T. P. Your professional associations. *The Physical Educator* 26 (May 1919): 79.

Cotten, D., and Paul, T. L. A unique undergraduate experience. *The Physical Educator* 43 (Dec. 1972):205.

Crisafulli, R., et al. What professional involvement really means. *JOHPER* 44 (Jan. 1973):69.

Davis, H. What does the future hold for a black physical educator? *JOHPER* 43 (Jan. 1972):65.

Eveits, C. Firsthand experiences for future physical educators. *JOHPER* 43 (Oct. 1972):72.

Fallon, D. Undergraduate community experience. *The Physical Educator* 29 (May 1972):61-62.

Finn, P. Career education and P. E. *JOPER* 47 (Jan. 1976):29-30.

Hall, D. North Carolina student majors hold convention. *JOHPER* 42 (Jan. 1971):77.

Herbert, B. Student physical education day in Vermont. *JOHPER* 43 (Sept. 1972):81.

Laughlin, N. A. Time for a change: A look at the professional preparation of physical educators. *The Physical Educator* 28 (Oct. 1971):150.

Louck, D. H. An educational device for developing the well-rounded physical education major. *The Physical Educator* 27 (Dec. 1970):147.

Neal, J. M. Student involvement in the administration of sports programs. *JOHPER* 41 (June 1970):57.

Robb, M. D. Cortland provides research grants for undergraduate students in physical education. *JOHPER* 42 (Apr. 1971):82.

Rothstein, A. Involving undergraduates in research. *JOHPER* 44 (Mar. 1973):71.

Taylor, M., and Lewis, P. Every student a teacher. *JOHPER* 46 (Mar. 1975):47.

Teitelbaum, B. R. A friend from Lehman. *JOHPER* 44 (Jan. 1973):24-26.

Thomas, C. F. Do we practice what we preach? *JOHPER* 32 (Oct. 1961):21-22.

Walsh, N., et al. Undergraduate students seek to improve physical education major offerings. *JOHPER* 41 (Apr. 1970):69.

Wells, M. A new physical major and minor club. *JOHPER* 42 (Feb. 1971):65.

Student Activities

1. If you have decided to remain in the discipline of physical education, indicate that this is a rational and planned decision by submitting an essay which includes this information:
   a. Whether you will major, minor, or earn one of the certificates
   b. A listing of those courses that you have yet to take to earn the degree or certificate which you seek
   c. A discussion of specific professional experiences which you honestly believe you will participate in before graduation. These might include:
      (1) Intramural and athletic experiences you will participate in while in college
      (2) Work experiences you expect to gain
      (3) Professional groups you will most certainly join
      (4) Professional meetings, conferences, conventions, etc. (with locations and dates, if possible) you plan to attend
      (5) Professional books and/or periodicals you will subscribe to
      (6) Names of professional workers whom you might observe and talk to from time to time
2. If you have decided that, at least for the near future, the discipline of physical education does not provide a career interest for you, indicate that you have gained some knowledge about our field by submitting an essay which discusses:
   a. How have the physical education experiences (classes, intramurals, and/or athletics) taken to this point helped you physically, socially, and/or emotionally?
   b. How will physical education experiences that you might participate in while in college be of help now or in the future?
   c. What type of physical education program will you help your children experience as they progress through grades K-12?

The second project asks you to submit an essay on your feelings toward physical education. This is not a "busy work" assignment, because you will be affected through life by this discipline. Presently, you are probably in a college situation which offers (even requires) you to take physical education courses. These probably should be selected for the benefit you can derive both now and in later life. Some of you will eventually raise a family, and your children will be taking physical education as a part of their education. You should know the objectives of our discipline (Chapters 5-10) and what constitutes a good school program (Chapter 11). This knowledge should aid you in ascertaining (demanding, if necessary) that your children receive the greatest possible benefits from physical education. Even as your children take school physical education, you will be faced with many choices related to our field. Chapters 6-10 have indicated some of the facts and concepts related to biological development, psychomotor learning, personal expression, mechanical forces, and social, political, and economic forces of sport. These are all related directly to the present and the future. It is logical to expect that knowledge of many of these facts and concepts might enrich your lives and theirs. Wise use of leisure time is, according to some, the greatest challenge facing Americans today. We hope you have been helped in meeting this challenge.

Sources of Professional Growth

Professional groups.

American Alliance for Health, Physical Education and Recreation, 1201 Sixteenth Avenue N.W., Washington, DC 20036. (Ask for information about student memberships, major's clubs, addresses of state HPER groups.)

Canadian Association for Health, Physical Education and Recreation, 703 Spandina Avenue, Toronto, Ontario, Canada M5S 2J4.

Delta Psi Kappa fraternity. Business Office, c/o Mrs. John W. Schroll, Rt. 1, Box 125, Winneconne, WI 54986. (Ask for name of nearest chapter, or if there is a possibility of beginning a local chapter.)

Phi Epsilon Kappa fraternity. Business Office, 6919 East 10th, Suite E4, Indianapolis, IN 46219. (Ask for name of nearest chapter, or if there is a possibility of beginning a local chapter.)

Professional periodicals.

Athletic Journal, 1719 Howard Street, Evanston, IL 60202.

Coach and Athlete, 1421 Mayson Street N.E., Atlanta, GA 30324.

Scholastic Coach, 50 West 44th Street, New York, NY 10036.

Sports Illustrated, 541 North Fairbanks Court, Chicago, IL 60611.

(Almost all colleges and universities have student subscription advertising cards available on bulletin boards. Use them for substantial savings.)

Specialized periodicals.

Bow and Arrow, 550-A South Citrus Avenue, Covina, CA 91722.

The Modern Gymnastics Magazine, 410 Broadway, Santa Monica, CA 90401.

Swimming World and Junior Swimmer, 12618 Killion Street, North Hollywood, CA 91607. (*Swimming Technique* magazine published at this address also.)

World Tennis, 200 Madison Avenue, Suite 1104, New York, NY 10016.

Catalogs of professional literature.

AAHPER, 1201 Sixteenth Avenue N.W., Washington, DC 20036. (Ask for latest catalog of publications.)

Athletic Institute, 805 Merchandise Mart, Chicago, IL 60654. (Ask for latest catalog of publications.)

INDEX